Abstract Sex

ABSTRACT SEX
PHILOSOPHY, BIO-TECHNOLOGY AND THE MUTATIONS OF DESIRE

LUCIANA PARISI

continuum
LONDON • NEW YORK

Continuum

The Tower Building, 11 York Road, London SE1 7NX
15 East 26th Street, New York, NY 10010

www.continuumbooks.com

© Luciana Parisi 2004

British Library Cataloguing-in-Publication Data
A catalogue record for this book is available
from the British Library.

ISBN: 0-8264-6989-2 (HB)   0-8264-6990-6 (PB)

Typeset by Acorn Bookwork Ltd, Salisbury
Printed and bound in Great Britain by MPG Books Ltd, Bodmin, Cornwall

Contents

THE STRATIFICATION OF ABSTRACT SEX

LAYERS	INFORMATION TRANSFER MODE	RULES OF ORGANIZATION	MICRO-FEMININE LINE	DATES	SEX MACHINE
BIODIGITAL	CLONING	RECOMBINANT DESIRE	EGG	LATE 20TH CENTURY	MOLECULAR SEX
BIOCULTURAL	SEXUAL REPRODUCTION	PLEASURE	FLUIDS	19TH CENTURY	HUMAN SEX
BIOPHYSICAL	BACTERIAL SEX	TRADING	MITOCHONDRIA	3,900 MILLION YEARS AGO	MEIOTIC SEX

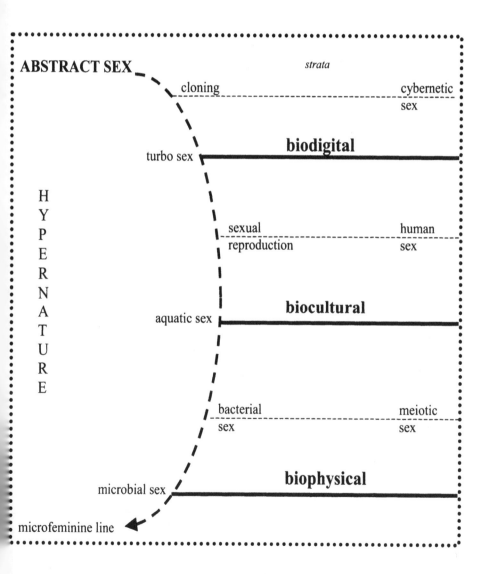

Acknowledgements

The concepts in this book are linked to an interdisciplinary research project involving many people sharing a method of analysis and perception of cultural mutations. This common method has been crucial to the engineering of this book.

I wish to thank Keith Ansell Pearson for his constant support and encouragement. His scrupulous comments and attention to earlier and final drafts have been essential for the completion of this work.

I am also very grateful to the Five College of Women's Studies Research Centre Award (Mount Holyoke College, Massachusetts) for giving me the opportunity to meet Lynn Margulis in 1997. Thanks to her generosity, I was able to access research material in the laboratory at Amherst College, and was involved in the various and exciting activities in her research study group.

My gratitude also goes to the Department of Cultural and Innovation Studies at University of East London for supporting my research and granting me a sabbatical to complete the book.

Finally, I wish to thank Nick Land for inspiring the diagrammatic conception of my work, and the Cybernetic Culture Research Unit (CCRU) where some of the key concepts in this book were generated collectively.

My special thanks go to Tiziana Terranova for her friendship and daily discussions. Her comments and advice enormously stimulated my writing. I am very grateful to my friend Steve Goodman for his precious contributions and immediate receptiveness that helped to convey concepts in my production. I also thank Stefania Arcara for her kind meticulousness and friendship. My love and gratitude go to all my friends everywhere.

I especially wish to thank Stephen Samuel Gordon for his indispensable loving presence, inspiring conversations and ability to listen.

I thank my family for their affectionate and practical support in all my adventures abroad. In particular, I thank my mother to whom this book is dedicated.

Introduction: Abstract Sex

In the age of cybernetics, sex is no longer a private act practised between the walls of the bedroom. In particular, human sex no longer seems to involve the set of social and cultural codes that used to characterize sexual identity and reproductive coupling. In the twentieth century, political movements, such as feminism, challenged the conventions that associate sex with sexual reproduction, freeing feminine desire from the biological function of procreation. At the turn of the twenty-first century, developments in information technologies have profoundly accelerated the separation of sex from natural reproduction. Human sex has now entered a cyberspace of information where everyday bodily contacts and sexual encounters have given way to long distance rendezvous. The emergence of cybersex defines a new prosthetic extension of human sex, the prolongation of sexual pleasures outside the limits of the body. In the last ten years, Internet-mediated communication and simulation of sex, cyberpractices such as gender swapping and cybererotics have been at the core of important debates about this transformation of human sex – as sexual reproduction involving two parents.

This increasing diffusion of mediated sex has been accompanied by contrasting views about the new blurring of the boundary between artificial and natural sex. Most commonly, for example, it has been argued that cybersex defines the cybernetic age as the age of the disappearance of the body and corporeal difference. With cybersex, male fantasies and mental projections have replaced physical appearances, material touch and fluid exchange. Artificial sex calls for the ultimate separation of the mind from biological limits, the simulated experience of being free from physical constraints in the immersive matrix of information celebrated by the cowboys of cyberspace. This triumph of artificial sex is said to crown the achievements of the male model of sex defined by the drive towards discharge, the channelling of all flows towards a final climax, the pleasure of self-satisfaction. Finally detached from the biological body by transcending all fleshy ties, this dominant model of sex realizes the most classical of patriarchal dreams: independence from matter. Leaving behind the heavy meat of physical presence and floating free in cyberspace, the triumph of artificial sex is equated to the triumph of the economy of pleasure (the discharging model of patriarchy).

The transformation of human sex in relation to technology has reopened the question of gender and power in cybernetic capitalism. In particular, feminists and cyberfeminists have criticized cybersex and its erasure of corporeal presence because it reinforces male pleasure. The pursuit of male self-satisfaction is continuously perpetuated in the disembodied world of simulation far removed from physical and biological ties. The expansion of mediated projections ensures the constant exorcism of the physical world of dark matter incarnated in the woman's reproductive body. Cyberfeminism has pointed to the problematic implications of the newly blurred distinctions between natural and artificial sex for feminism and beyond. The acclaimed autonomy of cybersex from reproduction, of sexuality from sexual reproduction entails a double bind that on the one hand liberates female identity from biological destiny but, on the other, realizes the patriarchal dream of liberation from flesh. Cybersex remains caught up between these two poles creating an impasse between disembodiment and embodiment highlighting the ultimate triumph of male pleasure over feminine desire, the socio-cultural disappearance of natural or material difference in cybernetic capitalism.

Nevertheless, the question of cybersex goes even further if we consider that the disappearance of natural sex is also linked to the disappearance of the male and female functions of reproduction increasingly threatened by the success of human cloning. In February 1997, renowned scientific journals such as the *New Scientist* and *Nature* reported the final accomplishment of the first mammal cloning by the Roslin Institute of Biotechnology in Edinburgh, announcing an unprecedented modification of reproduction that would have profound impacts on human sex. Scientific articles and reports on adult mammal cloning explain that this procedure involves a new understanding of reproduction, no longer determined by sexual mating but entailing a duplication or copy of genetic material extracted from one single parent. Since 1997, new debates about the transformation of human sex have been stirred up by the real prospect of cloning humans. Articles on the redundancy of sexual reproduction, but in particular the redundancy of the male and female sex for reproduction, are recurrent not only in scientific journals but also in magazines and newspapers.

In the February 2001 edition of *Wired* magazine, a report on human cloning entitled '(You)^2' discussed the prospect of cloning humans as an imminent possibility already partially achieved in 1999 by a South Korean team that voluntarily cut short the experiment. This report discusses how the latest advances on mammal cloning technique, the reduction of laboratory costs and the emergence of pro-cloning groups – such as the Raelians, a Quebec-based New Age religious group and the Human Cloning Foundation, a New York- and Atlanta-based group – are facilitating the opportunities for cloning humans. The increasing demand for cloning people from parents who have lost their child, from terminally ill people and from infertile men and women will soon find adequate supply in this newly constituted market. Not only does this report discuss how cell biologists, animal cloning specialists and fertility doctors believe that human cloning is an inevitable substitute of in vitro fertilization – cloning cows, pigs and people will soon become more efficient than natural reproduction – but it also highlights the newly discovered plasticity of genes. The novelty of Dolly, the cloned sheep, was not that you could clone an adult mammal, but that our genes and organs can be designed and shaped. The point is not solely that it is now possible to reproduce artificially, but that human beings can be reproduced from scratch. Artificial wombs, sperms and eggs are under construction and not only fathers but also mothers are about to become redundant. Artificial sex and reproduction marks the apex of the Brave New World where humans overcome death through the proliferation of identical copies.

Nevertheless, as asserted in the *Scientific American* in January 2002, in the exclusive 'The First Human Cloned Embryo', the clone is not a mere copy, but a new type of biological entity never seen before in nature. Artificial sex and reproduction not only replaces human functions of procreation but also engenders diversity by accentuating the genetic and somatic differences commonly experienced by identical twins. These controversial implications of human cloning and human design bring into question the power of science, capitalism and gender relations. As demanded by feminism, the female body is now free from the biological destiny of procreation. Yet, at the same time, the patriarchal dream of independence from nature and from the female body is also completely reached. The liberation from anatomy, from the identification of women with sexual reproduction, contrasts strongly with the liberation from the material body, the accomplishment of Cartesian disembodiment in the cyberspace of information.

The increasing investment in technologies of reproduction announces the new economic and cultural frontier of bio-informatic (or bio-digital) capitalism where artificial sex and reproduction define the new tendencies of power in the cybernetic age. The contrasting binarism between ultimate disembodiment on the one hand and the return to the fleshy body on the other coincides with the dichotomous boundary between technology and biology continuously scrambled into pieces by our biodigital capitalist culture. If it has become increasingly problematic to distinguish natural from artificial sex, then it may be superfluous to investigate the blurring of the biological and the technological from the perspective of a fundamental dualism between embodiment and disembodiment. The implications of cybersex point to a new direction for thought that requires the elaboration of an alternative understanding of sex.

We propose a third way out of the binarism between embodiment and disembodiment to engage with the biodigital mutations of human sex. This third way maps the emergence of a new (but ancient) kind of sex and reproduction, linking these mutations to microcellular processes of information transmission that involve the unnatural mixtures of bodies and sexes. The speeding up of information trading, not only across sexes, but also across species and between humans and machines, exposes the traits of a non-climactic (non-discharging) desire spreading through a matrix of connections that feed off each other without an ultimate apex of satisfaction. This new way points to the dissipation of the male model of pleasure by exploring the implications of a biodigital intensification of bacterial sex: the non-linear merging and copying of distinct information sources accelerating the emergence of unprecedented entities. As one scientist recently put it, it is increasingly evident that, since their appearance on Earth, humans have been living in the 'Age of Bacteria'. The mutual feedback between biology and technology marks an unpredictable proliferation of molecular mutations that poses radical questions not only about human sex but also about what we take a body, nature and matter to be. This new approach investigates the imminent pervasion of mutant species, bodies and sexes by the engineering of an altogether different conception of sex, femininity and desire – abstract sex.

CHAPTER 1

Virtual Sex

INTRODUCTION

Since 1997, when Professor Ian Wilmut of the Roslin Institute of Biotechnology in Edinburgh created the first mammal clone, Dolly the Sheep, animal cloning has been undergoing rapid bio-technological innovations. In June 1998, the American scientist Ryuzo Yanagimachi, from the University of Hawaii, announced the cloning of the first artificial mouse. In September 1999, Italian researchers accomplished the cloning of the first male mammal, a bull. Since then, several cloning experiments on cows, pigs and monkeys have been successfully carried out. The expansion of an artificial mammal world populated by replicant animals has seen the rise of debates about the limits that should be set for science in the manipulation of nature. When in July 2001 the Australian doctor Orly Lachman Kaplan declared open the experimentation on mammal fertilization without sperm, the debate quickly shifted towards the new implications for human sex, suggesting the superfluous activity of the male sex for human procreation. In the last five years, therefore, the impact of bio-technology on human sex and reproduction has more strongly influenced cultural and ethical debates about the power of science to engineer life.

Between 2001 and 2002, newspapers around the world reported several attempts at cloning adult humans on behalf of groups of scientists, despite the opposition of the Church, mainstream scientific communities, the government and public opinion. After helping a 62 year-old woman to become pregnant, the Italian fertility expert Severino Antinori declared that his plans to clone humans and assist the birth of the first human clone were about to become reality. The echoes of this news acquired more credibility once, together with with Dr Panos Michael Zavos he presented his plans to clone humans to the Academy of Science in Washington, during the International Conference on Cloning in 2001. The most debated gynaecologist in the last ten years, Antinori intends to carry out his project without the consent of the European Community or the American administration, but with extreme confidence in the two hundred couples on his waiting list, in private sponsors, laboratories and clinics around the globe. Recently, the Italian scientist claimed that a secretive global network of scientists, sponsors and surrogate mothers collaborated to create the world's first cloned human embryos. Although there is no evidence of recent births of human clones, according to Antinori at least three secret pregnancies in different countries have resulted from human cloning techniques.

As a fertility expert, Antinori's project of cloning humans mainly aspires to enable infertile couples to procreate their own genetic offspring without turning to surrogate wombs or foreign genetic material from sperm and egg donors as required by the procedures for in vitro fertilization. On the other side of the spectrum, the acclaimed project of cloning humans has also seen, in recent years, the diffusion of companies, such as Southern Cross Genetics, an Australian start-up that offers the service of storing DNA for future cloning. These companies follow the example of now popular cloning companies such as Clonaid, founded in 1997 by the Raelians, a pro-science religious group – a mixture of religious scientists and surrogate mothers. These groups also hint, together with the Human Cloning Foundation, to the more sinister attempts to clone dead offspring and relatives. In the year 2001, newspapers around the world reported the story of an anonymous couple willing to finance the Raelians to clone their one month-old dead boy from his frozen cells.

Although the success of human cloning is still liable to high rates of improbability, in December 2002, the head of Clonaid, chemist Brigitte Boisselier, claimed the successful birth of the first baby girl, Eve, cloned from the DNA of a 31-year old American woman. The group also expected four more cloned babies to be born in North America, Europe and Asia from one lesbian couple and from two couples using preserved cells of their own children before their deaths. As several experts on cloning point out, in order to perform human cloning it is sufficient to have access to large numbers of eggs, expert cell biologists, chemists and scientists, and well-equipped laboratories. With more than 50 women members, scientists and private benefactors, the Raelians are considered among the most likely candidates to pioneer human cloning.

As anti-cloning scientists have recently declared, even though Antinori or the Raelians fail to pioneer the scientific achievement of cloning humans, radical changes in human sex and reproduction are imminent. Although unaccepted by mainstream science, minor extravagant phenomena such as the Raelians' group or the Human Cloning Foundation together with Antinori's claims on cloning humans, incite profound anxieties about the mutation of the body and sex in our cybernetic age. In particular, rapid developments in bio-technologies, entailing the engineering of bodies from scratch through genetic design, are constantly blurring the traditional boundaries between life and death, natural and artificial. As often pointed out, far from ensuring the copying of the 'identical', genetic engineering accelerates the proliferation of molecular mixtures. The plasticity of genetic material enables the copying of genetic variations but it does not guarantee predictable results in the long run. The imminent expansion of cloned and designed bodies announces an increasing proliferation of mutant species and sexes that profoundly challenge our assumptions about what the body is and what it can do.

THE BIO-TECHNOLOGICAL IMPACT

Artifice is fully part of nature.

Deleuze (1988a: 124)

In 1985, Donna Haraway's Cyborg Manifesto highlighted the new mutations of the body–sex in bio-informatic capitalism. For Haraway, the convergence of bodies and technologies marked the emergence of the new metamorphic world of the cyborg, a hybrid blending of animal, human and machine parts. No longer embedded in the nuclear Oedipal family (the natural ties with the mother and the father), the cyborg was, for Haraway, the offspring of the post-gender world of genetic engineering where biological or natural sex no longer determines the cultural and social roles of gender. Cybernetic communication and reproduction enable the prosthetic manipulation of the physical bonds of gender stretching the limits of Mother Nature. Artificial sex permits the unprecedented transformation of our gender identity, the construction and reconstruction of sexual forms and functions of reproduction.

The post-gender world of the cyborg brings to the extreme postmodern claims about the end of certitudes where biological destiny is threatened by the saturating proliferation of technologies of communication and reproduction in our daily life. As opposed to the postmodern nostalgia for a lost world of stable boundaries between nature

7

and culture, the cyborg embraced the challenge of bio-informatic technologies affirming that our assumptions about nature are the results of
intricate cultural constructions articulated by specific technoscientific
discourses.[1] The equation between sexual identity and sexual reproduction at the core of our understanding of human sex is nothing natural.
Quite the contrary, it is embedded in the historical and cultural roots
of the Western metaphysical tradition of essentialism. Far from
reflecting a given unquestionable truth, the cyborg revealed that the
natural essence of a body rather derives from specific historical and
cultural constructions (or representations) of nature establishing a
natural association between feminine sex and sexual reproduction.
Rather than being determined by sexual identity and sexual reproduction, the artificial world of the cyborg announces the new historical
and cultural conditions of the posthuman body no longer able to find
shelter in the natural world.[2] For the post-gender world of the cyborg,
there is nothing natural about the human body, sex and reproduction.

Haraway's seminal text has strongly influenced debates about the
impact of bio-technologies on the body, sex and femininity. In particular, in the last ten years, debates about the convergence between
biology and technology have problematized the new tension between
natural and artificial sex, the disappearance of biological difference
and the celebration of artificial disembodiment.[3] It has been argued
that the post-gender world of the cyborg risks dissolving the biological
differences of the body, the ties with the corporeal world of sex,
celebrating the disembodied model of male pleasure (the independence
from matter celebrated by the closed economy of charge and
discharge). While liberating feminine desire from biological identity,
the cyborg also deliberates the ultimate detachment of the mind from
the body, the triumph of mental projections over material
constraints.[4]

These controversial debates about the implications of information
technologies for sexual reproduction tend to perpetuate a critical
impasse between biological essentialism and discursive constructivism.
Claims about the return to material embodiments (biological differences) are opposed to the emergence of a post-gender world of
cybersex where variable meanings and shifting discourses enable us to
perform our gender identity beyond biological anatomy. In this framework, gender no longer depends on sex – the form of sexual organs
and the function of sexual reproduction – rather it is sex that depends
on the constructions of gender, the signifying signs that constantly
change the nature of sex.[5] In recent years, the idea that you can

perform your own gender by changing your sexual identity has strongly clashed with the feminist argument of maintaining biological ties among women in order to resist the accelerating disembodiment of difference in cybernetic capitalism.

Yet this critical impasse is nothing new. The constitution of binary oppositions between what is given (the natural or biological realm) and what is constructed (the cultural or technological world) is entangled with the traditional Western model of representation. As often argued, the model of representation does not entail the exact reflection of reality or truth, but is more crucially used to refer to a system of organization of signs where structures of meaning arrange gestural, perceptual, cognitive, cultural and technological signs through the hierarchies of the signifier.[6] The model of representation reduces all differences – biological, physical, social, economical, technical – to the universal order of linguistic signification constituted by binary oppositions where one term negates the existence of the other. The binary opposition between embodiment and disembodiment is caught up in the binary logic of representation that disseminates the dichotomy between materiality and immateriality, the separation of the inert body from the intelligent mind. Embedded in the Platonic and Cartesian metaphysics of essence, the logic of representation subjects the body, matter and nature to the transcendent order of the mind,[7] suppressing the network of relations between nature and culture, sex and gender, biology and technology, rapidly transforming the way we conceive and perceive the body–sex.

Neither the politics of embodiment nor disembodiment provides alternative conceptual tools to analyse the recent bio-informatic mutations of posthuman sex. This critical impasse is embedded in a specific conception of the body where a set of pre-established possibilities determines what a body is and can do. These possibilities are defined by the analogy between biological forms (species, sex, skin colour and size) and functions (sexual reproduction, organic development and organic death) that shape our understanding of nature and matter through principles of identity (fixity and stability). This analogy creates a direct resemblance between body and mind, sex and gender, skin and race where biological destiny determines the hierarchical organization of social categories. Feminists and cyberfeminists have strongly criticized this biological sameness that constitutes the patriarchal model of representation whereby the body is mastered by the mind. Nevertheless, recent debates about cybersex or artificial sex have failed to provide an alternative understanding of the mind–body binarism reiterating the opposition between biological presence and discursive absence of the body.

The liberation from the mind–body dualism through the displacement of signifiers from fixed meanings (the signifier sex from the signified gender) appears to re-entrap the body in a pre-established set of possibilities determined by linguistic signification. The post-gender feminist attempt at untangling feminine desire from nature, through the floating of free signifiers of sex in the new cyberspace of information, problematically reiterates the mind–body dualism by associating the body with a fixed and stable nature where matter is inert. In a sense, post-gender feminism risks confusing the biology of the body with the materiality of a body where the conception of nature and matter is determined by and reduced to biological discourses or universal systems of signification. The continuous displacement of the signifier 'sex' does not succeed in detaching feminine desire from fixed nature as it fails to challenge the fundamental problematic of the body, biological identity, the imperative of sexual procreation and ultimately the metaphysical conception of matter.

The bio-technological mutations of human sex and reproduction expose new implications for the separation of feminine desire from biological destiny requiring an altogether different conception of the body in order to challenge traditional assumptions (pre-established possibilities) about what we take a body to be and to do. Expanding upon the feminist politics of desire, abstract sex brings into question the pre-established biological possibilities of a body by highlighting the non-linear dynamics and the unpredictable potential of transformation of matter. Drawing on an alternative conception of nature, abstract sex embraces the Spinozist hypothesis about the indeterminate power (or abstract potential) of a body suggesting that 'we do not yet know what a body can do'. This hypothesis challenges the analogy between biological forms and functions (the pre-established biological possibilities of a body) pointing to the capacities of variation of a body in relation to the continual mutations of nature. Moving beyond the critical blockage between biological essentialism (embodiment) and discursive constructivism (disembodiment), abstract sex proposes a third route to widen the critical spectrum of our conception of the body–sex.

By proposing to re-wind the processes of evolution of the body and sex, abstract sex starts from the molecular dynamics of the organization of matter to investigate the connection between genetic engineering and artificial nature, bacterial sex and feminine desire that define the notion of a virtual body–sex. This notion is not to be confused with the immaterial body—sex as defined by the debates about the embodiment (materiality) and disembodiment (immateriality). The notion of the virtual body—sex primarily implies that a body is more than a biological or organic whole, more than a self-sufficient closed system delimited by predetermined possibilities. The virtual body—sex exposes the wider layers of organization of a body that include the non-linear relations between the micro level of bacterial cells and viruses and the macro levels of socio-cultural and economic systems. The collision of these layers defines the indeterminate potential of a body to mutate across different organizations of sex and reproduction producing a series of micro links between biology and culture, physics and economics, desire and technologies. The networked coexistence of these levels contributes to construct a new metaphysical conception of the body—sex that radically diverges from the binary logic of the economy of representation.

Abstract sex suggests that bio-technologies do not reiterate new or old dichotomies. Abstract sex displays the intensive connections between different levels of organization of a body—sex, where nature no longer functions as the source of culture, and sex of gender. The intensive concatenation between nature and culture entails a reversibility in the ways in which nature affects and is affected by culture. This mutual relation points to an alternative understanding of sex and gender that no longer depends upon the primacy of identity and its mind—body binarism, but lays out the reversal relations between parallel modes of being and becoming of a body. Sex is neither constructed as the pre-discursive or as the product of techno-scientific discourses. Primarily sex is an event: the actualization of modes of communication and reproduction of information that unleashes an indeterminate capacity to affect all levels of organization of a body — biological, cultural, economical and technological. Sex is a mode — a modification or intensive extension of matter — that is analogous neither with sexual reproduction nor with sexual organs. Sex expands on all levels of material order, from the inorganic to the organic, from the biological to the cultural, from the social to the technological, economic and political. Far from determining identity, sex is an envelope that folds and unfolds the most indifferent elements, substances, forms and functions of connection and transmission. In this sense, sex — biological sex — is not the physical mark of gender. Rather, gender is a parallel dimension of sex entailing a network of variations of bodies that challenge the dualism between the natural and the cultural. Adopting Spinoza's ethics or ethology of the body, it can be argued that sex and gender are two attributes of the same substance, extension and thought, mutually composing the power – *conatus* – of a mutant body.[8] This conception of sex diverges from the critical impasse in cyberculture between essentialism and constructivism and its negative principles of identity.

From this standpoint, the bio-technological disentanglement of sex from sexual reproduction does not imply the ultimate triumph of the patriarchal model of pleasure, a longing for disembodiment and self-satisfaction. This disentanglement suggests an intensification of desire in molecular relations such as those between a virus and a human, an animal cell and a micro-chip. As opposed to the dominant model of pleasure defined by auto-eroticism (the channelling of flows towards climax or the accumulation and release of energy), abstract sex points to a desire that is not animated or driven by predetermined goals. As explained later in this chapter, desire is autonomous from the subject and the object as it primarily entails a non-discharging distribution of energy, a ceaseless flowing that links together the most indifferent of bodies, particles, forces and signs. In this sense, the cybernetic muta-tions of sex expose a continuum between the cellular levels of sex (bacterial sex), the emergence of human sex (heterosexual mating) and the expansion of bio-technological sex (cloning) entailing a new conception of the body. This conception highlights an alternative meta-physics of matter–nature that enfolds the multiple layers of composi-tion of a body and sex, defining their potential capacity to differentiate.

Abstract sex points to the non-linear coexistence of the biophysical (the cellular level of the body–sex defined by bacteria, viruses, mito-chondrial organelles, eukaryotic cells); the biocultural (the anthropo-morphic level of the human body–sex defined by psychoanalysis, thermodynamics, evolutionary biology and anatomy in industrial capit-alism); and the biodigital (the engineering level of the body–sex defined by information science and technologies such as in vitro fertili-zation, mammal and embryo cloning, transgenic manipulation and the human genome in cybernetic capitalism) layers of the virtual body–sex. This complex composition of the body–sex exposes the continual and unpredictable mixtures of elements stemming from different layers that indicate the indeterminate potential of a body–sex to mutate. In particular, the bio-technological engineering of the body, the genetic design of life accelerates the recombination of different elements and the mutations of the body–sex by disclosing a new set of urgent ques-tions about the relation between feminine desire and nature.

The rapid innovations of cloning techniques seem to announce the ultimate achievement of Man over Nature, the ultimate power of Man to design Man. Yet, what might seem the final act of mastering nature by patriarchal humanism exposes in fact much more controversial implications. As pro-cloning and anti-cloning groups often point out, the genetic designing of life, involving the non-linear transfer of information between different bodies (animal, humans and machines), implies an acceleration of evolutionary mutations whose results are not yet known. The acclaimed final control of man over nature rather suggests the loss of human control on the unpredictable mutations of the body. The recent proliferation of mutant bodies radically brings into question the conception of nature where the acceleration of cloning, in the form of bacterial sex, suggests that artifice has always been part of nature. This rapid unfolding of artificial nature opens up new problematic questions in relation to bio-technological mutations of human sex and reproduction.[9] If cloning has always been part of nature, as bacterial sex demonstrates, then isn't it natural to clone humans? Are the new bio-technologies of the body already part of nature? What are the implications of this newly defined artificial or engineering nature in relation to feminine desire?

In order to investigate these questions, this book proposes to build up a new set of conceptual tools borrowing from the philosophical work of Gilles Deleuze and Felix Guattari, the metaphysics of nature of Baruch Spinoza and the scientific work of Lynn Margulis. By analysing the implications of the bio-technological mutations of a body, abstract sex maps a wider critical route to relate the (cyber)feminist politics of desire with the artificiality of nature.

ABSTRACT SEX

The logos is a huge Animal whose parts unite in a whole and are unified under a principle or a leading idea; but the pathos is a vegetal realm consisting of cellular elements that communicate only indirectly, only marginally, so that no totalization, no unification, can unite this world of ultimate fragments. It is the schizoid universe of closed vessels, of cellular regions, where contiguity itself is a distance: the world of sex.

Deleuze (1972: 174–5)

With machines the question is one of connection or non-connection, without conditions, without any need to render an account to a

third party. It is from that that the surplus value of encoding originates. The situation is like that of a bumble-bee which, by being
there, became part of the genetic chain of the orchid. The specific
event passes directly into the chain of encoding until another machinic event links up with a different temporalization, a different
conjunction.

Guattari (1984: 125)

The mutations of a body are not predetermined by a given ideal or an
infrastructure defining the realm of biological possibilities of a body.
On the contrary, these mutations designate the abstract or virtual
operations of matter. As Deleuze and Guattari argue, inspired by
Henri Bergson, the virtual is not to be confused with the realm of the
possible. The possible, in fact, is often the reflected image of an
already determined reality contained in a closed set of choices. Possibilities do not have a reality, as their reality is already determined.
Instead of denoting a possible reality, the virtual *is* reality in terms of
strength or potential that tends towards actualization or emergence.
Thus, the virtual does not have to become real. It is already real. It
has to become actual. The actual does not derive from another actual,
but implies the emergence of new compositions, a becoming that
responds to (acts back on) the virtual rather than being analogous to it.
Hence, virtuality and actuality do not coincide. They are two asymmetrical yet coexistent planes of difference that constitute the potential
of a body to become different, to mutate beyond principles of analogy
and resemblance.[10] Far from opposing matter to immateriality, abstract
sex points to the potential mutations of a body that are not defined by
a transcendent substance but by the incorporeal (abstract) transformations of matter.[11]

Abstract matter is not substance. In the Cartesian tradition,
substance corresponds to the non-extended God separated from the
physical world of nature. The Cartesian split between the mind and
the body originates from the separation of the cosmos from matter, of
the transcendent God (the power of the soul–mind) from nature (the
power of the physical body). In this framework, what we see in nature
was created by a non-physical God, a superior entity that has the
power to create and destroy the natural world. Contrary to Descartes's
ideal soul, Baruch Spinoza's concept of substance demonstrates that
nature is not separated from the cosmos. The body originates in God
as God corresponds to an intensive and extensive substance. God does
not create matter, but *is* matter able to manifest itself through the

14

ceaseless mutation of bodies and things in nature. As explained later in this chapter, far from starting from the unity of the One, Spinoza points to the parallel multiplicities of being and becoming, the continual relations between the cosmos and nature, intensity and extension, mind and body that define the primacy of potential over possible matter. Abstract matter questions the philosophical tradition that separates the corporeal from the incorporeal, nature from culture, the organic from the technical. It exposes the potential relations of change between the virtual body and actual body, the symbiotic merging of non-identical powers (the continual power or potential between substance and modes) unfolding the unpredictable mutations of a body.

From this standpoint, abstract (mutating) matter is *machinic* as it entails the heterogeneous composition or merging of different bodies of production. This machinic process has nothing to do with the celebration of technological determinism where technical machines are opposed to the organic body (technology versus biology). Drawing on Deleuze and Guattari, a machine is above all defined by a mixture of biological, technical, social, economic and desiring elements that compose and decompose a body at certain speeds and according to given gradients. These mixtures are productive concatenations or *machinic assemblages* constituting for example the biocultural organization of the body (the disciplinary order of human sex established by the virtual links between psychoanalysis, anatomy, evolutionary biology and thermodynamics) that unleash a potential transformation of all the elements participating in the composition (the transformation of evolutionary theories, the laws of physics and the anatomical perception of the body–sex). Far from reiterating the critical impasse between the natural and the cultural – the realm of the given and the constructed – Deleuze and Guattari's conception of abstract matter or machine suggests an isomorphic method of analysis that maps the different yet connected levels of order of a body (the biophysical, the biocultural and the biodigital organizations of sex).

In this book, the process of endosymbiosis constitutes the abstract machine of sex or abstract sex. Abstract sex maps the isomorphic process of organization of different modes of information reproduction and communication. Lynn Margulis, the molecular biologist and theorist of endosymbiosis, or SET (serial endosymbiosis theory), explains how heterogeneous assemblages of molecules and compounds, unicellular and multicellular bodies, proliferating through gene trading, cellular invasion and parasitism, produce new cellular and multicellular compositions of bodies.[12] In particular, merged bacteria that infect one another and symbiotic cellular associations reinvigorated by the incorporation of their contaminating diseases, map the potential mutation of bodies and sexes.

The Darwinian logic of evolution, resting on the centrality of sexual reproduction in order to engender species variations or differences, is substituted with a rhizomatic recombination of information expanding through viral hijacking of codes between singular machines of reproduction: a microbe and an insect, a bud and a flower, a toxin and a human. A far cry from organic unity and identity or from the original line of descent, endosymbiosis or abstract sex starts from heterogeneous assemblages where the parasiting web between hosts and guests produces new bodies–sexes. Far from determining a dualism between micro and macro levels of composition, for example between bacterial and nucleic cells, endosymbiosis exhibits a reversible feedback of information transfer that unfolds a continual variation of the body–sex, nature and matter.

This abstract machine provides a consistent method to analyse the manifold compositions of biophysical, biocultural and biodigital levels of modification of sex and reproduction. This isomorphic organization explains the dynamics of distinct machinic assemblages, cutting across micro and macro orders, and defines an immanent connection between bacterial sex and biodigital cloning, nucleic sex and disciplinary reproduction through singular points of mixture and differentiation of transmission. Abstract sex deploys the consistent relations between different machines of sex: from the autocatalytic association of cells to the association of multicellular bodies, from the society of bacteria to the social domain of disciplinary sex, from the digital culture of cloning images to the bio-technological proliferation of engineering cells. This consistency demarcates the autonomy of abstract sex – the endosymbiotic mutations of sex or desire – from the biological structures of the organic body and the cultural structures of signification, from the primacy of organic and linguistic totalities. It is not a matter of socio-cultural imitations of the natural or biological imitations of society. What comes first is neither a given essence nor the signification of essence. Rather, the abstract concatenation of bodies–sexes delineates the primacy of heterogeneous mixtures or symbiosis – biophysical elements, socio-cultural energies, economic trades, technical inventions, political forces and particles of desire – unfolding the potential of a body to become (mutate).

Instead of re-articulating sex within a post-feminist critical framework where difference is no longer material, abstract sex extends the feminist politics of desire by mapping the transversal mixing of information between bodies of all sorts (bacteria, vegetables, animals, humans and technical machines). Abstract sex proposes to tap into the kinetic ethology of tiny sexes that lay out a micropolitics of symbiotic relations between different levels of mutation of matter and desire. The biophysical (the cellular organization of bacteria, eukaryotic cells and multicellular bodies), biocultural (the techno-scientific organization of the human body) and biodigital (the informatic manipulation of the human body) mutations of the body explain the entanglement of sex with sexual reproduction, the emergence of the two sexes, and the sex–gender association beyond the biological essence and the discursive construction of the body–sex.

It could be argued that this micropolitics exclusively highlights molecular differences or mutations of the body–sex by discarding, for instance, the feminist commitment and engagement with the macropolitics of representation that still determines the identity politics of sexual difference. Similarly, it might be observed that the microcosm of differences is not sufficient to account for body politics where categories of difference (gender, race and class) are still crucial for the situated conditions of minorities in global capitalism. Without dismissing these objections, abstract sex suggests that the micro levels of variation of the body (nature–matter) are crucial to produce a non-reductive understanding of difference (i.e. starting from zero or the plane of pure difference) in relation to the bio-technological engineering of cultures, bodies and life. The bio-technological mutations of the body point to the emergence of a micro level of difference proliferating through the symbiotic engineering of information crossing not only species and sexes, but also humans and machines. Far from abandoning difference, abstract sex connects bio-technological mutations to the mutations of desire announcing a new phase in the symbiotic becoming of the body–sex.

Abstract sex is a machinic concept that is not full of meanings, but is above all full of potential variations of the body. These variations emerge from a concatenation of small causes unleashing vast indirect effects that lead to a new conception and perception of sex. Concepts are operators of forces whose deployment is not related to the realm of possibilities, but to the plane of invention of a new kind of reality. Concepts have a political resonance, but this is not an immediate or direct one. Rather, they have to be continuously re-engineered in order to map the emergence of novelty. For this reason, the bio-technological disentanglement of sex from sexual reproduction is not to be reduced to the traditional dichotomy between biological conditions (embodiment) and techno-scientific discourses (disembodiment), but needs to be related to the connecting layers of organization (or stratification) of matter affecting bodies–sexes, societies, cultures and economies. In particular, as explained in the following sections, in order to engage with the new implications of the bio-technological mutations of the body, abstract sex argues that sex, far from being signified or represented, is primarily stratified.

STRATIFICATION

The system of the strata has nothing to do with signifier and signified, base and superstructure, mind and matter. All these are ways of reducing the strata to a single stratum, or of closing the system in on itself by cutting it off from the plane of consistency as destratification.

Deleuze and Guattari (1987: 71–2)

In the plateau entitled '10,000 BC: The Geology of Morals (Who Does the Earth Think It Is?)', Deleuze and Guattari use the geological concept of stratification to map the formation of different levels of organization of a body (1987). Rather than starting from unity or totality (the whole that predetermines parts), stratification exposes the points of mixture or concatenation of different bodies (machinic assemblages) challenging the dichotomy between organic and inorganic, nature and technology. Stratification entails the auto-organization of molecular elements (unstructured particles) into molar compounds (structured aggregates) unfolding the isomorphic process of production of strata (the genetic and cellular strata, the multicellular and social strata).

Strata are defined by at least two parallel levels of order, a twin or double articulation between molecular and molar organizations operating at all levels of material association (biological, social, economical and so on). Rather than a binary opposition between molecular and molar orders, establishing a hierarchical difference between the simple and the complex (the molecular dynamics of cells and the macro structures of society), stratification exposes the molecular dynamics of all molar aggregates. These aggregates are not simply the result or the sum of molecules, but emerge from the auto-catalysis of molecules selecting stable from unstable particles. The latter become statistically ordered through patterns of connection and succession that engender 'forms' (first articulation). For example, the auto-catalytic assemblage of DNA, RNA, protein statistically ordered in a sequence leads to the emergence of a cell membrane engendering a cell (bacterial cell without nucleus). These forms (cells) are functional and compact stable structures that are simultaneously actualized as 'substances' by their molar compounds (the aggregation of DNA, RNA and protein).

Forms are modes of coding and decoding matter entailing the organization of elements–particles into signs: a-semiotic encodings (RNA, DNA, proteins), semiotic signs (cultural signs such as gestures, sound–words, attitudes), signs of signification (the signifier). Substances are formed matters and refer to territorialities (milieus), degrees of territorialization and deterritorialization (occupation and alteration of milieus). Each articulation entails the double combination of codes (signs) and territories (milieus), forms and substances. Rather than a binary opposition between the first and the second articulation, there is a movement of association, division and intersection between molecular and molar layers of codes and milieus[13] emerging from a common plane of matter, defined by Deleuze and Guattari as 'the unformed, unorganized, nonstratified, or destratified body and all its flows', the Body without Organs (BwO), the Body of the Earth or the plane of consistency (the Planomenon).

Deleuze and Guattari adopt Louis Hjelmslev's distinction of *matter*, *content* and *expression*, *form* and *substance* from semiotic substances (signifiers) in order to define stratification through the autonomy of matter, particles and signs from signifying semiologies.[14] Different from the Saussurean and post-Saussurean structures of signification, Hjelmslev's study of unformed matter – the amorphous thought-matter or *purport* – breaks with the form–content dualism, but also with the signifier/signified duality. These structures of signification are self-referential and reduce the world of signs to words produced by a negative binarism between already determinate terms. They presuppose the primacy of universal signifiers over processes of composition and transformation of signs. As Deleuze and Guattari argue, Hjelmslev's linguistics provides new insights in the formation of signs as related to unformed flows: a field of algebraic signs (or immanent glossematics) liberated from the transcendent surveillance of the signifier. The plasticity of signs deploys the primacy of the mutual relationship between expression and content of matter over the relation of subordination between signifier and signified.

As Deleuze and Guattari explain, *content* corresponds to formed matters. The *substance* and *form of content* entail the selection of formed matters into substances (territories) according to a certain order that gives matters forms (codification) (1987: 43). For example, as discussed in the third chapter, on the biocultural level of organization of the body, the *matter of content* corresponds to the biophysical mass of bodies stratified as *substances of content* when the biophysical mass is chosen or selected to constitute the human body as an organism, and as *forms of content* when this mass is chosen in a certain order – according to species, gender, race, class. Conversely, the term *expression* concerns the functional structures of matter entailing the specific organization of their form, and the formation of compounds constituting their substances (*forms and contents of expression*) (43). On the same biocultural level of organization, the form of expression involves the set of codes and regulations that define for example the rules of human sex. The substance of expression rather corresponds to the letters and phonemes composing words and expressing rules.[15]

The relation between content and expression exposes the distribution of molecular machines in molar aggregations as 'two variables of a function of stratification.' (44). Both articulations involve the double coexistence of molecular and molar levels of order where forms of expression on one level (the biophysical level of cellular sex) become forms of content for another level (the biocultural level of scientific organization of sex), defining the heterogeneous assemblages of the abstract machine of sex or endosymbiosis. In this book, the symbiotic connection between different levels of content and expression indicates the parallel modes of existence of the abstract machine of sex on the strata and outside the strata.

This abstract machine delineates the unity of the stratum when mapping the auto-organization of elements–particles into signs – a-semiotic encodings (genetic codings), a-signifying semiotics (phenotypic expressions, gestures, mimetics, sounds, speech), and semiologies of signification (the signifier) (Guattari 1984: 148–50). Deleuze and Guattari define this unity of the stratum as the *Ecumenon*, the process of binding all particles–flows through different degrees of territorialization, deterritorialization and reterritorialization (substances), and codification, decodification and overcodification (forms). Endosymbiosis displays the ecumenical unity of the stratification of sex through the complex organization of different layers – from genetic to cellular sex (biophysical), from meiotic sex to human sex (biocultural), from heterosexual mating to bio-technological sex (biodigital). Each level of organization is actualized by machinic assemblages unfolding the layers of a vast machine of connection – the endosymbiotic machine. This machine lies outside the stratum or on the *Planomenon* when the endosymbiotic connection of singular orders designates the intensive continua (the non-climactic connection and intensification of desire) between all machines of sex. This continual movement unleashes the unpredictable potential of a body to mutate (differential difference) through the micro variations of sex: 'lines of flight or destratification' of desire from all layers of organization. As suggested in the last two sections of this chapter, abstract sex points to the potential mutations of all bodies of information implying an immanent relation between non-climactic desire and artificial nature (or hypernature).

Of the infinity of strata formations, this book distinguishes three main agglomerates – the biophysical level of cellular bodies and sexes, the biocultural level of scientific organization of the human body and sex, and the biodigital level of cybernetic organization of the body and sex. There is no fundamental difference between these strata. Their difference entails a singularity: the long-term tendency of a trajectory in a physical system that individuates or actualizes through the trans-duction (conversion) of information from one layer to another, from one stratum to another. As Gilbert Simondon argues (1992: 313), transduction denotes an activity of individuation of a physical, biolo-gical, mental or social process emerging from the metastable relations between two disparate realities (the pre-individual state of being and the individuated state of becoming).[16] Transduction explains the non-linear dynamics of connection between strata defined by their potential capacity to affect and being affected (to impact and being impacted) by singular levels of actualization of a body–sex.[17]

Interlocking strata

The strata are phenomena of thickening on the Body of the earth, simultaneously molecular and molar, accumulation, coagulations, sedimentations, folding. They are Belts, Pincers, or Articulations. Summarily and traditionally, we distinguish three major strata: the physiochemical, organic, and anthropomorphic (or alloplastic).

Deleuze and Guattari (1987: 502)

Expanding upon Deleuze and Guattari's use of stratification, this book discusses the biophysical, biocultural and biodigital strata of sex in the second, third and fourth chapters respectively. Each stratum will single out and link events from one stratum to another outlining the points of connection and differentiation between different orders of sex. For example, the biophysical organization of multicellular sex or meiotic sex will be linked to the biocultural overcodification of sexual reproduction, constituting the model of human sex and reproduction, and to the biodigital decodification of linear reproduction and sex. Far from entailing hierarchical progress, this *metacommunication* between strata lays out the non-linear or endosymbiotic connection between the multicellular organization of the sexed body, the disciplinary sexed/ gendered body and the cyborg, exposing the continual mutations of a body–sex.

Abstract sex starts from the biophysical agglomerate of strata discussed in the second chapter through the analysis of cellular and multicellular machines of stratification of sex. Questioning the critical emphasis on the discursive production of sex as a pre-discursive phenomenon, this chapter demonstrates that sex lies neither before nor after discourse. Sex is constituted by assemblages of microbodies that hyperlink the most divergent forms and functions of reproduction. The biophysical stratification of sex proposes an anti-genealogical analysis of the emergence and variation of genetic and cellular modes of reproduction suggesting that sexual difference is neither given nor culturally constructed. Quite the contrary, sexual difference and sexual reproduction emerge from parallel processes of transmission of information among diverging microbial bodies. The biophysical organi- zation of sex questions the accounts of a human-centred evolution that assimilates sex to sexual reproduction and sexual organs determining the progressive evolution of the body – from bacteria to humans – and sex – from unicellular to multicellular sex. The composition of the organic machines of sex entails the micro-organization of molecules and compounds (of modes of information transfer) leading to the emer- gence of the multicellular body, sex and reproduction.

The biophysical stratification of sex entails an ecosystem of molecular aggregation of bodies. It thus departs from the zoocentrism of evolu- tion (based on species) or Darwinian and neo-Darwinian evolution where the law of the fittest (the best adapted individual to an external environment) determines progress and ensures survival through rampant competition. As opposed to Darwinian and neo-Darwinian evolution that defines natural selection as the hand of God able to order nature by exterminating non-adapted species or genes, the process of stratification exposes the autonomous emergence of networked relations between codes and milieus, where selective pres- sures act upon molecular particle-flows able to engender new aggregations. The biophysical order of matter is not dictated by a transcendent force of abolition, but emerges autonomously out of collective assemblages where particle-forces collide at the edge of chaos. Such assemblages constitute a multicellular body as a multiplicity of microbodies defining the bacterial composition of new modes of information transfer. The understanding of this composition is indebted to Lynn Margulis's theory of endosymbiosis that suggests a rhizomatic conception of the evolution of sex proceeding by contagion rather than filiation.

From this standpoint, the multicellular body, evolved by the acquisition of inherited bacterial symbionts, generates a new molecular distribution of substances and forms of content and expression, new genetic and cellular processes such as mitosis and meiosis. These processes produce new patterns of sex and reproduction such as the meiotic machine of sexual reproduction: the doubling and reduction of chromosomes, the entanglement of reproduction with sex (heterosexual mating), and the genetic specificity of multicellular sex. The endosymbiosis of cellular reproduction presents a continual variation of microbial activities of contagion that are not replaced by molar aggregates – the eukaryotic cell and meiotic sex – but expand upon new levels of organic stratification.

The third chapter discusses the anthropomorphic agglomerate of strata defining the biocultural order of matter. The machinic organization of this order entails a leap of intensity between the organic stratification of sex and socio-cultural and politico-economical organizations of the body. On these strata the multicellular body becomes a convector of the new bio-social machines of sex and reproduction. The leap from the organic to the biocultural levels of stratification corresponds to the process of overcodification that Deleuze and Guattari explain as a translation on a new level of organization (1987). Overcodification involves a transduction (viral conversion or mutation) of the organic patterns of multicellular communication and reproduction – meiotic sex – on the biocultural level, spreading the biophysical entanglement between sex, reproduction and death (meiotic sex) across social and economic spheres. This diffusion is not primarily determinate by the scientific and cultural discourses of modernity.[18] Rather, it deploys the impact of the organic stratum on the biocultural order of the body—sex exposed by the entropy of equilibrium, the evolutionary variations of populations, technical reproduction, the anatomical and psychoanalytical integration of sex and death. Such an impact defines the complexity of the biocultural strata able to affect social and economic organizations by being affected by the organic entanglement between sex, reproduction and death (meiotic sex) enveloped within the body.

Rather than analysing the disciplinary discourses on sex, excluding the non-discursive relations between bodies (human body, social body, capital body, technological body), this chapter will highlight the biocultural constitution of new machinic assemblages of desire–power that define, as Foucault also argues, the sadist eroticism of disciplinary society. In particular, Foucault refers to the sadist obsession of disciplining sexual behaviour through the proliferation of deviancies in all spheres of organization – from the architecture of institutions to the rules in the family house, at school, the factory, the army etc. Yet, this sadist machine of sex governed by the entanglement between sex and death only defines one of the aggregates of desire–power or machines of sex that constitute the multifaceted layers of the biocultural stratum.

The machinic assemblage between the physics of thermodynamics, the biology of variation in evolutionary theory, the inorganic reproduction of industrial machines and the psychoanalytical and anatomical study of sex, maps a double process of overcodification and decodification of the entanglement between sex, reproduction and death deployed by the organic stratum. The entropic relation between energy–information (more energy, less information and vice versa) defines the model of pleasure and sexual reproduction through the tendency towards inorganic death and the transmission of information or life. The disciplinary horror and fascination with compulsive death (localized in the woman's pathologies of sex and sexual reproduction) does not only spread the overcodification of sex (the order of meiotic sex), but also introduces a decodification of desire unleashing an altogether different kind of sex and reproduction, masochism or parthenogenesis. The disciplinary obsession with regulating excessive flows, normalizing sexual behaviour and correcting perversions is of a different order of desire compared to masochist parthenogenesis. The last, as Deleuze argues, rejects the law of the phallus and sexual filiation, the identification of sex with genitality (1989a). Insofar as sadism defines the disciplinary biopower of the body–sex, masochism exposes the composition of a non-genital desire independent of disciplinary processes of reproduction and filiation: flows escaping stability, energy running towards dissipation, species mutations, instruments and machines of reproduction (producing new audio-visual perception).[19]

The biocultural bifurcation between distinct machinic assemblages of sex (sadist and masochist) highlights the primacy of a non-discursive (affective) transformation of sex expanding through all spheres of disciplinary society – cultural, economical, political. On the one hand, the sadist disciplines of sexual filiation (psychoanalysis and anatomy) distribute the entropic entanglement between pleasure and death through all aspects of reproduction of a body. On the other, the masochist machines of parthenogenesis – ante-posing variations to linear repetition – entangle non-filiative sex with inorganic reproduction beyond the entropic principle of pleasure. The impact of entropic dynamics of equilibrium on the reproduction of information introduces a new perception and conception of the body–sex on the biocultural stratum where the mutations of desire exceed the discursive representations of sex.

The fourth chapter discusses the emergence of a new level of order able to double-fold the biophysical and biocultural machines of sex through the technical capitalist recombination of information (the biodigital order of sex). The capacity to accelerate the time and space of reproduction and communication on an increasingly molecular scale suggests a transformation of the organic and disciplinary machines of sex. No longer do sexual reproduction and the sexed body determine the model of reproduction and communication of energy–information. The biodigital order does not rely on the extraction of surplus value of codes and the suppression of fluid forces, but on the recombination of excessive flows, modulating their microvariations into fluxes – laminar flows.

The passage from the biocultural to the biodigital stratum does not mark an arbitrary break between self-contained systems of stratification. This passage is a threshold of connection between one stratum and another entailing the intensification of biophysical and biocultural machines of sex. This threshold is not determined by technological developments, but by new machinic assemblages of modes of communication and reproduction – from the Internet to virtual reality, from cloning images to cloning humans – that are rapidly changing the conception and perception of sex.

Bio-informatic capitalism, thus, marks the threshold towards a new recombination of information transmission: the engineering of all useless flows at far from equilibrium conditions producing unprecedented forms of capitalization. Rather than repressing the capacity of a body–sex to reproduce, the biodigital order commercializes the unpredictable (the virtual and not the possible) power of mutations marking a new bifurcation between the molecular control of sexual reproduction and the molecular proliferation of bacterial sex.

If post-industrial capitalism is constituted by decodified flows (flows of money, culture, populations, information) then the recent investments in the mechanics of fluids and the chaos of turbulence is key to grasp the mutations of sex and reproduction. According to Deleuze, the disappearance of disciplinary walls has not dissipated bio-disciplinary power, but has extended its effects onto the microscales of the body–culture, body–politics and body–desire. The post-disciplinary organization of sex and reproduction entails a Superfold that modulates the smooth space of information flows, multiplying the channels for information transmission (transgenetic sex, bacterial and viral sex, cloning and so on).[20] Short-term investments in molecular information outside the logic of linear reproduction enable bio-informatic capital to overcome the limits of death, turning organic finitude into indefinite recombination. No longer is it necessary to exorcise death through reproductive procreation. Death has been extended to unprecedented reproductions: cellular and embryonic cloning, artificial life, sperm, egg, embryo, organ and cell banking constitute the new scenario of a ribosomal capitalist culture.[21] Genetic engineering and cybercommunication are the new channels of capitalization that connect turbulent flows of information to flows of money. In particular, the cyber-economic investments in the molecular level of the egg cell expose the commercial parthenogenesis of bio-informatic capitalism able to re-engineer reproduction through the cloning and patenting of genes and cells. This recombination of indifferent bodies (a human body, a bacterium, an animal and a technical machine) extends the diffusion of unpredictable mutations of sex and reproduction. Bio-informatic capitalism ceaselessly selects variable mutations of information. This selection is neither conservative nor transcendent, but immanent to molecular variations. It operates like a sieve whose variable meshes fish in the molecular reservoirs of a body, intensifying its indeterminate capacities to transmit, receive and recombine information producing new channels of capitalization. But mutations of information are neither calculable nor controllable. They emerge and proliferate without warning.

The collision of different layers of stratification of sex in the biodigital stratum induces a virtualization (an intensive expansion) rather than a disappearance of biophysical and biocultural machines of stratification. From bacterial trades to nucleic exchange from sexual reproduction to genetic engineering, from the sexed body to recombinant sex, the essence of the body comes to correspond to a mutating difference. This body–sex is composed of the symbiotic relations between

26

parallel levels of order (biophysical, biocultural and biodigital). It is a mutating or abstract essence exposing a continuum between the micro and the macro machines of organization of sex and reproduction.[22] By drawing on Deleuze and Guattari and Baruch Spinoza, the following sections elaborate on the concept of abstract essence, the immanent relations between nature and the body that point to the mutant essence of feminine sex discussed in more detail in the fifth chapter.

THE ESSENCE OF A BODY

Extension exists when one element is stretched over the following ones, such that it is a whole and the following elements are its parts. Such a connection of whole–parts forms an infinite series that contains neither a final term nor a limit.

Deleuze (1993: 77)

Essences, do not in turn form a unity or totality: one might say rather that a universe corresponds to each, not communicating with the others, affirming an irreducible difference as profound as that of the astronomic worlds.

Deleuze (1972: 143)

The process of stratification suggests that the materiality of a body–sex is defined neither by a given essence nor by socio-cultural conditions. A body is composed and decomposed by the activity of molecules and particles, forces and energies. It is not simply biological or cultural. A body is defined by metastable relations between microcellular and multicellular bodies, the bodies of animals and humans, the bodies of society and technological bodies merging and unleashing new mutating compositions (differential difference). Deleuze and Guattari suggest that a body arises from the collision of pre-individual particle-forces or collectivities. These are not the properties of the transcendent Being creating extended bodies while remaining itself un-extended. Rather, they are themselves bodies constituting an intensive matrix of singular actualizations. Every actualization entails a prior metastable state, 'the existence of a "disparateness" such as at least two orders of magnitude or two scales of heterogeneous reality between which potentials are distributed' (Simondon 1992: 246).

The distribution of potentials entails a continuum (intensive degree of power) between pre-individual and individual bodies where the actual (extensive) mutations of a body are entangled with the mutations of pre-individual (intensive) bodies. Actualizations unfold the differential degrees of power (intensive potentia) of a body, a genetic body, a cellular body, a multicellular body, a social body, a cultural body and a cloned body. Rather than to a predeterminate cause, these bodies are linked to 'quasi or meta causes' unfolding the capacity of a body to enter a new composition by precluding the body to acquire definite forms and functions.[23] This preclusion does not suggest that the power of a body is relative as established by the logic of identity absorbing all potentials into predeterminate power. The power of a body is not exhausted by the power of existing but is connected to an intensive body that is productive (produces new bodies) and comprehensive (comprehends of all that is produced).

The postmodern challenge to the essentialist tradition (Platonic, Aristotelian and Cartesian) has generated a negative relativism of the body that eliminates (negates) potentials by detaching causes from effects. Hence, the power of a body is defined by socio-cultural and economic structures and post-structures of signification opened to the relativism of interpretation. The elimination of a given cause is reiterated by already given effects (universal signifiers). The emphasis is different but the method is identical as it imposes the disqualification of the potential capacities of a body to mutate without being subsumed to a transcendent power (Ideas, God or signifiers). The postmodern analysis of the body as no longer shaped by modern technoscientific discourses (organic biology and evolution of the species), fails to explain the biodigital mutations of sex involving intensive–extensive variations rather than a shift from one discourse about the body to another.

In order to analyse these mutations without dismissing the potential of the body, it is necessary to apply an ontology of co-causal relations (non-linear feedback between causes and effects) rather than reiterating a given unity. These relations will enable us to map the mutations of a body–sex through the plasticity of material signs rather than signification, singularity rather than specificity, abstraction rather than generalities. This ontology requires the elaboration of *abstract materialism* (a symbiotic and multifaceted matter) as a method that unpacks the connecting layers of composition of a body: the continual variations of matter. Abstract materialism does not involve the analogy between the general (ideal) and the particular (individual) body or between pluralistic (many) and specific (one) categories of the body defined by the principles of identity (analogy between inert nature and body). Quite the contrary, this method produces a map of the non-linear movements of connection between causes and effects unfolding the potential (force) of a body to mutate through an ecosystem of indefinite mixtures. Abstract materialism entails the symbiotic networks between the most disparate bodies where singular layers of composition constitute a mutating essence of a body. As opposed to biologism, organicism or existentialism, this essence is linked to the far-from-equilibrium dynamics of matter: the emergence of unpredictable mutations generating from the auto-assemblage of diverse bodies.

Abstract materialism expands upon Baruch Spinoza's ethological study of a body. This body is not primarily an organism or an organization. It is an immanent assemblage of kinetic particles and anonymous forces, motion and energy that constitute every body: a bacterial body, a eukaryotic body, a multicellular body, a cultural body, the body of machines, etc. . . . A body is primarily defined by associations and splittings of particles and forces defining its immanent trajectories of transformation: longitudinal and latitudinal lines intersecting at every point.[24] This is not a Cartesian axis. These lines are the attributes of a matter-matrix whose longitudinal extensive parts fall under a relation of motion and rest (kinetics) and whose latitudinal intensive parts fall under a capacity to affect and be affected (intensity). The latitude of a body corresponds to the affects of which a body is capable at a given degree of velocity. The longitude of a body includes the extension of matter, the composition of particles, their kinetic pace.

According to Descartes a body is not capable of thinking. The body is extension. The mind pertains to the divine un-extended substance that is transcendent to the body–nature–matter. This substance is a God invested with the power of a tyrant (potestas) that masters the body, setting order in nature through the taxonomic organization of the body in species, classes, sexes. This God is external to nature. It creates bodies but it is not composed of bodies. It does not comprehend the mutations of a body because it is of another world, the spiritual world without matter opposing the active mind to the passive body. This God is imbued with an exterior power of selection that determines the essence of a body according to the capacity of the mind to transcend the world of bodily passions, the chaotic and contaminated world of nature. Hence essence is measured through the mental power to disembody from matter that distinguishes the animal from the human body and constrains the reproductive body (the female body) to a lower degree of power determined by its dependency on matter.

Spinoza explains that the Cartesian conception of un-extended substance is rooted in the Judaeo-Christian moralist God, detaching nature from cosmos by negating the participation of God in nature and of extended bodies in God. In particular, Spinoza points out that God (Substance or The Thing) has any mastering power (potestas) according to which God corresponds to an immutable and eternal essence that puts order in nature through the control of the mind on the body. Spinoza argues that God has no potestas but only potentia corresponding to an indeterminate power to produce and be produced by bodies.

This God is inseparable from nature (Ethics I, D. 3). Not only is it extended, but also its power (potentia) coincides with the extension of nature. This is a continuum rather than a dualism: a 'machinic phylum' of matrices and bodies without transcendent control or mastering.[25] Rather than an external cause detached from effects, Spinoza's substance is immanent to all that exists in nature.[26] Nature is composed of two parallel processes: Natura Naturans and Natura Naturata (Ethics, I, 29, Schol.). Nature is a dynamical and collective ecosystem of intensive and extensive bodies – growth. Natura Naturans indicates the activity of nature, the intensive capacity to produce. Natura Naturata implies the passivity of being produced. Nature exposes the coexistence of the process of producing while being produced where an infinity of attributes (expressing a multiplicity of essence or potential qualities that are not identical to God) unfolds a unity without equivalence (continuum) between the essence of substance and the essence of modes.[27]

For Spinoza, of the infinity of these attributes we know only two that constitute our essence, thought and extension. The mind, a mode of thinking and the body, a mode of extension. Between these two attributes there is neither separation nor reduction, but a strict parallelism or connection affirming that 'God's power of thinking is equal to his realized power of action' (Ethics II, 7, Corollary). For Spinoza, all power is inseparable from a capacity to affect (potentia) and a capacity of being affected constituting the mutating essence of substance corresponding to the essence of modes (affections of a substance).[28]

All modes are thus constituted by a mode of thinking and extension, mind and body involving dynamics of affect and velocities of composition between particle-forces: the molecules composing a microbe, the microbes composing a human, the populations of cultures composing a society are all modes of an engineering nature. The essence of modes defines a degree of power, a modification of

the indefinite capacity to think and to extend constituting the potential extension of God in nature. Being a physical intensity and not a
possibility, this modal essence does not dissolve itself into existence,
but preserves potentia in existence by expanding through an infinity
of extensive parts (from bacterial to eukaryotic cells from multicellular to bio-technological bodies) falling under relations of affect: the
capacity of a human body to be affected by a viral population. Once
essence (potentia) passes into existence to become a modal essence
then it is defined as conatus or appetite (Ethics, III, 7) as intensive
power tends to persevere by enduring and maximizing its capacity to
be affected by other existing modes. Bacterial endosymbiosis is a good
example of a mode of sex and reproduction persevering in existence
by increasing the capacity to be affected by other modes (atmospheric
pressures, viruses and eukaryotic cells) that have also increased its
capacity to expand its dynamics of information transmission through
mutations.

Spinoza distinguishes between pure modal essences, which are all
compatible as intensive degrees of the power of Substance, and the
conatus of an existing mode, whose extensive parts are combined in
relation to its intrinsic essence or degrees of power.[29] The direct
agreement among pure modal essences does not coincide with the
power relations among extensive modes. Here, in fact, essence turns
into conatus, the preservation of physical intensity in existence that
can always induce the parts of another mode to enter a new relation of
affect. Affects entail the colliding of particle-forces delineating the
impact of one body on another: the passion of the body–mind, the
capacity to feel before subjective emotion.[30] For example, the impact
of a poison on a human body entails the production of 'common
notions' between disparate bodies:[31] their immediate commonality of
extension provokes a reaction of the human body against the poison
increasing or decreasing the power (conatus) of this body to absorb or
expel the poison, which may or may not produce a mutation.

Spinoza argues that the preservation of conatus (the intensive essence
of an existing mode) depends on the capacity of a body to be affected
and to organize encounters among extended modes that increase its
capacity to affect (to explicate potentia through mutations). For this
reason, we do not yet know what a body can do, what are the affects
of a singular composition, how can these affects enter in a new composition with the affects of another body, either to destroy or to be
destroyed by it or to produce a more powerful body. In other words,
a body is never to be considered as a unity in isolation. It is never one

individual but a collective power: conatus. It always emerges out of infinite sets of affects entering into relation of movement or rest, turmoil or stationary state. As Deleuze underlines, conatus conveys 'an affirmative conception of essence: the degree of power as an affirmation of essence in God; the *conatus* as an affirmation of essence in existence' (1988c: 102). Conatus defines an abstract essence spreading through non-linear relations between intensive and extensive modes where not only can a body not be separated from the mind but also all extended bodies from God (potential affect). This essence exposes a machinic composition of a mode, whose power relies upon a continual colliding with other modes marking new degrees of mutation of a given assemblage. In this sense, the impact of bio-technologies on the body unfolds a series of micro affects between singular modes or machines of sex and reproduction (bacterial sex and human sex) merging to produce a new body while destroying another. This impact defines a new relationship between the biophysical and the biodigital machines of sex where a mutating essence (intensive and extended) suggests a new conception of feminine sex.

MICROFEMININE PARTICLE-FORCES

We oppose epidemic to filiation, contagion to heredity, peopling by contagion to sexual reproduction, sexual production. Bands, human or animal, proliferate by contagion, epidemics, battlefields, and catastrophes. Like hybrids, which are themselves sterile, born of a sexual union that will not reproduce itself, but which begins over again every time, gaining that much ground. Unnatural participations or nuptials are the true Nature spanning the kingdoms of nature.

Deleuze and Guattari (1987: 241)

Desire is not in the subject, but the machine in desire – with the residual subject off to the side, alongside the machine, around the entire periphery, a parasite of machines, an accessory of vertebromachinate desire.

Deleuze and Guattari (1983: 285)

[. . .] all elements are contained in all things and pervade everything: since not only is meat a constituent of bread, but bread of vegetables; and all other bodies also, by means of certain invisible pas-

sages and particles, find their way in and unite with all substances in
the form of vapor.

Diogenes in Deleuze (1990a: 130)

The feminist critique of the economy of representation has questioned
the identification of sexual difference with sexual reproduction, the
analogy between biology and culture. This identification assigns sexual
difference to a negative regime of presence and absence, full and void,
abundance and lack. In her work, Luce Irigaray questions the economy
of representation founded on the transcendent conception of matter
and the binarism of sex.[32] In her re-conceptualization of femininity,
sex is not determined by the biological form and function of sexual
organs, but becomes a fluid dimension of a matter–matrix that is
autonomous from the law of filiation. In 'The Mechanics of Fluids'
(1985b), Irigaray challenges the identification of femininity with inert
matter, matter with passive constancy and feminine desire with the
death drive. Femininity is disentangled from the binary system of
equivalence between the sexes dictated by the transcendence of the
symbolic phallus. Feminine desire becomes uncoupled from the sexed
organism, the phallic mother and hysteric woman, the passive receptacle
of reproduction where desire is reduced to the pleasure of discharge,
sex to genitality and (collective) affect to (individual) emotion.

Irigaray opposes the Freudian theory of entropic pleasure to multidirectional flows escaping the constancy of reproduction and exposing
the turbo-dynamics of a matter–matrix, a feminine sex outside all
claims of identity. Fluid dynamics defines a body not by its achieved
forms and functions (identity) but by its processes of composition and
transformation that exhibit the metamorphosis of fluids able to acquire
any shape. This metamorphic body–sex is not regulated by the cycle of
accumulation and discharge, but displays a ceaseless flow of desire that
leaks out of genitality and genealogy. Irigaray provides a non-transcendent conception of sexual difference that emerges from a 'matter/
mater/matrix continuum', the fluid embodiment of difference irreducible to the representation of 'women's experience'. For Irigaray,
experience does not belong to identities. Experience is always in
motion and entails a mutation of femininity. Nothing remains the same
on the fluid scale of matter. Femininity stops being represented to
expose the hydrodynamics of desire running parallel to a body without
contour; a sex without organs. Irigaray's fluid conception of sex and
femininity refutes the essentialist tradition of ideas and forms shaping
matter and anticipates some of the novelties of cyberfeminism encom-

33

passing the relationship between femininity and machines of reproduction and communication.

For recent feminist cultural theorists, the tradition of essentialism also constitutes the ultimate spectre of the metaphysical belief in nature as a space of unity and integration, serving as a model to culture and to the politics of difference. Donna Haraway's 'Cyborg Manifesto' (1985;1991), explicitly rejects the unity of the body, the metaphysical bliss of nature, the essential truth of femininity. Careful in exploring the new sets of power in the cybernetic age, Haraway does not hesitate to emphazise the deviations that the cyborg offers to the linearity of reproduction and sameness.[33] Haraway's cyborg expresses antipathy for Marxist idealism and for the claustrophobic triangle of identification rooted in the Oedipal complex. The cyborg shows no nostalgia for the model of exchange and reproduction, reality and pleasure. It embraces the crisis of the ontology of the self and other as an opportunity to become something else in feedback loops of information codes. Contrary to Baudrillard, Haraway realizes that the automation of genetic codes does not simply limit the body to self-reproduction and sex to autoeroticism.[34] The flow of codes traversing a body no longer defines the essence of form and the aims of sexual organic functions. Rather, it puts into contact a body with another body alongside non-linear transmission of information. With cybernetics, as Haraway puts it: '[b]iological organisms have become biotic systems, communication devices like others' (1991: 177–8).

The identification of women with nature, stemming from ideals of creation, motherhood, emotion and spontaneity, and opposed to the artifice and rationality of men, has for too long colonized the understanding of sexual difference, providing a symbolic model for gender. The overcoming of this dualism is crucial to Haraway's work on technoscience and the body. As a biologist and cultural theorist, Haraway contests the realms of nature and culture and the ontological evolution of the species where sex and reproduction are rooted in the humanist stories of competition, scarcity, balance and variation. Her work challenges the patrilinear system of evolution with descent embedded in colonialism and capitalism, refuting the ontological metaphysics of the one and the multiple. The historical project of humanism starts with the constitution of gender and sex as objects of study, the reproduction of the problem of genesis and origin (1991: 78). Thus, for feminism, an unproblematic re-proposal of the sex/gender dualism, a sterile analysis of the representation of nature and

culture only reinforces the structures of separation and negative oppositions at the core of the Western metaphysics of essence.

There is no innocent shelter for women to return to. Haraway
argues that the scientific association of sex with reproduction is central
to the ontology of the modern subject. Since the eighteenth century,
sex appears as 'the principle of increase (vitality) in biological stories'
where 'biology has been a discourse about productive systems, or,
better, modes of production' (1991: 106). The hylomorphic recapitu-
lation of the genesis of humanity, through the study of primates, indicates the main task of modern or disciplinary evolutionary science. In
modernity, the sex-reproduction association produces the body in the
form of the organism, the whole constituted of predetermined parts.
This organism establishes a model for modern bio-politics, the incarna-
tion of the transcendent Self/I into an already given body.

Although aware that the biological conception of sex is reduced to
linear reproduction, Haraway does not dismiss sex in favour of gender
but focuses on 'theories of embodiment where nature is no longer
imagined and enacted as resource to culture or sex to gender'(148). In
order to intervene against the nature/culture, sex/gender split, the
metaphysical re-birth of the One is here questioned through an
ontology of regeneration and integration of differences. This ontological model draws on the semiotics of cybernetics, immunology and
genetics that arrange phenomena of incorporation through flexible
boundaries of exclusion, opposition, access and resistance.

The refusal of totalizing doctrines for a feminist body politics parti-
cularly invests the question of difference and the necessary heterogeneity embodied by the cyborg. This is a body, which synthesizes the
morphologies of matter and the dynamics of discursive power, re-
processes the nature/culture, sex/gender splits according to non-
hierarchical patterns. The cyborg proposes a post-gender body politics
of transversal coalitions and alliances, emerging out of affinities, rather
than identities, among bodies as a 'poetic/political unity without
relying on a logic of appropriation, incorporation, and taxonomic identification' (1991: 157).[35] Animal, human and machine are the forms
that the post-gender cyborg contains in the most unrecognizable
fashion.

Although crucial for the cultural study of technoscience, the narra-
tives of the cyborg preclude an engagement with the processes of
mutation of a body–sex linked to the metaphysics of nature since
Epicurean atomism and Lucretius's notion of the *clinamen*, discussed in
On the Nature of the Universe. Lucretius rejects the mechanistic law of

cause and effect implying a passive view of the body-nature, determined by a transcendent power. Epicurean philosophy affirms that everything that exists is made up of matter and empty space. Matter is composed of tiny invisible and indivisible elements called 'atoms' (in Greek 'indivisible') which are the building blocks of everything that we see around us, including our bodies. For Lucretius, atoms are always flying off the surface of objects and forming fresh compounds. They descend at the same speed, swerving occasionally from the straight vertical path to one side or the other, and thus they collide. There is no causal explanation for this swerve. It is indeterminate, as is the emergence of a vortex. The unpredictable behaviour of molecular particles composing complex systems — atmospheric, biological, physical as well as social, cultural and political — has been recently studied by quantum mechanics where quanta are an infinitesimal quantity that escapes exact measures. Lucretius called the indeterminable swerve of atoms the *clinamen* or declination. Chaos theory will call it turbulence.[36]

By dismissing the conception of nature as always already constructed according to the metaphysics of the given, the post-gender world of the cyborg excludes a more productive engagement with the material politics of a body–sex proposed by Irigaray's early work. The cyborg re-inscribes on the body the identity questions about feminine embodiment and disembodiment, experience and actualization opposing without radically challenging Cartesian metaphysics. Far from representing nature, the digital impact on nature exposes the way the hypernatural has taken the place of the supernatural. No longer the battle between extension and intensity, cause and effects, mind and body, god and things. Hypernature envelops and is enveloped by all bodies of communication and reproduction exposing a machinic phylum of unnatural associations. Hypernature expands on and is expanded by modes of connection and recombination of information. As discussed in the last chapter, this network of bodies connects the biophysical and the biodigital groups of strata unfolding the machines of destratification of sex cutting across the parallel levels of material order previously analysed. These machines emerge from an immanent plane of nature — hypernature — as the composition of free intensities, molecular populations of flows that are autonomous yet coexistent with the processes of organization of matter constituting the biophysical, biocultural and biodigital strata.

Machines of destratification are then engineering component pieces of hypernature that produces while it is produced by abstracting molecular forces and distributing capacities of differentiation. Hypernature is not pre-programmed and is not produced by simulations. It is not more natural than nature as it never starts from the knowledge of nature, the primacy of representation over the processes of intensive conjunction between material flows and bodies. Hypernature subtracts nature from the transcendence of the material and the ideal, unfolding a machinic essence of a body–sex composed of intensive relations between the most disparate modes of communication and reproduction. The biodigital reconfiguration of the body partakes of a hypernatural plane, where particles, and not parts, recombine, where forces, and not categories, clash. Such a reconfiguration poses new problems for the conception of feminine sex and the politics of difference. How can feminine sex be disentangled from the sex/gender problem of embodiment and disembodiment? How does the politics of desire operate in this newly defined artificial nature or hypernature?

Spinoza's ethology of nature provides a new route to engage with these problems. For example, the pragmatics of affect is a pragmatics of desire whose tendencies of composition are induced by encounters between the most different modes. This desire is machinic as it entails the association of heterogeneous particle-forces running at different speeds and entering different kinds of relations. Far from being primarily repressed, desire ceaselessly flows and produces modes of power that are neither primarily good nor bad. Modes are ethical dimensions of an engineering substance whose intensive bodies extend through kinetic and affective encounters between non-identical particles. These encounters define the capacity of an always collective body to increase or decrease its capacity to act, its power to become.[37] Spinoza's ethics suggests that the relation between substance and modes is primarily productive as it is also produced – and transformed – by new assembling modifications. Essence is no longer relegated to the transcendent morality of depth and a priority, but is produced by an immanent relation between the explication of intensities and the construction of encounters between bodies.

Insofar as desire involves positive productions and joyful encounters constituting a phylum of relations between substance and modes, Spinoza's ethics also includes sadness and poison as ethical dimensions. The difference is that these are merely reactive responses to the desire of encounters. In this sense, fascistic desire is a dimension of desire, a reactive dimension in the incessant flow of production where desire lends itself to the production of death. The latter creates a blockage of flows, the dread of being engulfed by holes of nothingness, the transcendence of lack and scarcity, the paranoiac or hypochondriac desires that block flows by abolishing lines of flight in favour of secure shelters. Yet reactions and suppressions are not primary but emerge from the encounter with actions and productions, the actual impact of potentia, the far from equilibrium circuits of a virtual-actual becoming. The Spinozian explanation for sadness and evil corresponds to a biophysical reaction to poison spreading from encounters between chemically altered bodies or from the molar aggregation of molecules able to diffuse a micro-fascism that expands on the most minute dynamics of order.

Spinoza defines desire as appetite (*appetitus*) 'accompanied by the consciousness thereof': the awareness of a passage, information of the state of the affection of the body. The causes pass quickly while the effects are amplified on the body to mark the passage. It is not that we are not aware of what we desire. Awareness mainly involves information of the state of a body whereas desire exposes an incessant appetite '[W]e do not endeavor, will, seek after or desire because we judge a thing to be good. On the contrary, we judge a thing to be good because we endeavor, will, seek after and desire it' (*Ethics*, III, 9, scholium). Desire should never be subjectivized. It is always already part of a composition, a machinic assemblage, the encounter and the collision of particles and forces. The subject is an appendix to the machine in desire, an accessory that does not determine ethical relations but only positions of will. Desire is detracted from individual pleasure and climactic purposes to become part of a machine in production: an endosymbiotic multiplicity.

On the Spinozian immanent plane of nature, essence becomes an intensive modification of substance, the proliferation of a joyful desire that changes through the encounters with other modifications or modes. The emergence of a singular mode defines the preservation of essence in existence, the intensive extension of potential – or conatus. The essence of a body is not defined by its properties but by its power to connect or not with other bodies, to assemble to create a more powerful body, to merge to increase or decrease potential. Such an intensive essence maps a multiplicity of levels of transmission that operate at parallel times and spaces and construct new modes of connection. These modifications indicate a molecular nature upon which strata organize and single out sexual orders of reproduction and communication.

The process of stratification of sex enfolds molecular bodies that produce the sexed body by entangling sex with sexual reproduction. If feminine desire has been confined to biological sex, then the process of stratification unpacks the singular potential of desire, the variation of modes of connection and transmission. The biology of sex does not determine modes of connections 'in which form is constantly being dissolved, freeing times and speeds' (Deleuze and Guattari 1987: 267). Sex is disentangled from genital sex and sexual reproduction, the symbolic representation of sexual difference. Sex is abstracted from the already sexed body to proliferate through infective transmission, molecular contacts. Sex no longer individuates the body but becomes a machinic construction of a multiplicity of modes of information transmission. Sex is *transductive*: it webs bodies of all sorts, exposing the power or desire of a body to become in a network of matrices.

Femininity no longer remains specific to one mode of sex. It is not localized in one body or another, in one composition or another. It is not an identity, an individual unity. Feminine desire can only be defined by a pack of relations where microfeminine particle-forces spread at every kinetic and affective encounter.[38] These relations produce a micropolitics of becoming where particle-forces combine or disintegrate, activate or react against new encounters. These relations enable the construction of a molecular ethics of affect that flees away from the politics of representation. The latter congeals the micro-changes of relations into one structural aggregate that is erected as a delegate of multiplicity. Macropolitics will always ask femininity to represent the subject woman and biological sex to represent desire. Yet molecular dynamics of power are not subsumed to their molar organization, but remain consistent with their effects. Micropolitics ceaselessly breaks through despotic aggregates with incorporeal lines of differentiation. Lines of flight, as Deleuze and Guattari argue, are not reactive to molar or macro organizations. Rather they are leaking flows that are prior to and independent of structures of organization. Organizations emerge from flowing flows and not the other way around. Macropolitics only corresponds to one of the levels of organization of micropolitical compositions of desire–power that affect – and transform – the very constitution of macropolitical projects.

Micropolitics, then, involves the becoming-molecular of femininity, the consistent – synthetic – production of machinic desire that destratifies (swerves from) the Oedipal woman, organic sex and filiative reproduction by constructing a collective body–sex, letting desire run parallel in all dimensions of communication and reproduction without isolating sex from the rest. The construction of a microfeminine desire is not exclusively addressed to women. This is a micropolitics that diffuses beneath the binarism of masculinity and femininity to traverse all compositions and proliferate in all spheres: biophysical, socio-cultural, politico-economic, techno-scientific. Deleuze and Guattari also define this micropolitics as involving the construction of 'molecular sexes' or 'n-1 sexes' at each encounter of bodies: the intensive expansion of desiring flows reaching critical phases of mutations by composing and decomposing assemblages between the most unnatural bodies.

Far from being a spontaneous force, microfeminine particle-forces emerge from non-linear relations between the potential and the actual desire–power of essence involving singular modifications of reproduction and communication in the process of stratification of sex. Each stratum lays out the micropolitics of composition and decomposition of particle-forces involving the emergence of new bodies of transmission.[39] The next chapter, for example, will discuss the biophysical level of stratification of sex, the micropolitical relations between molecular particles and compounds, cellular and multicellular bodies that have determined the entanglement of sex with reproduction. On this stratum the micropolitics of cellular mergings exposes microfeminine particle-forces fleeing from the meiotic order of sex and producing unprecedented implications for the conception and perception of femininity on the biocultural (disciplinary society) and biodigital (control society) strata. This emission of feminine particle-forces suggests a micropolitics of passions and actions of a body–mind that is not ready made, but needs to be decrypted and constructed.

The following strata-analysis of sex is not exclusively interested in what blocks desire and what encloses femininity in identity, the signifier of lack in desire. Quite the contrary, it maps microfeminine lines spreading through the machinic compositions of bodies. These compositions are viral and proliferate by contamination rather than linear filiation. They unfold a process of becoming and not positioning. On the micro-dimensions of power, becoming involves the mixture of a population of bodies able to produce more powerful assemblages or to disintegrate and create new ones. It is a process of engineering proximities by desire, passions and actions of a body–mind immersed in the appetites of particle-forces running through genetic strings and cellular bodies, multicellular organisms and biodigital assemblages. This may seem as a new anthropomorphism of the body – the extension of a cultural conception of femininity onto the unknown – the interpretation of random matter. Yet the relation between micro-feminine desire and matter diverges from the post-feminist relativism of difference, where the politics of desire is reduced to ready-made understanding of power and difference perpetuating the essentialist conception of a body–sex. Micropolitics requires the *engineering* of abstract sex (symbiotic desire) where bodies of connection are not determined by the identity of sex but by incorporeal mutations of desire or the machinic compositions of essence (difference).

Notes

1 D. J. Haraway argues that the convergence of biological and technological systems involves the emergence of a common language of codification produced by cybernetics. See Haraway 1991: 149–201; on the cyborg see also C. Hables Gray, (ed.) 1995; D. Bell and B. Kennedy (eds) 2000; G. Kirkup, L. Jones, K. Woodward, F. Hovenden (eds) 2000; M. Flagan and A. Booth (eds) 2002. See also the literature developed in feminist studies of science and technology. N. Tuana (ed.) 1989; A. Fausto-Sterling 1992; L. Birke 1986; R. Hubbard 1990; E. Fox Keller 1992; E. Fox Keller 1995; S. Harding 1991.

2 On the posthuman, see K. N. Hayles 1999.

3 On the dissolution of corporeality in cyberspace, see A. Balsamo 1996; A. R. Stone 1991; C. Springer 1995; S. Turkle 1995; J. Squires 1996: 194–216; R. Braidotti 1994.

4 For a recent insight in these debates see M. Flagan and A. Booth 2002; K. N. Hayles 1999. See also, S. Plant 1997, 1998, 2000.

5 Cyberfeminism has been influenced by Judith Butler's concept of 'gender performance'. See Butler 1990, 1993. Although I do not discuss Butler's concept of performativity, I will indirectly refer to this discursive understanding of sex.

6 See F. Guattari 1984: 73–81.

7 On the critique of the economy of representation and the metaphysical notion of essence, see G. Deleuze 1990a, 1994. On the critique of Plato's and Aristotle's essence in Deleuze, see M. DeLanda 2002. See also L. Irigaray 1985a.

8 On Spinozist ethology see G. Deleuze 1988c. See also M. Gatens 1996a: 162–87.

9 These questions will be discussed in relation to Spinoza's ethology of nature. Unlike the moralist and transcendent perspective, Spinoza's ethics proposes an immanent conception of nature. See Spinoza 1992.

10 The word 'virtual' is derived from the Medieval Latin *virtualis*, itself derived from *virtus*, meaning strength or power. In scholastic philosophy the virtual is that which has potential rather than actual existence. See H. Bergson 1991: 127–31; 210–11. See also G. Deleuze 1988a: 42–3, 55–62, 100–1.

11 See Deleuze 1990a: 4–11; 13–21; 23; 35; 12–22; 67–73; 52–7. See also M. Foucault 1977: 165–99; see also G. Deleuze and F. Guattari 1987: 80–3; 85–8; 107–9.

12 See L. Margulis 1981; see also J. Sapp 1994.

13 The distinction between molecular and molar is not a question of scale, but of

mode of composition involving quality rather than quantity – there are molarities of every magnitude as, for example, the nucleus of the atom. While molecular multiplicities define local connections between singular particles, molarities imply the aggregation of local singular particles already grouped and rigidified into a whole. See Deleuze and Guattari 1983: 89; 342–3; 1987: 208–31. See also B. Massumi 1992: 54–5.

14 See Guattari 1984: 148–50. See L. Hjelmslev 1969. On the importance of Hjelmslev's work for Deleuze and Guattari's schizoanalytic semiotics, see also D. Olkowski 1991: 285–305; B. Bosteels 1998: 145–74; G. Genosko 1998: 175–90.

15 See Deleuze and Guattari 1987: 44.

16 Gilbert Simondon applies the concept of transduction to the notion of information. Cybernetics (especially the homeostatic cybernetics of Norbert Wiener) still defines information through the essentialist conception of form (hylomorphism). Wiener associates information with signals or vehicles of information determining identities rather than transformations. Simondon, on the other hand, adopts physical and biological models to understand communication as involving the pre-individual existence of being, the unpredictable emergence of difference Simondon 1992: 296–19. See also F. Guattari 1995.

17 Far from equilibrium patterns of communication outline a continuum between biological and physical models where the dynamics of information involve an intensive process of transmission, a bifurcation towards novelty. See DeLanda 2002: 78–9. My study on information theory mainly stems from Deleuze and Guattari's adaptation of molecular biology and chaos theory. Through their work, I understand information as intensity constituting differential scales of communication and reproduction including the biophysical, biocultural and biodigital scale. I also draw on Simondon's conception of information as involving a pre-individual plane of potentials. The scientific and philosophical debate about information theory has recently shifted towards genetic computations (DNA computing) and a new cybernetics of biology and mathematics resulting in the Omega theory of randomness. See G. J. Chatin 1999. I reserve the study of these theories for future research.

18 Isabelle Stengers problematizes the epistemological study of techno-science defining science as homogeneous and a-historical. Science is not primarily an institution that reproduces dominant knowledge, science is a 'historical adventure in knowledge' marked by a 'chance-event' linking scientific with non-scientific procedures. See Stengers 1997.

19 In particular, anatomical perception is entangled to the impact of sexual morphologies on the scientific apparatus of observation. See M. Foucault 1994.

20 According to Deleuze, modulation involves a continual variation. This concept will be explained in Chapter 4. See Deleuze 1995a: 178–9; Deleuze and Guattari 1987: 482–8.

21 On cyberpunk, see D. Cavallaro 2000. Ribofunk maps the bio-technological imaginary born out of the ribosomal and protein chains of engineered cells. See P. di Filippo 1996.

22 On the notion of the abstract, see Deleuze and Guattari 1987: 497–8. See also W. Worringer 1963: 33, 42.
23 See Deleuze 1990a: 109, 117, 142–7.
24 See Spinoza 1992: III, Preface.
25 The machinic phylum delineates a pure continuum of material particles: 'matter in movement, in flux, in variation, matter as a conveyor of singularities and traits of expression. . . . this matter-flow can only be *followed*' (Deleuze and Guattari 1987: 408).
26 See Deleuze 1988c: 52, 109.
27 '[Essences] have no parts but are themselves parts, parts of power, like intensive quantities. They are all compatible with one another without limit, because all are included in the production of each one, but each one corresponds to a specific degree of power different from all the others' Deleuze 1988c: 65.
28 On the difference between modes, see Deleuze 1988c: 92.
29 See G. Deleuze 1990b: 183.
30 On the difference between emotion and affect, see B. Massumi 1996: 217–39.
31 On common notions, see Spinoza 1992, II, Prop. 37–40.
32 My hypothesis of microfeminine micropolitics connects the work of Irigaray with the work of Baruch Spinoza and Deleuze and Guattari. Yet, it is important to consider Irigaray's critical intervention against Spinoza's monism, and her critique of Deleuze and Guattari's ontology of becoming. See L. Irigaray 1993: 83–94; 1985b: 140–1. See also E. Grosz 1994: 160–83. It is important to point out that there is no analogy between Irigaray's and Deleuze–Guattari's works. Rather, there is a 'common' engagement against the philosophical, scientific and political tradition of representation and essentialism in Western culture.
33 I need to specify that the work of Irigaray and the work of Haraway quite differently address the issue of femininity and desire. Irigaray's early work engages with the material manifestation of femininity and female desire. Haraway's cyborg no longer recognizes desiring flows traversing the body. It is numb to matter, passion and sex. I bring together very few aspects of Irigaray's and Haraway's works as they both produce a critical intervention against essentialism moving towards two different directions. Irigaray's later works emphasizes the necessity to construct a new subject woman (1993). Haraway appears to rely on epistemological criticisms without exploring the ontological materiality of a body–sex and nature. Although crucial in feminist politics, both interventions risk reiterating the economy of representation to invalidate their political programmes. Although molar, institutional politics is not detached from material politics of organization of matter-sex-body, my intervention focuses on the importance of the molecular level of affect to expose the concept of femininity to a metaphysical immanence of matter.
34 See J. Baudrillard 1994a, 1994b.
35 Haraway argues: 'The cyborg is a creature in a post-gender world; it has no truck with bisexuality, pre-oedipal symbiosis, unalienated labour, or other seductions to organic wholeness through a final appropriation of all the powers of the parts

into a higher unity. In a sense, the cyborg has no origin story in the Western sense. . . . An origin story in the 'Western', humanist sense depends on the myth of original unity, fullness, bliss and terror, represented by the phallic mother from whom all humans must separate, the task of individual development and of history, the twin potent myths inscribed most powerfully for us in psychoanalysis and Marxism. . . . The cyborg skips the step of original unity, of identification with nature in the Western sense' Haraway 1991: 151.

36 I. Prigogine and I. Stengers 1984; I. Prigogine 1997.

37 On the immanent constituency of a collective body as an ethical–political pragmatics of action and intervention, see T. Negri 1991a.

38 Some questions might be asked about the notion of microfemininity, such as 'What is the relation between microfemininity and feminine desire?' 'Why is microfeminine desire important for women?' 'Doesn't the relation between hypernature and femininity risk re-essentializing the body?' I will address these questions in the conclusion.

39 Each stratum deploys a micropolitics of sex. The study of the biophysical stratification will point out the affects stemming from the organization of bacterial sex in meiotic sex and sexual reproduction. The analysis of the biocultural stratum will discuss the affects of the overcodified body or of disciplinary sex in relation to sex and death. The analysis of the biodigital stratum will consider the affects of decodification of organic sex and death. The final chapter will investigate the connection between the machines of destratification of sex unfolding the relations between nature and microfemininity.

CHAPTER 2

Symbiotic Sex

[. . .] every individual animal of every species is a whole composed of various parts – bones, blood, veins, heat, moisture, flesh, sinews: and these are all widely different, being formed of differently shaped atoms. Again, whatever can be set on fire and burnt must conceal in its body, if nothing else, at least the matter needed for emitting fire and radiating light, for shooting out sparks and scattering ashes all around. If you mentally examine anything else by similar procedure, you will find that it hides in its body the seeds of many substances and combines atoms of various forms.

Lucretius, *On the Nature of the Universe*, II, 668 (1994: 54).

Symbiotic bacteria and transfer virus – naturally occurring in all animals and specific for each species – are implanted with molecular memory transcribed from the intron. They exit the individual and pass on to another individual, 'infect', transfer the memory to somatic cells. Some of the memories are then returned to chemical storage status, and a few return to active memory. – Across generations? – Across millennia.

Bear (1985: 224–5)

INTRODUCTION

This chapter discusses the modes of reproduction that compose the biophysical order of sex.[1] In particular, it questions models of evolution, such as Darwinism and neo-Darwinism, that identify sex with sexual mating, sexual organs and sexed genes. These models conform to the hierarchical shape of the tree, where difference corresponds to gradual variations descending from the same pool. Sex remains a function of mating or the motor of preservation and production of variations that can be traced back to the same origin or source. The invisible hand of natural selection that exterminates ill-adapted organisms, the weaker

45

competitors for survival, guarantees the transmission of the fittest traits. These models, based on natural selection, scarcity, individual competition and gradual adaptation are at the core of the understanding of the organization of nature, society and economics. They define reproduction as finalized to the preservation of individual variation: the genealogical function of meiotic sex (sexual mating) determining the biological binarism of the sexes.

This chapter proposes an alternative conception of sex and reproduction. It explores the dynamics of evolution by drawing on Deleuze and Guattari's geological model of the organic strata, Lynn Margulis's endosymbiotic theory and far from equilibrium processes of coevolution. The chapter constructs an abstract map of the molecular mutations that lead to the emergence of meiotic sex.

The chapter is divided into four sections. The first section points to an immanent notion of natural selection that accounts for the (metastable) coevolution of the individual and the environment. The second section combines the Deleuze–Guattarian concept of organic stratification with Lynn Margulis's hypothesis of endosymbiosis to map the events of sex on the biophysical strata as machinic modifications of the relation between milieus and codes. The third section discusses the molecular organization of the meiotic order of sex, reproduction and death. The fourth section suggests that the organic stratification of sex entails a micropolitics of bacterial recombination and symbiotic composition of cellular and multicellular modes of sex and reproduction. This micropolitics exposes an anti-genealogy of sex that generates difference without linear descent. Meiotic sex is not the ultimate determinant of variations. Rather, meiotic sex emerges from a continual variation of microbial sexes.

GENEALOGICAL DIFFERENCE

The conception of difference – especially sexual difference – is related to the hypothesis of evolution of the organism. Before Darwin's theory of branching philogeny defining the genealogical tree of evolution, theories of evolution emphasized the existence of a universal logic or mechanism generating variations in all forms of life.[2] Linnean taxonomy defined the natural order of all living things, the place of diversities in a hierarchical scale of analogies. Yet, Darwin's study of evolution did not seek general laws but historical and accidental contingencies leading to the generation of variations. Variations between populations did not correspond to the Platonic eternal forms or Aristotelian immanent types. The Great Chain of Being does not define the essence of a species, where all variations stem from one universal form: the identical form of all origins.[3] According to Darwin, the variation of species needs to be related to contingent relations between populations and territories that involve a transformation of variations arising within one species and spreading across species. Darwin's theory of evolution defines the passage from typological to population thinking, substituting individual types for codes in a population and degree of development for differential relations between populations.[4]

In *Difference and Repetition*, Deleuze argues that Darwin introduces the thought of individual difference as the organization of free-floating and unconnected differences into singular and determinate differences (1994). Individual differences are not predetermined but are formed through a process of differentiation and selection of accumulating variations. Darwin's study of individual difference is inseparable from sexed reproduction that defines the ' "incessant production of varied individual differences" ' (Darwin quoted in Deleuze 1994: 248–9). Sexed reproduction exposes the existence of three biological differentiations – that of the species, that of organic parts and that of the sexes (249). The interlink between sexual reproduction and individual difference is at the core of the Darwinian theory of 'modification with descent': every individual being is part of a genealogy of beings open to variations through breeding and intercrossing. As Darwin states, '[t]he real affinities of all organic beings are due to inheritance or community of descent' (1809; 1993: 634).[5] This theory of continuity and variation (evolution) relies on natural selection – the source of order in the biological world – acting upon the reproductive individual that preserves the phylum from extinction. Individual differences are slight modifications of a common pool of variations that are preserved through adaptation and sexual mating.

In *The Origin of the Species* (1809), the principles of evolution and variation define the action of natural selection upon organic adaptation.[6] Herbert Spencer translated this function of adaptation with the notion of the 'survival of the fittest', according to which natural selection acts upon organisms competing in an environment of lack and scarcity – disorder – to preserve the best adapted organism of reproduction. According to Darwin, natural selection is the principle by which each slight variation is preserved through heredity to benefit the individual's adaptation to an ever-changing environment (88).[7] Natural selection acts as an invisible hand: a blind force of order that remains external to the degrees of variation within populations and between populations and territories. It intervenes as a regulator of differences ensuring the reproduction of a common descent through slight changes. The genealogical tree of evolution guarantees the self-preservation of the species through its capacity to adapt to environmental changes and its capacity to sexually reproduce (preserve) variations in a competitive environment. Natural selection compels organisms and species to strive for stability while sexual mating guarantees branching philogeny (the preservation of the lineage).

The Lamarckian model of inheritance of acquired characteristics defines individual difference as the result of the pressures of the environment on the organism (passive adaptation). Conversely, Darwinism considers difference as an internal capacity of the organism to survive defined by the capacity of adaptation and transmission of variation. Mendel's atoms of heredity and Weismann's doctrine of the germ plasm contributed to formalize this internal process according to the germline of heredity.[8] Hence the model of descent came to define individual difference through the function of sexual reproduction. The principle of inheritance depending on the transmission of the most adapted variations through sexual mating (meiotic sex) directly relies on the ability of sexual selection to preserve variations. Unlike natural selection, sexual selection does not exterminate the ill-adapted but determines the system of inheritance of the species. Sexual selection is intrinsically linked to the laws of inheritance and variation of individual traits confirming the centrality of sexual reproduction (mating) for the transmission of the germ plasm (sexed chromosomes).

Neo-Darwinism extends this model of evolution to genetic units of selection, reformulating the relation between the organism and the environment, the randomness of variation and the cumulative and conservative process of heredity on the level of the genotype. In particular, Richard Dawkins's notion of the *Extended Phenotype* (1983) suggests that the arbitrary category of the organism upon which natural selection acts is the genotype, the germline of transmission discovered by Weismann.[9] The genetic unit, and not the organism, constitutes the selected individual. Genes are more durable than the organisms they inhabit for their capacity to store and transmit information. According to Dawkins, DNA information passes through bodies and affects them, but, conversely, bodies do not affect information in its own way through them.[10] In this frame, the struggle that counts for survival takes place at the level of individual genes that determine (cause) individual difference.

For neo-Darwinism, natural selection exercises an arbitrary action on accumulated and random variations in favour of genetic units or parts, which work for their auto-replication.[11] This cumulative and conservative evolution relies on the notion of heredity, which crucially designates the economy of self-propagation of the genetic unit (the cause of all differences). Heredity confirms the autonomy of genes from the environment (the genotype from the phenotype). This understanding of heredity has been mostly influenced by Weismann's model of transmission of hereditary particles in sexual reproduction. Weismann argues that the development of the somatic body (i.e. the phenotype, the environment) has a very limited affect on the hereditary function of genetic material. Genes determine the growth of an individual organism. The environment within which the organism is born cannot re-programme the hereditary function of genetic material. Neo-Darwinism argues that external factors cannot be direct causes of changes inheritable through generation. It defines a unidirectional transmission of genetic information, which excludes the feedback relations between environment and genes.

Neo-Darwinism affirms that the potential for variation is built into the organism as part of its species-heritage; variation is therefore contained within the original germ-plasm. The 'Weismann Barrier' between germ-plasm (genetic unit of selection) and soma-plasm (environment, phenotype) demonstrates that the genome acts as an independent, self-controlled unit. The split between the germ-plasm, associated with the internal force of evolution and variation, and the soma-plasm, the external force of the environment, resonates in neo-Darwinism with a divorce of the body (or soma/environment/matter) from the mind (or the organic unit of selection). The germ-plasm ensures the transmission and reproduction of genetic information. The soma-plasm only provides the environment for the formative force to reproduce. The hereditary line of the germ-plasm allows the fittest genes to survive and differentiate. The environment is destined to die as an irrelevant, inert and passive context of development.[12] Neo-Darwinism professes a nucleocentric view of evolution, identifying formative forces with the nucleic unit of selection (germline).

The neo-Darwinian conception of evolution perpetuates the understanding of genealogical difference substituting genetic codes for species or organisms. Sexed difference still remains attached to meiotic sex or sexual reproduction: the chromosomal reshuffling of nucleic genes (sexual mating) preserves the fittest genes (the most adapted genetic differences). Sexed difference is defined by the sexual function of reproduction determined (caused) by nucleic genes. The Darwinian and neo-Darwinian hypotheses of evolution entail a genealogical conception of difference that is based on the linear transmission and preservation of genetic variation (the inheritance of the germline) through meiotic sex (sexual reproduction). These hypotheses reiterate a binary system of identification of the sexes (male and female) that has enormous implications for the understanding of sexual and gender differences.

In particular, the analogy between biological sex and socio-cultural gender based on the centrality of sexual reproduction permeates the understanding of power relations in natural, cultural and technological systems. This model of evolution has become representative of all modes of organization of society, economy and politics. The analysis of such powerful perspectives informs the feminist critique of science according to which models of evolution infiltrate the meaning of sex and gender, through the rhetoric of competition, survival and adaptation.[13] Although useful to track the universal causality that defines these models of difference, these critical insights focus on the power of signification of meiotic sex (the discursive construction of sex-gender identity and sexual reproduction) without engaging with the biophysical, socio-cultural and techno-economic dynamics of evolution. The epistemological critique of techno-science, with its attention to language and representation, does not provide alternative conceptual tools for a definition of biological difference beyond the essentialist tradition of forms and types, blind selection and competitive nature.[14]

Molecular selection

In *Creative Evolution*, Henri Bergson argues against the teleology of evolution. Differences do not derive from (pre-existing individual) parts. Difference does not correspond to already actualized differences. Actualized differences partake of a process of differentiation between heterogeneous particle-flows moving in inverse direction, exposing the tension of forces between the *élan vital* and matter. Difference emerges as an actualization of multiplicity: a singular stoppage of the running flow (*élan vital*) whose potential surpasses individual differences through infinitesimal deviations.

> [. . .] the difficulty arises from this, that we represent statically ready-made material particles juxtaposed to one another, and, also statically, an external cause which plasters upon them a skil-

fully contrived organization. In reality, life is a movement, materiality is the inverse movement, and each of these two movements is simple, the matter which forms a world being an undivided flux, and undivided also the life that runs through it, cutting out in it living beings all along its track. Bergson (1983: 249).

Drawing on this process of differentiation, Deleuze suggests that the real causes of experience, unlike the universal notions of representation, do not resemble their effect in any way, anymore than an organism resembles its genetic material, even though the causes are virtually present in their effect.[15] For real causes are not universal and a priori rules that the effect merely represents the way in which a member represents a species (or the genotype represents the phenotype). Real causes are as determinate and particular as the effect, with which they are as if they were synergetically coexistent. The forces that actually produce experience are for the most part without form or law. Thus, an actual difference, conveying the contingency of experience, is constituted through a chance concatenation of forces: converging and diverging fluxes that together produce something new and unpredictable. Deleuze defines the emergence of a new actuality as the *event* of actuality.[16] An event is a mixture of the necessary and the abstract: the necessary production of an effect by its cause or the contingent effective presence of those causes at that particular moment.[17] Rather than a transition from the possible (the genotype) to the real (phenotype), the emergence of difference involves the production of something new through virtually present forces that enter a new actual relation through chance encounters. In this sense, the actualization of difference is entangled with a virtual variation never confined to organic or social actuals. As a singular intensity, the emergence of difference zigzags across planes of actualization through dynamics of genetic drifting and parallel communication.

Arguing against Darwinian evolutionary mechanism, Bergson suggests that the internal principle that explains genetic change and adaptation is not at all a result of selection from purely contingent variations, but involves a continuum of genetic energy. Such a continuum resides in the intuitive perception of time as duration, which does not confine the past in the past and the future in the advent to come. Rather, it exposes the coexistence of the past with the future through a passing present. The perception of time is attributed neither to natural resemblances nor to cognitive speculations. Perception does not derive from the phenomenological chain of signification. Perception constitutes the catalysing forces of an autonomous processuality, never representing something else. Perception entails movement of light-energy particles, the continual variation of matter that sediments, doubles, intersects and folds back. Similarly, according to Bergson, evolution does not proceed through the addition of substances (from simple to complex), but by the doubling and disassociation of time–matter. 'Evolution requires a real continuity of the past in the present', an infinite splitting of time rather than the juxtaposition of segments of time that determines the inheritance of the past through a frozen present (linear heredity).

Evolution is not the realization of a programme involving the competition and preservation of possible variations (actualities). As Bergson observes, Darwinism is unable to relate difference to evolution, as it does not explain movement in itself: a motor of non-possible but potential differences. The energetic conception of motion as merely stemming from a point or source of contact – a leveller – needs to be substituted with another movement: an action of particles that has no points, no centre of anchorage and yet ceaselessly moves, passing and traversing different states, expanding through thousands of tendencies.

> While, in its contact with matter, life is comparable to an impulsion or impetus, regarded in itself it is an immensity of potentiality, a mutual encroachment of thousands and thousands of tendencies which nevertheless are 'thousands and thousands' only when regarded as outside of each other, that is, when spatialized. Matter divides what it is, and what does not cease to be a 'virtual multiplicity' (Bergson 1983: 258).

Bergson questions the Darwinian concept of natural selection as a negative force that abolishes non-adapted species and does not produce new ones. The selection of the most adapted organism or fittest genes demands nothing else but an effort of adaptation that subsumes the productive autonomy of particle-flows to a blind power of elimination (transcendent power). Selective pressures, far from preserving individual variations, deploy a movement of actualization of virtual multiplicities (potentials): the emergence of novelty. The movement of selection entails a process by which molecular particles productively respond to immanent selective pressures out of which individual differences emerge. Deleuze and Guattari draw on Nietzsche to explain this process.

> When Nietzsche says that selection is most often exerted *in favour of the large number*, he inaugurates a fundamental intuition that

will inspire modern thought. For what he means is that the large numbers or the large aggregates do not exist prior to a selective pressure that might elicit singular lines from them, but that, quite on the contrary, these large numbers and aggregates are born of this selective pressure that crushes, eliminates or regularizes the singularities. Selection does not presuppose a primary gregariousness; gregariousness presupposes the selection and is born of it. (1983: 343)

The nature of selective pressures is creative and active in a Nietzschean sense.[18] It defies the metaphysics of negativity – aiming at selecting the fittest by eliminating the ill-fitted. Indeed, selective pressures or forms of selection 'are not to be explained in terms of any goal or end' according to which modes of communication and heredity are always already associated with molar organic aggregates, such as sexual reproduction (meiotic sex). Rather, selective pressures depend upon an immanent given degree of capitalization of molecular forces leading to a limited yet unpredictable number of molecular compositions in molar aggregates. Selective pressures do not maintain order by producing a chain of cause and effects based on linearity. Jacques Monod pointed to the arbitrary activity of selection according to which molecules regulate metabolic functions through the modifications of the input from the output – for example the regulatory molecule that binds different enzymes bears no resemblance to the substrates or products of the enzyme (1971). Such a conception of selection does not sort out order from chaos by deducting effects (phenotype) from causes (genotype). Rather, it is immanent to the metastable feedback between the individual and the environment.

Questioning this negative role of natural selection, contemporary evolutionary biology characterizes basic living organizations as autopoietic systems (from the Greek self-producing). According to the biologist Francisco Varela, an autopoietic system is organized as a network of processes that produces components continuously regenerating and realizing the network that produces them. These components constitute the system as a distinguishable unity in the domain in which they exist (1991: 81). Autopoiesis explains the non-linear dynamics of composition of an individual that is ever fully developed as it coexists with the ecosystem in which individuals are localized. Autopoiesis does not rely on self-created and self-generating organisms that define a harmonic whole. Rather, it indicates the codependence of the individual and the milieu. The poiesis – or doing – of the organism defines

the condition of its reproduction within a biosphere that is itself autopoietic. Franciso Varela affirms that a living system does distinguish
itself from its environment. At the same time, however, it maintains
its coupling with it. The bond between them cannot be untangled
since the organism rises in relation to the environment. The living
system does not exist for itself and in itself. Its emergence partakes of
a network of bodies (environment) upon which it depends and is
depended upon. As Gilbert Simondon argues:

> Individuation must therefore be thought of as a partial and rela-
> tive resolution manifested in a system that contains latent poten-
> tials and harbors a certain incompatibility with itself, an
> incompatibility due at once to forces in tension as well as the
> impossibility of interaction between terms of extremely disparate
> dimensions. (1992: 300)

This potential environment defines a network of differential (potential) relations between individual bodies regulated by far-from-equilibrium dynamics of organization (autopoietic processes of organization
marked by thresholds of change). In particular, Stuart Kauffman's
analysis of non-linear dynamics of evolution points out that rates of
variation accelerate at bifurcation points (critical thresholds of
change), challenging the assumption that natural selection sets the
gradual accumulation of variations in order.[19] The emergence of difference no longer concerns the selection of the most adapted individual,
but virtual processes of individuation. Difference indicates states of
becoming of a potential body-milieu relation exposing the microvariations between actualized differences.

As Manuel DeLanda points out, the concept of virtual difference
(differential relations between bodies) is linked to the concept of
intensive (micro) bifurcation in evolutionary rates indicating the
complexity of variation in processes of evolution (2002). For
Darwinism and neo-Darwinism evolutionary rates define a linear and
gradual accumulation of variations. The rate of accumulation varies
from species to species due to their different generation times, but
within each species the rate is supposed to be uniform. Nevertheless,
in contemporary evolutionary biology the role of acceleration and
deceleration in evolutionary rates has become crucial to understand
variations within the same population. The velocities of variation have
also indicated the phenomena of long jump adaptations 'where genetic
alterations jump beyond the correlation length of the landscape' or

beyond the margins of territorialization to produce new variations. Kauffman (1993: 117). From this standpoint, variations are not the outcome of natural selection, but emerge through the parallel network of relations between populations and territories poised at the edge of a phase transition from one state to another. Kauffman compares these points of transmission values to singular zones of intensity existing at the phase transition between gaseous and solid states (too little and too much chaos or order). He argues that ecosystems (composed of populations and territories) may need to be poised at the edge in order to maximize their emergent computational capacities (237).

Natural selection does not constitute the sole source of order in evolution. Order in evolution emerges from the auto-organization of complex systems of bodies exhibiting parallel processes of communication and reproduction of information operating on the chemical, physical, biological levels. Far-from-equilibrium dynamics, rather than involving individual variation and exterminating selection, exposes the coevolution and co-adaptation between organism and environment. These non-linear dynamics constitute ecosystems as composites that are themselves connected to one another through the molecular velocities of evolutionary rates. The target that selection achieves is not the individual, but complex aggregations of bodies poised at the edge between order and chaos. Selection does not impose an order of fitness to these networked systems. Rather, it is immanent to their regulatory circuits as it acts at their differential degrees of complexity. Kauffman suggests that at the heart of a living system is a network of channels that is able to catalyse its own reproduction. Hence, the genome, rather than a small aggregate of individual genes directly selected by a superior order, is a complex adaptive system composed of networks of genes and their production that interact with one another in regulatory circuitry.

In a genomic system, each gene responds to the various products of those genes whose products regulate its activity. All the different genes in the network may respond at the same time to the output of those genes which regulate them. In other words, the genes act in parallel. The network, insofar as it is like a computer program at all, is like a *parallel-processing network*. In such networks, it is necessary to consider the simultaneous activity of all the genes at each moment as well as the temporal progression of their activity patterns. Such progressions constitute the integrated behaviours of the parallel-processing regulatory system. Kauffman (1993: 442).

The network dynamics of genetic organization challenge Dawkins's model of evolution based on the unit of selection, the genetic material acted upon by natural selection. This dynamics reveals that even a single cell is a cooperative colony that is not independent of the environment, and does not emerge from a gradual accumulation of variations. The phenomenon of symbiosis also provides an example of complex co-evolution, co-adaptation and micro-deviations in evolutionary rates. Yet, symbiosis has not to be confused with altruism whereby kin selection can take place only on an interspecies level or with the neo-Darwinist conception of cooperative behaviour between different species in a competitive environment. Studies on symbiosis affirm that cooperation is not simply the exception to the rule of competitive individuals. Symbiosis shows that the distinction between environment and individual is violated by the intersection of widely divergent species that have no genetic relation and that do not simply cooperate but combine, merge for long periods and generate novel metabolic systems. Symbiosis defies the neo-Darwinian conception of natural selection as a source of order reacting upon units of information that compete to adapt to a detached environment.

Symbiotic relationships are not the end result of altruism or competitive individualism. Symbiotic novelties emerge out of networked organizations that involve chance interlinks between populations and territories. Symbiosis as a source of novelty occurs at many levels of scale. The cellular level of the food chain producing photosynthesis through the symbiosis of micro-organisms and the larger scale of autonomous communities of bacteria that allow legume to fix nitrogen (DeLanda 2002: 55). Symbiosis entails the meshing of two or more heterogeneous populations of bodies followed by the eventual co-evolution of the partners. It exposes the dynamics of a molecular (virtual) selection that defines difference as potential emerging from a mutual web of relation between different bodies and milieus. Individual difference is inseparable from a molecular composition of bodies unfolding the capacity of a body to become something else in relation to an ecosystem of bodies.

The evolutionary model of sexual reproduction, ensuring the genealogy of difference through the inheritance of the fittest variations, needs to be re-worked through the far-from-equilibrium dynamics of molecular selection and the symbiotic networks of cellular bodies. Drawing on Lynn Margulis's model of endosymbiosis and Deleuze–Guattari's stratification, the following sections argue that meiotic sex emerges from the symbiotic network of microbial sexes – the micro fluctuations of bodies and territories that constitute the potential complexity of individual difference. Thus, meiotic sex does not preserve individual variations through sexual reproduction (genetic inheritance), but indicates the cloning of bacterial variations enfolded in every cellular and multicellular body.

CRACKS ON THE ORGANIC STRATA

The organic stratum is not a whole composed of parts. Deleuze and Guattari argue that a single abstract machine – the *Ecumenon* – produces the unity of the organic stratum through metastable ruptures between codes and milieus. They use this term to define a body of relations specific to a stratum: the virtual coexistence of differential potentials from which actual differences emerge in a distributive pattern across the stratum and serially over time to compose individuations as regulated interactions. Individuations may change in nature while continuing to belong to the stratum: the metabolic and reproductive functions of carbon-based chemistry, RNA > DNA information storage, the genetic code for RNA > protein pathways, are examples of molecular regulated interactions constituting the unity of the organic stratum. The strato-dynamics of the Ecumenon thus define a regime of common principles (e.g. the terrestrial biosphere) that might nevertheless differ radically from alternative biological organizations (e.g. non-carbon based bacterial cells). The Ecumenon maps the ideally continuous belt or ring of the stratum in its organic forms and functions: the bio-geological unification of the 'inhabited earth'. It delimits the organic stratum through the unity of 'exterior molecular materials, interior substantial elements, and the limit or membrane conveying formal relations'.[20]

This machine is different from the *Planomenon*, the machinic plane of consistency, which has no regime. The Planomenon is the body without organs cutting across all strata. It unfolds the autonomy of differential potentials from the strata that themselves actualize. Here, individuations are becomings that fall out of strata altogether, as though falling in the cracks between the strata. This is either tantamount to suicide (the 'line of abolition') or it leads to the emergence of a new form of individuation (with a new stratum). The Ecumenon and the Planomenon are not separate. They are two sides of a coin or two folds of the same fabric. The Ecumenon is the Planomenon as enveloped (selected from, accessed for limited actualization) by a particular stratum. The Planomenon is the collective Outside of the strata (where they meet virtually by distributing their potentials) that designates processes of destratification.[21]

The Ecumenon is composed of territorial and code modifications that are never internal to a specific system, but depend on interactions. Territories are patterns of movement (substance), constituting the active traits of the environment as phenomena of territorialization (occupation), deterritorialization (uprooting) and reterritorialization (re-implantation). These movements are modes of differentiation intertwined with codes. As Deleuze and Guattari suggest, a territory is neither a milieu nor a passage between milieus. It is rather defined by elements that compose every milieu (interior, exterior, intermediate or annexed milieu) constituting the 'indexes' of a territory: genetic material, atmospheric pressures, metabolic functions and energetic sources. Each milieu has its own code and the passage between milieus involves a continuous transcoding (passage and mutation of codes) between milieus that 'are essentially communicating' (1987: 313). Milieus in a territory are products and marks of territorialization. 'The territory is in fact an act that affects milieus and rhythms, that 'territorializes' them' (314).

Territories emerge on the free margin of the code and impact on cellular compounds. Territorialization thus involves a decoding: a change in the repeated patterns of the code (genetic code) that affect the territory. This change enables the emergence of new variations in a species that are not generated by mutations internal to the code. Rather this change occurs on the margins of the code (the margins of its milieus) and defines another kind of mutation involving extra-chromosomes that are outside the genetic code. For example, as later discussed, the emergence of respiring bacteria is linked to a decodification of non-respiring bacteria involving a new territorial relation between aquatic and atmospheric marginal codes. This relation produces a new kind of cell (nucleated cell) as a new degree of microbial differentiation.

Codes define an order of molecular functions (form). Codes can be envisioned in relation to more or less molar compounds (hierarchical aggregates),[22] depending on the code's ability to propagate in the milieu or create for itself a new associated milieu – 'parastrata'. The modified code will propagate in the new milieu as it occurs with the modified code of anaerobic bacteria producing a new milieu in which it becomes aerobic. The emergence of new associated milieus leads to a modification in the code that does not involve a translation from one code to another, but processes of decoding. By drawing on François Jacob, Deleuze and Guattari gloss: '[t]here is no genetics without a genetic drift' (1987: 53). Decodification propagates through a surplus value of code (extra codes) that Jacob defines as 'side-communication', exposing the molecular composition of the organic stratum (1973: 290–2; 310–12).

Deleuze and Guattari argue for a fluctuating disjunction (metastable relation) between codes and territories defining the emergence of new coded milieus. The Ecumenon is composed of layers moving from a centre to a periphery and the other way around deploying a multiplication of intermediate states. These intermediate states are defined as 'epistrata': outgrowths and levels emerging 'between the exterior milieu and the interior element, substantial elements and their com-pounds, compounds and substances, and between the different formed substances (substances of content and substances of expression)' (50). For example, as discussed in the following sections, the constitution of bacterial cells implicates the multiplication of the intermediate state between unorganized genetic material and atmospheric pressures (interior element and exterior milieu). Similarly, the emergence of bacterial sex indicates the intermediate state between damaged DNA in the composition of a new bacterial compound (substantial elements and their compounds). Furthermore, bacterial sex marks an intermediate state between anaerobic and aerobic bacteria (substance of content – nonrespiring cell – and substance of expression – function of respiration).

In addition to the relative interior/exterior relations of the epistrata, formal relations (the limit or membrane between interior/exterior) introduce a new milieu on the stratum: the parastrata. This is an 'annexed or associated milieu' delineating the incorporation of new energy sources different from alimentary materials. Deleuze and Guattari point out that the organism, before these sources were obtained, nourishes itself, but is in a state of suffocation. The alimentary activities of its constituting elements and compounds introduce a rupture on the stratum through the production of new energy sources (e.g. oxygen). As discussed in the following sections, the relations within and between the epistrata and the parastrata map the machinic organization of sex and reproduction on the biophysical strata.

The implosion of sex

We do what you call genetic engineering. We know you had begun to do it yourself a little, but it's foreign to you. We do it naturally. We *must* do it. It renews us, enables us to survive as an evolving species instead of specializing ourselves into extinction or stagnation.

Butler (1987: 39)

The stratification of sex draws on the theory of endosymbiosis or SET (Serial Endosymbiosis Theory) re-elaborated by Lynn Margulis in the 1960s.[23] According to her thesis, the classical evolutionary explanation of the development of life, based on differences of degree (increasing complexity) and types (species) and on random mutation (Darwin's theory of natural selection), dismisses the symbiotic aggregation of cellular bodies forming new modes of communication and reproduction. Endosymbiosis displaces the 'zoocentrism' of the theories of evolution (the a-priority of *Homo sapiens*) and demonstrates that 'each eucaryotic "animal" cell is, in fact, an uncanny assembly, the evolutionary merger of distinct prokaryotic metabolism' (Sagan 1992: 363). This theory focuses on the emergence of life across differentiated lines, novel alliances among unrelated bacteria integrated by 'more or less orgiastic encounters (eating, infecting, engulfing, feeding on, having sex and so on)' (366). The symbiotic assemblages of heterogeneous bodies entails a process of 'a-parallel evolution' along movements of deterritorialization and decodification of molecular assemblages on the biophysical stratum. Margulis's conception of life as an autopoietic and dissipative system offers a complex picture of the physico-chemical and biological organization of matter. Her work on the microbial origins of sex explains the transformation of molecular sexes (bacterial trading) into molar aggregates (nucleated cells) indicating 'how things [molecular sexes] get into them [the strata] in the first place' (Deleuze and Guattari 1987: 57).

The symbiotic assemblage of molecular elements or compounds into larger cellular bodies involves the bifurcation of matter into two parallel machines of organization. These machines define the double pincer between content (formed matter) and expression (functional structures), according to which molecules sediment (1st articulation) and fold back (2nd articulation) to produce new levels of order – new machines of reproduction. As already observed, Deleuze and Guattari use Louis Hjelmslev's notions of *matter*, *content* and *expression*, *form* and *substance* in order to define the operations of the double articulation – the virtual-actual circuits of differentiation of bodies – distributing regulatory patterns of order (1987: 44).

From the standpoint of stratification, the emergence of bacterial cells (the first autopoietic system)[24] indicates a split between content and expression according to the activities of the double articulation. The 1st articulation involves a process of sedimentation of chemical catalysts from unstable flows (the pre-biotic soup or *matter of content*) out of which metastable units emerge, such as self-bounded chemical systems based on long-molecules, nucleic acids and proteins (*substances of content*). A statistical order of connection and succession is imposed on these units to form a membrane (the chemical system never stops metabolizing and reaches a critical point resulting in the formation of a membrane – *form of content*). The 2nd articulation establishes functional stable structures or forms such as protein synthesis, RNA and DNA (*forms of expression*) and constructs molar compounds in which these structures (protein synthesis nucleotides) are actualized: the membrane-bounded cells or bacteria (*substance of expression*). The two articulations involve the mutual dynamics of sedimenting matter of content, formed matter on a territory (e.g. long-molecules, nucleic acids and proteins, and membrane), and folding matter of expression – unformed molecular functions (e.g. protein synthesis, RNA and DNA metabolic functions of bacteria). This bacterial autopoietic body is stratified matter: the actualization of virtual heterogeneous flows or the selection of pre-individual particle-forces through gigantic lines of bifurcation. The emergence of bacteria (non-nucleic cells) points to this double organization of matter that defines a micromap of the symbiotic modifications of sex and reproduction.

Margulis and Sagan's research of microbial fossils attests that the first membrane-bounded cells, bacteria, emerged soon after a solid crust formed on the Earth, and that sex[25] – as a mode of transmission and reproduction of information – is almost as ancient as the body of the Earth *herself*. Before the composition of a cellular system, the networked dynamics of information transfer already characterized the function of the RNA molecule. Margulis and Sagan indeed argue that RNA is a 'supermolecule' constituting early cells metabolism that only later used DNA transmission (1995: 63–6). RNA is the first 'sexy molecule' that metabolized genetic material before DNA deployed its capacity to process information for cellular life (1997: 70–1).

During the Archean Aeon, in the Pre-Phanerozoic, 3900 millions of years ago, bacteria (non-respiring membrane-bounded cells) invented genetic engineering as a mode of sex and reproduction (transgenesis or cloning). The Pre-Phanerozoic geological period followed the time of the Moon and Earth's formation (called Hadean Aeon, 4600 million years ago), when anaerobic bacteria suffered from the damage of their DNA caused by intensive solar radiation, intense UV irradiation and bombardment of cosmic rays.[26] Under this setting, the chemical substratum composed of water vapour, nitrogen, carbon dioxide (exterior code-milieu or form and substance of content), entered a new relation with the membrane-bounded DNA, RNA and protein composing the bacterial cell (interior code-milieu or forms and substances of expression), damaging some of the codes (2 thymine bases of the DNA) of anaerobic bacteria. In particular, photosynthetic bacteria damaged their DNA by extending their exposure to sunlight energy. Thus, they invented genetic engineering (bacterial sex) as a mode of repairing the damage. These bacteria activated the enzymatic process of DNA repair by borrowing genetic material (forms of content and expression) from different bacteria. This new intermediate (epistratic) relation between interior and exterior codes-milieus led to the emergence of bacterial sex, the sexual trade of microbial DNA across unrelated bacterial cells.

> [E]arly in the planetary life, one bacterium used its repair enzymes to integrate foreign DNA from a mate or from water. Ultimately, the DNA sequence from the other bacterium instead of its own was used: sex, as recombination, had begun. [. . .] Sex, then, as genetic infusion, permitted survival in a chemically chaotic and irradiated world. Such successful bacterial DNA transfer rescued bacteria, preparing them to repeat and refine their salutary sex acts
> (Margulis and Sagan 1997: 67).

Margulis and Sagan explain that the emergence of bacterial sex is linked to the capacity of cyanobacteria to capture sunlight energy through photosynthesis. By incorporating carbon dioxide and carbohydrates (substances and forms of content) through metabolic processes, these bacteria also expelled oxygen – a poisonous gas – in the atmosphere. According to the geologists Mark and Dianne McMenamin, this metabolic process of carbon dioxide by photosynthetic cyanobacteria initiated an irreversible process: 'the clock began ticking for the day when oxygen, the waste-gas they produced, would effectively poison the planet' (1994: 38). This oxygen infusion corresponds to the greatest pollution the Earth has ever known.

> The Oxygen Revolution is that moment in geological time when significant quantities of free oxygen first accumulated in the atmosphere and in the sea. Before then, oxygen was absorbed and rendered harmless by chemical combination with marine iron and other substances common in sea water. But these oxygen sinks eventually reached the limit of their ability to chemically combine with oxygen, and continuing photosynthesis by cyanobacteria meant that the waste gas had 'no place to go'. Oxygen began to accumulate in the atmosphere (1994: 38).

The interior substantial elements (bacterial un-bounded DNA) and exterior molecular materials (carbon dioxide and carbohydrates) defining the epistratic metabolism of aquatic anaerobic bacteria were forced to turn to less 'convenient material', i.e. oxygen. The distribution of contaminating oxygen in the atmosphere introduced the interior/exterior milieu to a 'third figure: [. . .] an *annexed* or *associated milieu*' (Deleuze and Guattari 1987: 51). Oxygen deterritorializes the organism from its 'state of suffocation' offering a new opportunity for cellular life to engineer information in a new milieu of relations between bacterial codes. This opportunity deployed a new layer in the organization of sex (a new articulation of the forms and substances of content and expression). The increasing of oxygen in the atmosphere (associated or annexed milieu) jeopardized non-respiring bacteria. Yet, this immediate danger (the spreading of poisonous oxygen) turned into a new engineering opportunity for bacterial anaerobic sex. Anaerobic bacteria merged with respiring bacteria defining the first symbiotic parasitism of one bacterial cell inside another: hypersex.

This machinic composition of codes and milieus (non-respiring and respiring metabolic processes and aerobic and aquatic milieus) does not imply a progressive development from the anaerobic aquatic environment to the aerobic and terrestrial one. Conversely, this composition introduces a new substance of content (oxygen molecules) and expression (aerobic bacteria) on the stratum. According to the McMenamins, the emergence and differentiation of oxygen induced microbes to move from the sea to the harsher environment of land intensifying biochemical and parasitic relationships that gave rise to a superentity: Hypersea (1994). In order to pass nutrients, microbes had to build a web of connection relatively thicker than the food chain built in the sea. Thus, land organisms: 'evolved together as part of a greater interconnected mass of living cells. In moving out of marine waters, complex life has taken the sea beyond the sea and folded it back inside of itself to form Hypersea' (1994: 5). The appearance of complex life on land is an event in which a kind of 'bacterial sea' invaded the land surface and imploded in respiring bacteria.

Margulis stresses that the explosion, differentiation and increase of oxygen in the atmosphere contributed to the engineering of a new cellular assemblage with fermenting bacteria acquiring as partners a number of smaller oxygen-respiring bacteria. The sexual merger of anaerobic and aerobic bacteria entails a sort of permanent parasitism producing a new cellular compound – the protista, the first cell with membrane-bounded nucleus or eukaryote. This endosymbiotic formation does not only involve a deterritorialization of milieus (aquatic and anaerobic) but also a decodification of codes (metabolic functions and structures) impacting on bacterial sex and reproduction. This symbiosis involves a fusion between codes (anaerobic and aerobic genetic metabolism of bacteria) and milieus (aquatic and land reservoirs) that generates a new mode of sex and reproduction: *hypersex*. Hypersex defines a double parasitism between one bacterium entering another, growing and reproducing (cloning) in its inside forever. This unnatural merging of originally separated bacteria (aerobic and anaerobic) distributes the modifications of aquatic codes and milieus on land biota.

Recent research suggests that the permanent symbiosis of anaerobic and respiring bacteria involved the merging of a large anaerobic host, the Thermoplasma (that became the nucleocytoplasm and eventually the nucleus-bounded membrane of the eukaryotic cell) with oxygen-respiring microbes, (purple bacteria, ancestors of mitochondria) that were ingested but not digested by their Thermoplasmic host. As Margulis states: '[e]ventually the small aerobic bacteria became the hereditary guests of their hosts: these were the first mitochondria' (1970: 10). By feeding off its mitochondrial guests (organelles), the Thermoplasma evolved in the eukaryotic a successful lineage that combined the nucleus-bounded membrane with the mitochondrial oxygen processing. The endosymbiotic engineering of unrelated bacterial cells does not only involve the transgenesis or cloning of genetic information (bacterial sex), but also the incorporation of two or more bacterial bodies. The anaerobic thermoplast captured respiring bacteria or mitochondria as the substances and forms of content (elements and codes) of a new level of expression: the nucleic rules of DNA transmission (form) and nucleic DNA (substance). However, respiring bacteria or mitochondria can also define the substance and form of expression of the eukaryotic cell as they constitute its metabolic rules and express its protein synthesis in the cytoplasmic body (the body of the cell outside the nucleus). The matter of expression of one microbial scale of order becomes the matter of content on another scale. The forms and substances of expression of bacteria become the content of eukaryotic cells. Yet bacteria and mitochondria are not only the content but also define the multi-levels of expression of eukaryotic cells. The double articulation is not dialectical. It is an index of the machinic engineering and folding of microbial bodies co-adapting with an environment of immanent pressures through parallel processes of communication and reproduction (bacterial sex or trading, and bacterial merging or hypersex).

The implosion of anaerobic bacteria into respiring bodies maps the emergence of hypersex as an incorporeal variation of microbial trading that bursts out the previous arrangements of cellular contents and expressions. The emergence of hypersex exposes a machinic phylum of heterogeneous modes of sex and reproduction from where new content and expression of molecular sexes eventuate. Novel patterns of information appear through relative deterritorialized milieus and decodified genes splitting the unity of the organic stratum – the Ecumenon – and constituting new assemblages of reterritorialization: the eukaryotic cell (the nucleated cell). The hypersexual permanent incorporation of anaerobic into aerobic bacteria cracks the integrity of the stratum into a multiplicity of molecular relations moving within and among epistrata and parastrata.

This crack defines the emergence of different molecules (oxygen, carbon, nitrogen), specific substances (bacterial and eukaryotic cells), and irreducible forms (mitochondrial DNA and nucleic DNA), conveying a reterritorialization of sex through a microbial implosion into the eukaryotic cell.[27] As such, the eukaryotic cell incorporates microbial modes of information – bacterial sex (the trading of genetic material) and hypersex (the cellular merging of different bacteria) – not as a container of previous forms, but, more strikingly, as a multiplier of parallel orders of sex. These new internal membrane-bounded nuclei define a new threshold of relations between the 1st and 2nd articulation of cellular order entailing the nucleic-bounded process of mitosis (genetic doubling and cellular splitting or a-sexual reproduction), and meiosis (genetic fertilization and reduction or sexual reproduction). The membranic relationship between nucleic material and the cytoplasmic body of the eukaryotic cell deploys the micropolitics of mitochondrial and bacterial cloning folded inside a new machine of sex.

NUCLEIC EXPRESSION

[. . .] starting from this domain of chance or real inorganization, large configurations are organized that necessarily reproduce a structure under the action of DNA and its segments, the genes, performing veritable lottery drawings, creating switching points as lines of selection or evolution, this, indeed, is what all the stages of the passage from the molecular to the molar demonstrate, such as this passage appears in the organic machines.

Deleuze and Guattari (1983: 289)

You are hierarchical. That's the older and more entrenched characteristic. We saw it in your closest animal relatives and in your
most distant ones. It's a terrestrial characteristic.

Butler (1987: 37)

The organic stratification of sex defines a machinic order of molecular
codes'–milieus' connections. The code of anaerobic bacteria becomes
incorporated into aerobic bacteria with a modification where codes
become enclosed within the nucleus – a new milieu – separated from
the rest of the cellular body by a membrane. This endosymbiotic
fusion deploys the coexistence of singular machines of sex and reproduction in the eukaryotic cell. This cell is defined by a nuclear
membrane that divides the nucleic genome from the (extra) genome
outside (the body of the cell). The latter is composed of mitochondria:
organelles that do not share nucleic modes of sex and reproduction.
Mitochondria recombine like bacteria. The nuclear-bounded organization of genetic material introduces a new machine of reproduction,
meiotic sex. In order to map the emergence of such a machine, it is
necessary to consider first its prerequisite, mitosis or the organization
of the eukaryotic genome into chromatin and its transmission to
offspring cells.

Mitosis is related to the deterritorialization of genetic material that
constitutes the nucleic genome as the interior milieu of a eukaryotic
organism. As Deleuze and Guattari state, '[t]he more interior milieu
an organism has on its own stratum, assuring its autonomy and bringing
it into a set of aleatory relations with the exterior, the more deterritorialized it is' (1987: 54). Not only does the interior (bounded)
genetic milieu of the nucleic cell disassociate from the exterior material of the cell itself (cytoplasmic genes, mitochondrial DNA or plastids), but it also becomes relatively autonomous from the more
exterior energetic and genetic material (bacterial and viral populations). Margulis and Sagan observe that the process of interiorization is
specific to cellular life itself, which preserves and increases an interior
order only by adding to the 'disorder of the external world' (1994:
26). Cellular life enfolds a dissipative autopoietic process that moves
through orders of complexity by means of deterritorialization and
decodification.

Hypersex, the parasiting integration of independent bacterial cells,
also involves a process of deterritorialization from bacterial sex: the
incorporation of anaerobic bodies in the interior milieu of a new autonomous aerobic cellular organism. However, the deterritorialization of

the nucleated genome of the eukaryotic cell displays a further autonomy of the interior milieu (the nucleic membrane). Such movements of deterritorialization are always counterbalanced by a reterritorialization on the stratum that assigns new roles to molecular material and substantial elements. For example, the deterritorialization from the anaerobic milieu of bacterial sex (the damaged DNA repair chain) through the explosion of oxygen, is followed by the reterritorialization of substances through hypersex. This permanent symbiosis forms the nucleic cell that constitutes a wide group of cellular bodies: 'from unicellular amoebas to plants and animals with billions of such cells apiece' (Margulis and Sagan 1997: 79).

To the movement of deterritorialization and reterritorialization in the epistrata, the process of coding and decoding in the parastrata adds new layers to the eukaryotic assemblage. The emergence of eukaryotic cells includes a capture of bacterial sex transforming its forms (free DNA, RNA and protein synthesis) and substances (bacterial genome) of expression into eukaryotic content connected to new forms and substances of expression (DNA > RNA > protein and nucleic genotype). The form of expression of the nucleic cell becomes autonomous and relatively independent of the content (free DNA and bacterial cell) constituting a unidimensional genetic machine of information. The decodification from the bacterial genome displays the capacity of the nucleated genome to abstract codes from its substantial milieus. Bacterial forms and substances of expression implode into the serial chromosomal numbers of the nucleated expression able to flatten the genome into a unidimensional order of transmission.

> In short, what is specific to the organic stratum is this alignment of expression, this exhaustion or detachment of a line of expression, this reduction of form and substance of expression to a unidimensional line, guaranteeing their reciprocal independence from content without having to account for orders of magnitude (Deleuze and Guattari 1987: 59).

The relative autonomy of DNA from RNA and protein defines the unidimensional line of expression, where the nucleated code uncouples from the epistratic relations (RNA and protein) demonstrating that '[t]he essential thing is the linearity of the nucleic sequence' (Deleuze and Guattari 1987: 59).[28] According to Erwin Shröndinger, DNA can be conceived as an 'aperiodic crystal' since it presents structural characteristics of 'repetition' and 'periodicity' (1944: 60–1). It implies a mechanism of variation (e.g. the variation in the sequence of nucleic basis: Adenine, Guanine, Cytosine and Thymine), through which this 'macromolecule' contains and transmits information.[29] This macromolecule marks a bifurcation between the nucleic and cytoplasmic body (DNA and protein). DNA's capacity of replication and control of the proteic synthesis has led molecular biologists to define nucleic DNA as the 'Master molecule'.

Yet, the autonomy of nucleic DNA entails a wider process of abstraction (symbiotic synthesis) of microbial codes-milieus. According to Margulis and Sagan, the study of the symbiotic emergence and organization of chromosomes, defined as mitosis or 'the dance of chromosomes'[30] is crucial to understand the relevance of the microbial substrata.

This mitotic apparatus is composed by two correlated and yet separable series of microbial aggregations: the mitotic spindle and chromatic transformations.[31] The mitotic process of genetic replication and cellular doubling exhibits a double ancestry: the microtubule-motile complex (MTOC) or the protein system inherited from spirochete bacteria, and the nucleochromatin complex, stemming from a parasitism between organellar genomes (1994: 142). Endosymbiosis attributes the emergence of mitosis to the ancient microbial parasitism between eukaryotic hosts and motile symbionts called spirochetes. These motile symbionts – spirochetes – merged entirely with their eukaryotic hosts that abducted their capacity for replication and motion. The formation of chromosomes by the condensation of chromatin evolved when the eukaryotic host co-opted and utilized the spirochete motile protein system. The function of replication of the MTOC in mitosis is owed to the remnant spirochete genome, which is now involved in the division of each chromosome. The mitotic apparatus exposes a new bifurcation in the microbial assemblage establishing new functional and stable structures of expression (chromosomal duplication and chromosomes) or the autonomy of nucleic genotype from forms and substances of content (non-nucleic genome and spirochetes).

As a new machinic order of genetic transmission, '[. . .] mitosis ensures the orderly distribution of at least one set of genes to each offspring cell' (Margulis and Sagan 1986: 124). The mitotic deterritorialization from microbial substances defines a new mode of packing genetic information: nucleic DNA is condensed, wrapped up, folded in around sets of histone proteins. This deterritorialization produces a genetic programme that enables mitotic divisions through a chromosomal motility incorporating the regulatory networks of bacterial microtubule systems and the nucleochromatin complex (content).

Meiotic sex: the fold of microbial bodies

Hazel had gone on a sidetrack with her E. coli cultures, trying to prove that sex had originated as a result of the invasion of an autonomous DNA sequence – a chemical parasite called the F-factor – in early prokaryotic life forms. She had postulated that sex was not evolutionarily useful – at least not to women, who could, in theory, breed parthenogenetically – and that ultimately men were superfluous.

Bear (1985: 27)

The machinic composition of the eukaryotic cell involves the symbiotic assemblage of bacterial codes and territories marked by membranic thresholds. The eukaryotic pattern of genetic replication (mitosis) is 'an evolutionary advance of a kind fundamentally different from discrete mutation' (Margulis 1971: 9). The bacterial implosion in the nucleated cell entails a new mode of packaging genetic material through the parallel-processing of regulatory networks that double codes, align segments and functions in order to condense the widest pool of genetic information into one dimension (the flatline of expression, the genotype). Mitosis defines only a first step towards the invention of new machines of information transmission leading to meiosis and sexual reproduction.

During the Protocist evolution (1500 million years ago), the bacterial symbiotic organization of genetic material and cellular bodies gave rise to the eukaryotic cell, which, after a long period of perfection of mitotic doubling (a billion years of Precambrian time), engineered the reproductive cycle of meiosis. The mitotic cellular process of doubling chromosomes underwent a symbiotic re-arrangement of genetic and cellular forms and substances through a new cellular process of doubling (fertilizing) and breaking up (reducing) chromosomes: meiotic sex.

The Darwinian and neo-Darwinian models of natural and sex selection define the emergence and maintenance of meiotic sex as the essential principle of biological differentiation in and between species, organic parts and sexes. Yet, the entanglement of sex with reproduction (sexual mating), far from being the fruit of selection, is linked to the meiotic process of cellular doubling and reduction. These models

point out that sexual reproduction or meiotic sex requires major energetic expenditures that are functional to the production of genetic
variations. Meiotic sex serves as a leveller of variations between
species. This understanding of sex and reproduction – relying on scarcity, effort and gratification – fails to consider meiosis as a cellular
assemblage that is independent of sexual mating, but consistent with
the endosymbiotic production of the eukaryotic cell and its a-sexual
machine of reproduction (mitosis).

For endosymbiosis, meiotic sex is a programme that conveys a new
order of genetic sequence able to differentiate forms and functions of
cells, tissues, organs, sexes and species. Meiotic sex has not been
directly selected as the most successful mode of reproduction. Rather,
it is a symbiotic variation of eukaryotic a-sexual reproduction – mitosis
– favoured by immanent selective pressures. According to Margulis and
Sagan, under harsh conditions, protists (eukaryotic cells) were forced
to cannibalism: they ate without digesting each other, engulfed
without eliminating their extra cellular body. Lacking immune system,
protists incorporated each other without rejection. This cannibalism
led to cellular and genetic diploidy: the doubling of the nucleated cell
and DNA. The eater, instead of killing, incorporated the prey (or the
prey survived in the eater) establishing a new parasiting permanent
fusion. '[A]t this time sex, rescue from death, cannibalism, and lack of
digestion were the same thing' (1986: 152). This cannibalism, corresponding to mitotic reproduction, induced eukaryotic cells towards a
cancerous metastasis that was at some point re-balanced by a new
synthesis of genetic material. The eukaryotic doubling was followed by
a reduction of chromosomal duplicity developed through the
temporary delay of chromosomes from replicating.[32] This delay introduced a genetic reduction giving way to meiosis. Meiosis enabled the
reduction of nucleic bodies and saved the 'lineage from dying out'. As
a new machine of reproduction, meiotic sex constitutes a 'balancing
act between our existence as bodies with two sets of chromosomes
that inevitably die, and sex cells made by these bodies with one set of
chromosomes which enjoy the possibility of continued life in the next
generation' (Margulis and Sagan 1997: 83).

Once meiotic sex became established, it persisted and flourished.
With a cellular deterritorialization, meiosis reduces, through symbiotic
fusion, chromosomal a-sexual diploidy into sexual haploidy – single sex
cell – able to double again. Both movements of deterritorialization and
decodification of mitotic duplication introduce a novelty: the establishment of a new machine of sex and reproduction, guaranteeing the

transmission of the germ plasm to the next generation. In particular, meiosis entails the processes of doubling the haploid egg and sperm – each equipped with 23 chromosomes in humans (XX for females and XY for males) – and reduction from the diploid (46 coupled chromosomes) to a single haploid state (23 shuffled chromosomes) permitting the heredity of the germline.

The eventual sophistication of meiosis involved new patterns of cellular aggregation, linked, for example, to physiological necessities (e.g. the tissue development in the hosts). According to Margulis and Sagan, the transfer of the genetic potential of the original microbes (spirochete) to each newly formed diploid cell was and still is crucial for the emergence of differentiated tissues in ancestral and present animals. As they suggest, we still live with the imperative of our motile cell inhabitants (spirochete) to elaborate cell differentiation. This imperative only befalls in the cells of the germline – sperm, eggs and spores – destined to repeat the cannibalistic act of their eukaryotic ancestors. From the symbiotic standpoint, the emergence of meiotic sex and its processes of multicellular differentiation are not individual instances, but partake of the parallel regulatory processes of microbial endosymbiosis (1986: 170). Meiosis is a topological machine able to pack and unpack complex genetic instructions imploded in the eukaryotic cell through bacterial parasitism. In particular, it displays the coexistence of parallel machines of reproduction – nucleic and cytoplasmic or the germline and somaline – that extend the physiological development of cells towards the differentiation of multicellular organisms. Genetic variations and sexual diversity are not the result of sexual mating as often maintained by evolutionary biologists.[33] The microbial implosion in the machinery of meiotic sex, rather than the mixture of haploid cells (two-parent sex), introduces variation or rejuvenation in eukaryotic cells. 'Meiosis as a cell process, rather than two-parent sex, was a prerequisite for evolution of many aspects of animals' (1995: 191).

> Meiosis, especially, the chromosomal DNA alignment process in the stage called prophase I, may be a sort of 'roll call' ensuring that sets of genes, including mitochondrial and chloroplasts genes, are in order before development of the plant or animal embryo ensues.
>
> Margulis and Sagan (1997: 117)

The eukaryotic machine of sex and reproduction – meiotic sex – ensures the ordered transmission of all information material (nucleic and cytoplasmic codes-milieus) in the cycles of growth of multicellular organisms. According to Margulis and Sagan, the meiotic check-up system cleanses all genetic excesses. Similarly to complex computer programs or stock inventories in every large merchandizing operation, meiosis also operates as a 'garbage collector', intervening to ensure the presence of at least one balanced, unshuffled, reproducible cell lineage (192). Meiotic sex involves a sort of numbers game in which the internal cellular populations, composed of nucleocytoplasmic, mito-chondrial, undulipodial, and sometimes plastids and other free-living bacterial constituents, reproduce at differential rates. In particular, the meiotic prophase, with its special DNA and protein synthesis, is a mechanism of intracellular control to ensure cells', tissues' and organs' differentiation in animals and plants. This control is a listing that checks and organizes an ancient microbial matrix. 'Cloned and differ-entiated, microbes eventually become plants and animals' (Margulis and Sagan 1986: 182).

The death programme

'[. . .] it has been several million years since we dared to interfere in another people's act of self-destruction. [. . .] we thought . . . that there had been a consensus among you, that you had agreed to die.' 'No species would do that!' 'Yes. Some have. [. . .] We have learned. Mass suicide is one of the things we usually let alone.'

Butler (1987: 14)

[. . .] death is what is felt in every feeling, what never ceases and never finishes happening in every becoming – in the becoming-another-sex, the becoming-god, the becoming-a-race, etc., forming zones of intensity on the body without organs.

Deleuze and Guattari (1983: 330)

Meiosis entangles sex – information transmission – with sexual repro-duction – meiotic fertilization – and introduces a new cellular content-expression on the stratum: death. Ageing, decline and death mark relatively recent acquisitions of the organic stratum. While bacteria, mitochondria and some protists do not die, eukaryotic cells and multicellular organisms experience death as a price to pay in order to transmit haploid sex cells or germ plasm to offspring cells. This is a 'programmed death': cells age and die as part of the life of the multi-cellular differentiated bodies. This death is also called apoptosis, from the Greek 'drop away', and is considered to be the cellular equivalent of suicide.

> Instructions for death are sent out by the DNA of the nucleus into the cytoplasm. The RNA message is converted into proteins, enzymes which, in turn, begin to cut the DNA into small fragments. Genetically shredded, the DNA can no longer be read. Once cleavage of the long strand DNA into small pieces begins, there is no return: the cell will die.
>
> Margulis and Sagan (1997: 135)

This irreversible process is instructed by nucleic DNA, the nervous apparatus of the eukaryotic cell, that contains the master plans for every protein the cell is equipped to make. Once a cell commits itself to death by suicide, it copies off one last set of instructions from the DNA in the nucleus and sends them to the cytoplasm. After processing the instructions, the cytoplasm sends back messages to destroy nucleic DNA that, once fragmented, can no longer transmit information. Programmed death appears as a requirement of multicellular organized life inducing the final dismemberment of nucleated DNA. When cells commit suicide they are responding to a programme that cannot alter in any way. This built-in programme of self-destruction defines every eukaryotic cell. The programme is intrinsically part of the dynamics of growth, development and differentiation of a nucleated multicellular body.

Since the Proterozoic (1500 million years ago), this bifurcation between information contents (somaline; cytoplasm) and expressions (germline; nucleus) maps the complex networked organization of eukaryotic organisms. The symbiotic cannibalism between protists during time of stagnation introduced death (the cancerous process of eukaryotic doubling or mitosis) in the eukaryotic lineage. 'Meiosis and fertilization return nucleated beings to a "zero point" from which they can begin anew their life cycle' (Margulis and Sagan 1997: 141). Meiosis promises the continuation of eukaryotic life through a pact with death. 'Death is the price we all pay for this ancient history of multicellular compounding, for this inability of hungry protists to undo their Proterozoic entanglements' (Margulis and Sagan 1994: 130). Meiotic sex is a time bomb. It prevents ageing by turning the clock backwards and organizing the transmission of genes and proteins for the development of eukaryotic organisms: the differentiation of cells, organs, sexes and so on. The emergence of meiotic sex conveys the imperative to organize microbial codes-milieus in the eukaryotic cell, to activate their differentiated processes of cellular growth and development. This process involves a somatic death for the transmission of the germline.

The short circuits between germline and somaline

Yet a simple metric change would not account for the difference between organic and inorganic, the machine and its motive force. The movement goes from fold to fold. Metamorphosis is more than mere change in dimension. Every animal is double – male and female – the ovule furnishes one part whose other is the male element. In fact, it is the inorganic that repeats itself, with a difference of proximate dimension, since it is always an exterior site which enters the body; the organism, in contrast, envelops an interior site that contains necessarily other species of organisms, those that envelop in their turn the interior sites containing yet other organisms.

Deleuze (1993: 9)

Weismann argued that germ cells transmit the hereditary substance through sexual reproduction. His theory, famously summarized as 'the Weismann Barrier', indicates a split between the germ plasm (forms and substance of expression – genotype) and soma plasm (forms and substances of content – phenotype) that specifically exemplifies the detachment of nucleic material from the cytoplasmic body. Only the germline can demonstrate direct progeny, while the soma has discrete life span and dies. Germ cells (sperm and eggs) have one specific function, the transmission of DNA from one generation to the next via sexual reproduction. The rest of the genome in the body cell receives the identical sets of chromosomal DNA, which will be used to carry out a-reproductive functions, such as metabolism. Somatic cells simply divide by fission (like bacteria) without exchanging DNA. Thus, the germ plasm (nucleus) is responsible for the preservation of variations in a species. This preservation goes beyond any environmental – or acquired – character or factor. The immortality of the germline, therefore, is determined by its autonomy with respect to the mortal environment of the cell or soma cells.

In *Beyond the Pleasure Principle* (1920), Freud hypothesizes that sexual reproduction re-balances the death tendency of living organisms in favour of the immortality of germinal life. In his articulation, sexual instincts or Eros, also defined as the 'preserver of all things' or as 'life instinct', aim at the coalescence of portions of living substance, which operates in opposition to death instincts 'brought into being by the coming into life of inorganic substance' (1920: 61). Freud underlines that the coalescence of germ-cells (between the chromosomes of the sperm's and egg's nucleus) is necessary for the immortality of the germline in multicellular organism. 'It is only on this condition that the sexual function can prolong the cell's life and lend it the appearance of immortality' (44). The immortality of cellular life through the sexual transmission of germ-cells is explained by the concept of Libido: a self-preservative instinct or narcissistic libido extended to individual cells.[34]

Freud connects his theory of life (organic) and death (inorganic) drives with Weismann's morphological theory in order to display the Libido of individual cells transmitted through sexual reproduction. Nevertheless, Freud disagrees with Weismann, who points out that mortality is a recent acquisition in the evolution of multicellular organisms, a manifestation of the cellular adaptation to external conditions, which was unknown to protozoa (bacteria). In order to affirm that sexual reproduction enables the transmission of life drives by overcoming the primal tendency to death in all living creatures, Freud appeals to bacterial conjugation, one of the many sexual recombinations among bacteria, where genetic material is transmitted from donor to recipient (44; 56). In bacterial conjugation, two-parents' mating − sexual reproduction − and death − the death of the soma − coexist and confirm his theory of the ancestrality of death in the process of evolution, the linear evolution from the inorganic to the organic (the evolution of life).

According to Freud, the balance of energy-heat dynamics also suggests the original cyclic tension between life and death. Drawing on the second law of thermodynamics, he affirms that the life process of the individual tends, for internal reasons, to an abolition of chemical tensions (increasing entropy or death). Conversely, the union with the living substance between different individuals increases those tensions and lets the substance live. The great cost in expenditure of energetic and chemical tensions (i.e. the cost of sexual reproduction) is compensated by the introduction of fresh 'vital differences' − the differences which, according to Freud, must be 'lived off' − bringing new amounts of stimuli in multicellular life.

According to this dynamic model, death (the inorganic) defines the tendency of life towards dissipation compensated by sexual coupling.

Similarly to Darwin, Freud considers evolution as a tendency towards disorder regulated by sexual reproduction that preserves variations by blocking the movement towards the inorganic (dis-organization). This blockage involves an act of discharging excessive energy: the channelling of increasing tension outside the system. Sexual coupling requires this energetic expenditure – charge and discharge – that serves to effectuate a strengthening and rejuvenating affect on germinal variations.

This hypothesis entangles sex with a thermodynamic cycle of expenditure (output) and re-balance, which ensures the rejuvenating variations of the living substance. The absence of the two-parent sex provokes a tendency towards an inorganic state or death (because of the increasing entropy in the system). Similarly, in Freud's words, '[t]he tendency of mental life is the effort to reduce – keep constant or remove internal tension due to stimuli [. . .] – the tendency which finds expression in the pleasure principle' (55–6). This libidinal tendency to reduce tension confirms that sexual reproduction (coupling) is necessary for the development of organic life in order to postpone the return of death or the inorganic.[35]

> If we take it as truth that knows no exception that everything living dies for internal reason – becomes inorganic once again – then we shall be compelled to say that '*the aim of all life is death*' and, looking backwards, that '*inanimate things existed before living ones*'.
>
> (38)

The priority of the inorganic defines the regressive point of life towards finitude, a compulsive return to death in order to reproduce life. Freud's theory introduces an analogy between cellular death and dissolution of difference and between cellular reproduction, life and differentiation. He associates the death of the soma (the body) with regression towards the inorganic and conceives of life as the constant balance of energy flows in a closed loop tending towards disorder and death. This cyclic return from death to life and death again only corresponds to the constancy of organic life and variations. This constancy is ensured by a mutual relation between sexual reproduction and the immortality of the germ plasm (the meiotic reduction of chromosomal doublings – mitosis – which enables the transmission of nucleated material).

Freud's investigation of sex, reproduction and death focuses on sexual mating as the model of variation of bodies defined by the linear transmission of the germ plasm (nucleic genes). The narcissistic libido of the germline (nucleic DNA) constitutes the order of life that exorcizes death – the return to the inorganic phase unable to produce difference. Freud's insistence on the presence of the death drive since the 'origin of life', re-appearing as a regressive repetition of the primordial (inorganic) state in the multicellular life cycle, exclusively concerns eukaryotic machines of nucleic transmission (mitosis and meiosis).

The endosymbiotic stratification of sex, however, challenges this constant cycle of life and death drives (the linear flow from inorganic to organic, simple to complex). The symbiotic folding of inorganic masses of bacteria in the organic smaller and polarized genetic chromosomes in the eukaryotic cell constitutes meiotic sex as a machine that envelops while being enveloped by inorganic soma. Somatic death does not indicate regression of organic life towards inorganic dissolution. Rather, the emergence of cellular death is linked to the molar (nucleic) organization of bacterial bodies in the eukaryotic cell introducing a cancerous metastasis in the lineage through the duplication of the nucleus. The emergence of meiotic sex does not exclusively ensure the reduction and the transfer of genetic material, but also the recombination of bacterial genes residing in the cytoplasmic body of the eukaryotic cell. The molecular network between the germline and the somaline in meiotic sex reveals that multicellular differences emerge from the cloning or repetition of microbial sexes.

As Margulis and Sagan observe, the body of the cell (cytoplasmic soma) is occupied by organelles, which symbiotically contributed to the formation of the eukaryotic cell. These organelles are genetically alien to the patterns of chromosomal wrapping and hereditary transmission of nucleic DNA; they partake, indeed, of a *different* phylum – a 'rhizomatic phylum'.[36] The cytoplasmic body of the cell is crowded with microbial cells, plastids and mitochondria.[37] The last possess an autonomous machinery of genetic replication (DNA, messenger RNA and ribosomes): a complete independent system that reproduces like bacterial cloning or gene trading.

> Unlike the DNA of the nucleus, but like bacterial DNA, mitochondrial DNA is not coated by histone protein. Mitochondria assemble proteins on ribosomes very similar to the ribosomes of bacteria. [. . .] mitochondria reproduce on their own timetable and in their own way, forgoing the complex mitosis of the nucleus for a simple bacterium-like division. They engage in the nonsystematic genetic transfer that characterizes bacterial sex. All in all, they behave like prokaryotic captives.
>
> Sagan (1992: 364)

Once autonomous respiring bacteria (specifically purple bacteria), mitochondria arose from larger anaerobic or inorganic archeobacteria incorporating aerobic bacteria. This hypersexual fusion, followed by increasing atmospheric oxygen, gave rise to the eukaryotic symbiont within which mitochondria became permanently captured. The integration of organelles (mitochondria and plastids) and their function into the eukaryotic cell constitutes a relatively recent process compared to the organelles' more ancient autonomy. Once captured, these bacteria turned 'into the matrilineally transmitted mitochondria – only the ovum bequeaths them to the human embryo – exploit[ing] oxygen's great reactivity', which enabled these bacteria 'to employ reactive oxygen to improve cell processes of energy transformation' (Margulis and Sagan 1994: 105). Since then, mitochondria became the energizer of all eukaryotic cells: 'the first order way that life banks for the future'(80).

From this standpoint, it can be argued that Weismann underestimated the wide capacity of many animals and nearly all plants to retain the master set of community genome outside the germline – the set of cells destined to become gametes, such as egg and sperm. Most species of eukaryotes can form gametes: clones and asexual organisms are able to grow through organs as occurs for the gemma of sponges. Meiotic sex ensures the retention and transmission of at least one copy of each gene including organelles – mitochondria. The inorganic soma, far from dying, is probably far more important for the evolutionary process than hitherto imagined.

Weismann's intuition about the germinal continuum should be extended to include at least one set of cytoplasmic genes for each of the reproducing organelles. For endosymbiosis, the germ plasm corresponds to a complete set of heterogeneous genomes (nucleic and cytoplasmic) contained within a membranous package separated by a plasmatic, rather than nucleic, membrane (Margulis and Sagan 1994: 176). Hence the distinction between the nucleus and the cytoplasm (germline and somaline) is not a boundary but a threshold between parallel networks of sex and reproduction (nucleic and mitochondrial). The nuclear membrane of the eukaryotic cell is part of a plasmatic synthesis or a microbial assemblage of heterogeneous genetic material. The implosion of microbial sexes in the nucleic and cytoplasmic milieus of the eukaryotic cell deploys an indefinite modulation of sex and reproduction through increasingly smaller folds constituting the multicellular organism as a network of microbial variations. As Deleuze points out: 'This organism is enveloped by [other] organisms, one within the other (interlocking germinal matter), like Russian dolls' (1993: 8).

The continuum between inorganic and organic variations involves an *intensive extension* of microbial sex and reproduction rather than inorganic regression. The tendency towards death involves a molecular mutation of microbes that far from dissolving all bodies—sexes (death) expose the inorganic continuum across organized life: a symbiotic aggregation of sexes (bacterial sex, hypersex) that *appears* contained in molar forms of sex (meiotic sex, sexual reproduction and organic death). The eukaryotic folding of microbial mutations catalyses the emergence of larger aggregates, multicellular bodies through the differentiation of tissues and organs that introduces the new dimensions of sex and gender. In particular, the new genetic structure packaged and transmitted through meiosis leads to the formation of sexed organisms in animals and plants. When meiotic sex first spread in protists, sexual patterns appeared nearly identical. Later on, in a watery environment, 'a host of different genders and their determining mechanisms evolved', by inducing a restoration of chromosomal numbers in fertilization varying across plants and animals (Margulis and Sagan 1986: 201).

Not only the chromosomal determination of gender varies and is irreducible to only two sexual forms (male and female), but also the morphologies of the gendered body have been changing in relation to the codes of the milieu it occupies. For example, the metamorphic transformations of sexual reproduction and sexual organs indicate the passage from aquatic to terrestrial modes of mating.[38] At a first glance, gender appears as univocally determined by genes, but machines of stratification of sex signal that interlinked variables of expression and content (genotype and phenotype) define a wide range of gender determinations (from single to multigendered populations in cells, plants and animals: fungi, dandelions and lizards). This range presents various degrees of order that define gender as a process of becoming: a molecular differentiation of bacterial sex, hypersex and meiotic sex.

> Gender-changing mutations occurred as heritable alternations in the genes of the original community of microbes that comprised the eucaryotic cells. Changes in the genetic basis of gender determination occurred as many times as speciation itself in the rise of obligately sexual species.
>
> Margulis and Sagan (1986: 203)

Although gender can be differently determined in plants and animal, in humans, as in all mammals, genes and, in particular, chromosomes, determine sex.[39] In humans, sex chromosomes are distinguished in XX 23 matched pairs in females, which are contained in the ova, and XY 23 matched pairs in males, contained in the sperm. Male haploids, or sperm, are small, motile and numerous. The female gametes, or eggs, are large and stationary.[40] The gendered sex is determined by the Y chromosome, also named 'testing-determining factor' (or TDF) developing its function only in the testis.[41] Its absence induces the gonad to 'remain' an ovary. The TDF adds a supplementary dimension to the embryo, which will otherwise remain female. The affect of genetic sex on the entire organism is actualized through hormones, which about the eighth week of embryonic development determine the gender of the organism. As Margulis and Sagan point out, '[a]lthough chromosomes entirely determine the genetically transmitted gender in vertebrate animals, hormones determine the actual functioning gender' (1986: 201). The sex steroid hormones or gonadal steroids do not directly affect genes. Rather, they enter into a complex apparatus where they become identified and 'bound by receptor molecules in the cells of the target tissues' (LeVay 1994: 25). Such receptors determine the specificity of sexed steroids: androgen receptors bind testosterone and similar steroids (androgens), progestins bind progesterone and oestrogen receptors bind oestrogen. Receptors influence the expression of genes in the target tissue that induces this tissue to develop as male or female.[42] The determination of gender implies a supplementary hormonal dimension: in foetal life the secretion of hormones establish the maleness of the embryo, while the imperceptibility of this secretion marks the embryo as female.

Although there is no space to explore the hormonal stratification of sex, suffice it to say that their biochemical presence is very ancient. They appear as receptors and communicators of early aerobic bacteria, which could regulate their sexual encounters through biochemical signals. The organization of hormones' response-stimuli in multicellular organisms entails complex feedback loops that constitute the 'endocrine system': an apparatus of regulation of networked hormonal signals. The endocrine system deploys a series of feedback loops giving instructions to the organism and receiving information from the environment, affecting the development of organs and sexual/gender orientations.[43] It forms an apparatus of regulation of thousands of biochemical inputs, stimuli, secretions folded inside the organism to maintain its metabolism and to check some fundamental organic functions. Among many, those linked to sexual cycles in women – puberty, pregnancy, menopause – are specific marks of the organic stratification of the female sex. These marks are not directly determined by sex chromosomes, but entail the folding of bacterial sex and mitochondrial hypersex into the eukaryotic machine of meiotic sex. Bacterial and mitochondrial sexes are not simply substituted but are incorporated in the chromosomal sex-gender machine of differentiation. The meiotic entanglement between sex, reproduction and death locates sexual reproduction in a wider stratification of sex and reproduction emerging from bacterial sex and cloning.

SYMBIOSEX

After a few hours she dozed off and dreamed of bacterial buildups inside the bodies within the trench graves. Biofilms, what most people thought of as slime: little industrious bacterial cities reducing these corpses, these once-living giant evolutionary offspring, back to their native materials. Lovely polysaccharide architectures being laid down within the interior channels, the gut and the lungs, the heart and the arteries and eyes and brain, the bacteria giving up their wild ways and becoming citified, recycling all; great garbage dump cities of bacteria cheerfully ignorant of philosophy and history and the character of the dead hulks they now colonized and reclaimed. *Bacteria made us. They take us back. Welcome home.*

Bear (1999: 34).

The symbiotic stratification of sex suggests that reproduction is a prerequisite of sex and differentiation. Reproduction does not correspond to sexual mating, but entails the autopoietic networks of a body in relation to milieus. These networks can be found at every level of biophysical organization, from single to assembled bacteria, from eukaryotic cells to multicellular organisms. In particular, the endosymbiotic evolution of sex defines sexual reproduction (meiotic sex) as a large aggregate of microbial symbiotic machines enfolded in the double body of the eukaryotic cell (genotype and phenotype, nucleus and cytoplasm). Endosymbiosis explains the emergence of sexual reproduction and sexed difference in relation to a metastable ecosystem of microbes cloning and mutating across thresholds of environmental change. In this sense, human sex and reproduction is neither the first nor the last mode of sex and reproduction. Sexual reproduction partakes of the endosymbiotic dynamics of information trading (bacterial sex) and cellular mergings. This dynamics exposes the velocities of mutation in the rate of evolution of a species.

The Darwinian conception of evolution concentrates on rates of changes or differentiation between populations, whose capacities of adaptation are determined by natural selection, the blind hand of order. In this framework, rates of changes correspond to gradual developments from simple to complex variations (from bacteria to eukaryotes). Natural selection acts upon already actualized forms, sorting out best from ill-adapted organisms. This gradual development of variations defines sexual reproduction as the sexual exchange par excellence (the exchange of male–female chromosomes). Sexual reproduction guarantees the preservation of genetic variations. It is a mechanism that serves to overcome the death drive, the compulsion to repeat death, the return to the inorganic (somatic) substrate in order to be born again (through discharge). Sex and reproduction remain subjected to the arborescent model of descent reducing difference to linear heredity and binary sexes.

Endosymbiosis challenges this genealogical difference. It maps the rhizomatic variations of sex and reproduction through the parallel networks of bacterial and eukaryotic machines. The endosymbiotic articulation of meiotic sex exposes a molecular mixture of bacterial contents and expressions (codes-milieus relations). This mixture questions the barrier between the germline and the somaline that defines sexual reproduction as the most successful model for the regeneration of genetic variations. Variations are far from being determined by the organic germline and the inorganic death of somatic bodies. Rather, they entail a repetition or doubling of inorganic sexes imploded in the meiotic machine of sex. In this sense, multicellular differentiations are folds of microbial mutations exposing differential degrees of sex: bacterial sex, mitochondrial hypersex and meiotic sex. Sexual reproduction is intensive; its microbial potential discloses human sex and reproduction to unpredictable mutations.

Symbiosex is not the end result of previous parasitic relations indicating a forced cooperation between different bodies to reach a shared goal or to survive in a hostile environment. These relations are not the effects of a primordial cause or the urge of individual organisms to gather in a competitive environment in order to increase possibilities of survival. Symbiosex maps the ceaseless assemblages of heterogeneous bacteria under given pressures without ultimate purpose. This is a machinic composition of singular components (atmospheric, genetic, chemical, cellular) generating a new assemblage under certain conditions on the biophysical stratum. This composition points to the micro-politics of bacterial sex and reproduction beyond identity.[44] Bacterial recombination and cellular parasitism challenge the identification of sex with sexual reproduction, reproduction with sexual organs and sexual difference with sexed chromosomes. Rather than competing for survival, bacteria distribute information through infectious recombination, parasiting cellular fusions and cannibalistic incorporations producing new modes of sex and reproduction. Symbiosex maps the biophysical stratification of sex as an ecosystem of microbial codes-milieus marked by critical thresholds of equilibrium.

Notes

1 On the cybernetic function and behaviour of reproduction characterizing the understanding of information patterns of transmission, see S. A. Kauffman 1993. In studies on biological computing and Artificial Life, information reproduction is defined by the concept of emergence. See C.C. Langton 1992.

2 Late eighteenth and early nineteenth-century biology focuses on the search for universal principles to explain the diversity of organisms. This biology was embedded in the Kantian distinction between organisms and mechanical devices. Organisms are self-reproducing wholes whose parts exist both for one another and by means of one another. Parts in mechanical devices exist only for one another as each marks the condition of the other's functions toward a common functional end. See S. Jay Gould 1977; W. Coleman 1977; J. H. Zammito 1992; Kauffman 1993: 3–26; M. DeLanda 2002.

3 The Darwinian theory of evolution challenges the Platonic and Aristotelian classical conception of an inert, pre-formed and passive matter that fails to auto-organize without intervention of the transcendent or immanent divine. The Darwinian emphasis on the variation of populations between territories also challenges the Cartesian belief in a non-extended substance that governs the instinctive body. The relation between animals' and plants' population across different milieus questions the belief in the exclusive capacity of the human being to engender social communities. See DeLanda 2002: 45–81.

4 Deleuze and Guattari's explanation of the complexity of the organic stratum also draws on Darwin's evolutionism. See 1987: 47–8. On population thinking, see F. Jacob 1974; E. Mayr 1982.

5 In the nineteenth century, Wallace associated Darwin's notion of descent with modification with the term evolution intended as organic evolution and organic progress. See Gould 1977; 1991.

6 Inspired by Malthus, Darwin defined natural selection as a mechanism whereby only few offspring of a given species would survive the competition for limited resources. See Gould 1991.

7 See K. Ansell Pearson 1997a: 117; 1999: 69.

8 See A. Weismann 1882.

9 The genotype is the set of genetic instructions or material in a cellular or multi-

cellular organism. The phenotype corresponds to the set of external manifested characteristics on the organism such as colour, size and behaviours.

10 See R. Dawkins 1989; 1991.

11 Replication is defined by Margulis and Sagan as a '[p]rocess that augments by copying the number of DNA or RNA molecules. Molecular duplication process' (1997: 248).

12 The cybernetic feedback of information questions the linear relation between genotype and phenotype (cause-effect) in evolution. See G. Bateson 1973.

13 On the epistemological critique of science, see S. Harding 1991; E. F. Keller 1992; D. Haraway 1989; 1991.

14 Isabelle Stengers argues that the epistemological critique of science is based upon Thomas Kuhn's conception of paradigms. This conception assumes that science is a human construction and that scientific objectivity is a social convention building on the agreement between scientists. She considers scientific hypothesis as situated in a vaster set of potential happenings: events. Stengers 1997.

15 See Deleuze 1988a: 95–7; 1994: 240; 1992b: 172; 232–3.

16 See Deleuze 1990a: 4–11; 13–21; 23; 35; 12–22; 67–73; 52–7; 1994: 94.

17 See Deleuze 1992b: 208–10; 212; 230; 238ff; 249–50.

18 See Deleuze 1983: 39–72; 1994: 22; 24; 40–2; 55. See also Ansell Pearson 1997a: 45–6; 147; 126–29.

19 The concept of molecular selection is related to Kauffman's study of the capacity of chemical, physical, biological systems to auto-organize through a web of parallel relations and engender novelty at the moment of suspension (poised state) between order and chaos. See Kauffman 1993: 173–236.

20 This relation between interior and exterior elements and material refers to the definition that Deleuze and Guattari assign to the three constitutive marks of the organic stratum: 1. molecular material, which is furnished by the substrata and becomes the exterior milieu for the elements or compounds of the stratum, also for those constituting the prebiotic soup – for example, solar energy and biochemical material which form the compound of hydrogen in the Hadean Aeon; 2. substantial elements, which marks the interior milieu for the elements or compound of the strata – for example catalysts, enzymes which appropriate materials and exteriorize themselves through replication even in the condition of the primordial soup (prebiotic synthesis of lipids). 3. formal relations, which define the limit or membrane between the interior and the exterior within the stratum. The membrane regulates exchanges and transformations in organization and defines all of the stratum's formal relations or traits – for example the prebiotic membrane, cellular bacterial membrane, the eukaryotic membrane. See Deleuze and Guattari 1987: 50. On the prebiotic evolution of molecular material, substantial elements and formal relations, see A. Lazcano, George E. Fox, and John F. Orò 1992: 237–95.

21 See Deleuze and Guattari 1987: 56. On machines of destratification see chapter 5.

22 See B. Massumi 1992: 54–5.

23 The theory of endosymbiosis has important precedents in the work of, for example, the German biologist A. F. Shimper (1893), the French biologist Paul Portier (1918), the American anatomist Ivan Wallin and the Russian scholar-biologist K. S. Mereschovsky, in the first quarter of the twentieth century. In particular, Mereschovsky (1855–1921) rejected the Darwinian theory of natural selection as a source of innovation and invented the term 'symbiogenesis' to explain that the appearance of new organisms stems from prolonged symbiotic associations. Although dismissed for a long time, symbiogenesis is increasingly acquiring scientific relevance. Its scientific importance has also been supported by molecular biology and biochemistry which have questioned the classical division between plant and animal kingdom and the classification based on this division, in favour of the most fundamental difference in life between eukaryotes (cells with nuclei, among which mitochondria and, in the case of algae and plants, plastids) and prokaryotes, also called monera or bacteria (cells without membrane-bound nuclei). See J. Sapp 1994; D. Sagan 1992: 362–85; L. Margulis 1981: 1–14.

24 According to Margulis and Sagan, the cell is the minimal unit of both autopoiesis and reproduction. Chemical systems or biochemical reactions are not auto-poietic. For example, the polishing of silver and the production of plastic involve chemical reactions, whereas the treatment of sewage and the production of beer involve autopoiesis as they require the metabolism and growth of organisms. See 1986: 11–12.

25 Sexual processes involve the production of genetically new individuals, but do not require an increase in the total number of individuals. Reproduction, instead, involves the increase in the number of living beings. Bacteria or prokaryotic cells, which contain free-floating strands of DNA comprising their nucleotids, repro-duce by splitting in two (fission). The newly and continuously synthesized DNA while attached to a cell membrane is distributed to each offspring cell. Bacteria transmit information by trading genes, passing genes from one donor to the reci-pient (bacterial sex). See Margulis and Sagan 1986: 54–7. On different forms of bacterial sex, see Margulis and Sagan 1997: 58.

26 See Pace 1991: 531–3. See also Margulis and Sagan 1986: 38–53.

27 On the distinction between prokaryotic and eukaryotic cells, see Margulis and Sagan 1986: 62.

28 On the importance of the genetic code on the organic strata, see Deleuze and Guattari 1987: 42.

29 This information is codified by the DNA, and in particular by the succession of triplets or codons, groups of three nucleic bases. Each triplet corresponds to an amino acid of the protein through a process implying a series of procedures: one of them is called 'transcription' and entails the flow of information from DNA to RNA; another one is called 'translation' and entails the flow from the RNA to the protein. Between the DNA and the protein there is a correspondence of information.

30 Chromosomes are defined as: '[g]ene (DNA)-bearing structure made of chro-matin, usually visible only during mitotic or meiotic nuclear division in stained

cells or cells with large chromosomes'. Margulis and Sagan 1997: 244. In mitosis, the dance of chromosomes refers to 'the formation of visible and countable chromosomes and their movement first to a plane in the center ('equator') and then to the poles of the spherical cell'. Margulis and Sagan 1986: 64.

31 On mitotis, see Margulis and Sagan 1986: 232.

32 Chromosome reduction has been explained as a delay in the time of reproduction of both kinetochores and DNA. Margulis and Sagan 1985: 185–90; 1986: 151–52; 1987: 37–9.

33 Margulis and Sagan question evolutionary theories that define sexuality as a single process (linking sex with reproduction). In particular, they challenge the 'Red Queen Hypothesis', which maintains that sexuality produces greater genetic diversity because of which the 'cost' of sexual mating becomes compensated. See, 1997: 118–21.

34 For Freud, libido is a regressive satisfaction bound up with the death instinct- the inorganic. For Deleuze and Guattari, libido operates as a productive impulse tending towards turbulent becoming, supermolecular declinations rather than circling in a self-enclosed cycle. See Deleuze and Guattari 1983: 333.

35 Freud identifies the death drive with a linear regressive repetition of the same inorganic material according to an entropic cycle assuring a return to the Identical. In his texts, Deleuze critically engages with Freud's homeostasic thought by contrasting his 'organismic' conception of life and death. For example, Deleuze discloses repetition to the creative production of novelty (1994). Similarly, in his work with Guattari, the death drive, rather than a regressive satisfaction linked to discharge implies a schizo-supermolecular becoming. Deleuze and Guattari 1983: 330.

36 On the rhizomatic or machinic phylum see Deleuze and Guattari 1987: 406–7, 409–10. See also DeLanda 1992: 129–67.

37 On mitochondrial endosymbiosis and the importance of organelles for the constitution of eukaryotic cells, see Margulis 1970: 178–205; 1971: 3–11. Margulis and Sagan 1986: 65–73. Sagan 1992: 362–85. Margulis and Sagan 1994: 104–10.

38 See E. Morgan 1990. The theory of the Aquatic Ape will be explained in Chapter 5.

39 The determination of sex occurs through the reading of the chromosome's DNA by the messenger RNA in the production of proteins. Then, proteins produce differentiated cells, and these engender small molecules, such as steroid hormones, that communicate to other cells. The steroid hormones enter their target cells, bind with chromosomes there, and permit the differential production of genes products, messenger RNA and protein. Margulis and Sagan 1986: 200.

40 According to Margulis and Sagan, the definition of male is simply an organism (gamont) that produces relatively small and moving gametes (or microgametes). The term female usually refers to those gametes, which stand still or those gamonts, which produce sedentary gametes. See 1986: 195.

41 See S. LeVay 1994: 18.

42 While the presence of the Y chromosome and its TDF genes enables a masculine development of tissues, the absence of these genes makes gonads turn into ovaries. The latter do not secrete perceptible amounts of sex steroids during foetal life, thus marking the development of the embryo as female. Only at puberty, the ovaries start to secrete high levels of oestrogens adding features to the differentiation of the organism as female, while for men, the secretion of testosterone at puberty completes their differentiation as male. See LeVay 1994: 29.

43 As many studies demonstrate, there is no linear correspondence between the chromosomal determination of sex and the phenotypic traits of gender linked to hormonal development. See N. Oudshoorn 1994.

44 The micropolitics of microbial sex will be addressed at more length in Chapter 5. The microbial differentiation of sex and reproduction defines a drifting tendency of information: a ceaseless de-differentiation of acquired states of difference.

CHAPTER 3

Parthenogenic Sex

Under no circumstances could desires be allowed to flow in their inherently *undirected* manner. Word of the ability to tie themselves to any *object*, then abandon it to form new ties in a powerful movement of affective intensities, couldn't be permitted to leak out. *Goals* had to be found, desires had to be channelled.

Theweleit (1987: 270)

INTRODUCTION

This chapter points out that the passage from the organic to the biocultural stratification of sex entails a process of 'overcodification' of the meiotic order of sex and reproduction. This process defines a new organization of the body–sex in disciplinary society. As Foucault argues, in disciplinary society, a new scientific conception of reproduction leads to the emergence of a new sex.[1] Yet, this conception is not primarily determined by modern discourses about the body. Rather, it involves a biocultural and socio-technical abstraction of the organic machines of sex, reproduction and death: meiotic sex (sexual reproduction).

The organic (eukaryotic) order of genetic and cellular sex now expands across socio-cultural, economic and technological dynamics of reproduction, introducing a new distribution of content and expression of matter on the strata. The multicellular forms of content and expression (the chromosomes and the genotype) are overcodified through 'regimes of signs' on the biocultural stratum. The multicellular substances of content and expression (the cytoplasm and the phenotype) are deterritorialized and decoded through 'technologies of power'.

According to Deleuze and Guattari, this new distribution of content and expression constitutes a new group of strata: the 'anthropomorphic stratum'.[2] The process of overcoding integrates different orders of magnitude (biophysical and biocultural) through a process of formal synthesis of all expressions, a phenomenon unknown on the organic strata: *translation*. Translation is not the linguistic possibility to represent language in other languages, but the ability to overcode (code on a new level) non-semiotic encodings (genotype and phenotype, nucleic and cytoplasmic reproduction) into a deterritorialized system of signs: linguistic signs.[3] Overcoding implies that the '[f]orm of expression becomes linguistic rather than genetic'.[4] On this new level of organization, expression no longer operates through genetic connections, but entails the emergence of a new order above the layers of the genotype. This new order of expression is constituted by comprehensible and transmittable symbols that convey a superlinearity: the capacity to synthesize all codes-milieus' relations into a sufficiently deterritorialized system of signs. In particular, this order defines the capacity of the scientific world to translate all particles, codes and territorialities of the organic strata into a new order of signs. This order does not correspond to the power of representation, the impositions of the signifier on matter. Overcodification does not work by principles of analogy and resemblance. It involves an abstraction (virtualization or potentialization) of particle-signs on a new level of relations, producing a new organization (decodification and deterritorialization) of forms and substances of content and expression.

On the one hand, the decodification and deterritorialization of substances of content and expression of a multicellular body (cytoplasm and phenotype) mark the emergence of the ability to touch, which, in a first instance, is deployed by the hand and the tool, and translated into a technological content. As Deleuze and Guattari argue, this content does not equate to the hand and tools. Rather, it indicates a technical social machine that pre-exists and exceeds the human hand and the technical instrument. 'Technologies of power' constitute the disciplinary assemblage of this machine. Technologies of power are machines of organization of bodies that define their rules and architectures. They mark a new entanglement between the forces of reproduction of the human body and the technical machine (substances of content and expression) in disciplinary society.

On the other hand, the decodification and deterritorialization of the forms of content and expression of the multicellular body (chromosomes and genotype) map the ability to see and speak, the intensive synchronism between facial and linguistic expressions that constitutes the 'regime of signs' (an abstract symbolic expression). This regime does not correspond to the regime of the signifier. The signifier only constitutes one of the levels of the semiotic stratification of elements, particles and compounds that mould a singular organization of power. Even when considering its relevance and operation, the signifier does not exist in isolation from a-signifying modes of organizations. The regime of signs defines a semiotic collective machine that pre-exists and exceeds facial and linguistic expressions. In Foucauldian terms, this machine forms 'knowledge' with its two forms of content and expression, the visible and the articulable (non-discursive and discursive multiplicities). It would be misleading to conceive of signs (forms of content and expression) through the hierarchy of words and things. As Deleuze and Guattari put it, 'the form of expression is reducible not to words but to a set of statements arising in the social field considered as a stratum (that is what a regime of signs is)'. Similarly, 'the form of content is reducible not to a thing but to a complex state of things as a formation of power'. Signs are composed by '[t]wo constantly intersecting multiplicities, "discursive multiplicities" of expression and "nondiscursive multiplicities" of content' (1987: 66). The disciplinary organization of signs exposes a mutual relation between scientific statements (in physics, biology, anatomy, psychoanalysis) constituting discursive multiplicities or forms of expression, and the architectures of the body (the human body, the technical body, the social body) constituting non-discursive multiplicities or forms of content.

The symbiotic aggregations of these new levels of substances and forms of content and expression entail an overcodification of the parallel orders of reproduction on the organic stratum: the nucleic machine of filiation (germline) and the cytoplasmic machine of recombination (somaline). These orders become folded inside the apparatus of biopower: the synthesizer of bodies–sexes into an organic unity. Biopower condenses these flows around the molar aggregations of signs: 'the Sovereign or the Law, in the case of the State; the Father in the case of the family; Money, Gold or Dollar in the case of the market; God in the case of religion; Sex in the case of sexual institution' (Deleuze 1988b: 76). Nevertheless, these aggregations do not cease to diffuse new flows of reproduction that intensify the double order of organic sex. This intensification generates a new bifurcation of the machines of sex on the biocultural stratum indicating the autonomy of new reproductive forces (the abstracted cytoplasmic somaline) from the filiative law of sex and the patriarchal order of reproduction (the abstracted nucleic germline) characterizing the disciplinary formation of sex.

As a new mode of reproduction, disciplinary sex is marked by what escapes (what differentiates from) the apparatus of biopower (or the negative binarism between the sexes determined by the self-contained system of norms and deviancies). Arguing against the Freudian pleasure principle, I will point to another kind of sex distributing across the disciplinary organization of reproduction. In particular, I will delineate the emergence of a masochistic assemblage of desire-power of reproduction to map the disciplinary entanglement of sex, reproduction and death outside the economy of representation.[5] The legacy of the Freudian pleasure principle accompanies the understanding of the relationship between sex and reproduction where the female body remains the depository of filiation and death. The Freudian interpretation of masochism defines the feminine instincts of death and destruction, passivity and inertia. Freud conceives of masochism as the correspondent inversion of sadism. However, according to Deleuze, masochism is irreducible to the sadist dynamics of death. It is autonomous of the law of the phallus and the principles of death and life. Thus, in masochism, femininity lacks nothing (1989a).

Masochism and sadism are not the correspondent poles of the same desire. Rather, as discussed in this chapter, they constitute a double (and irreducible) organization of the biophysical entanglement between sex, reproduction and death that generates a new assemblage of desire-power constituting heterogeneous machines of sex in the disciplinary formation (e.g. heterosexual reproduction, homosexual reproduction, parthenogenesis). As Foucault argues, the sadist tendency of biopower manifests itself through the disciplinary obsession with managing uncontrollable fluids, channelling information towards profit, ordering the body through the organic (nucleic) forms and functions of reproduction (1989b). Conversely, the masochist desire-power delineates the emergence of an autonomous kind of reproduction (the autonomy from sameness and filiation), distributing a new perception of sex (parthenogenesis) on the biocultural stratum.

This chapter is divided into four sections. The first section discusses the psychoanalytical overcodification of the organic order of sex, reproduction and death that define the disciplinary machines of sex. Drawing on Deleuze, I suggest that different compositions of desire entail different productions of sexual power – sadism and masochism – in the disciplinary formation. In the second section, I relate these compositions to the economy of reproduction of industrial capitalism, arguing that the entanglement between death (the inorganic) and reproduction (constant and variable capital) exceeds the logic of organic balance. The third section argues that the anatomical and gynaecological perception of the entanglement of sex and death marks the emergence of a new perception of sex and reproduction (i.e. parthenogenesis) that I will analyse through David Cronenberg's film *Dead Ringers*. The fourth section points to the diffusion of partheno-genic sex across all bodies of disciplinary reproduction: the female body, the body of industrial capitalism, and the biotechnical body. Parthenogenic sex interrupts the entropic cycle of pleasure and filia-tion: the sadist homo-erotics of biopower. It delineates a biocultural mutation in the process of stratification of sex and reproduction.

DISCIPLINARY ENTROPY

> If one can apply the term bio-history to the pressures through which the movements of life and the process of history interfere with one another, one would have to speak of biopower to designate what brought life and its mechanisms into the realm of explicit calcula-tions and made knowledge-power an agent of transformation of human life. It is not that life has been totally integrated into techni-ques that govern and administer it; it constantly escapes them.
>
> Foucault (1990: 143)

The disciplinary overcodification of the organic entanglement between sex, reproduction and death is enmeshed with the scientific conception of information-energy transmission and reproduction.[6] The shift from the classical to the thermodynamic conception of nature is crucial not only for physics and biology, but also for socio-cultural and economic organizations. Yet, the thermodynamic conception of reproduction, entangling sex with death, does not represent a paradigmatic shift following the crisis of the classical *épistème*. Quite the contrary, it marks the emergence of a trans-situational event that exceeds para-digms, structures and systems. The thermodynamic conception of life and death spills in and out of the scientific spheres to invade and be invaded by the socio-cultural and techno-economic changes of the nine-teenth century.[7]

For classical science the world reflected the order and stability of the universe. Newtonian physics presupposes equivalence and resemblance between the past and the future. An initial condition fulfils the expec-tation of its outcome. Particles have only to pass through without change. The laws of eternal reflection and immobility determine the essence of the universe and nature through the analogy and resem-blance of forms. In the nineteenth century, the thermodynamic conception of energy began to challenge this time-reversible perspective of the universe. In particular, entropy came to define the tendency of heat – energy – to diffuse and to waste. This tendency marked the irreversible gradient of time, the irreversible trajectory of flows of energy running towards chaos. Time symmetry was transmuted by time irreversibility, by that which escapes the manipulation of energy flows. Before its use in the second law of thermodynamics, in 1865, Rudolf Julius Clausius defined entropy as evolution, change and mutation. Yet, the Viennese physicist Ludwig Boltzmann reworked the thermodynamic sense of evolution affirming that the reach of equilibrium and uniformity distinguishes biology from physics. The problem of equilibrium was for the first time introduced as a problem of controlling, mastering the tendency of entropy to diffuse and disperse energy, the tendency towards organic self-destruction. According to Prigogine, Fourier's law of heat diffusion, the tendency of energy to escape manipulation became the new focus of scientific enquiry. Thermodynamics is set up in relation with irreversibility but also against it, seeking not to know change but to avoid it (1997: 36–7). Certainty, immutability and order no longer rule nature and the universe, which are now governed by entropic flows marking the mutating stages of equilibrium.

In the Foucauldian analysis of disciplinary biopower, entropy or death lies at the crossing of a new organization of power. The discipline of life subjects decoded populations to a regime of knowledge (the bifurcation between forms of expression or collective statements, the discourses of science, and forms of content or non-discursive codes) that constructs normality through the classification of diseases, pathologies and madness. Simultaneously, this discipline subjects forces of reproduction to technologies of power (the bifurcation between substances of content, the biomass of bodies and substances of expression, their organization in schools, factories, hospitals, public and private spaces), organizing the space and time of life through the constant threat of disorder. Biopower spreads lines of deviation from the discipline of life through technologies of reclusion – the clinic, the asylum, the prison, the factory, the house – and knowledges of perversion that point to the threatening presence of the morbid, the sick, the infected, the parasite in society. Biopower diffuses the traits of death through the policing of life by investing all modes of reproduction: from human reproduction to the reproduction of capital (variable and constant labour), from the reproduction of equilibrium to the function of reproduction in psychoanalysis, anatomy and gynaecology.

The notion of entropy, for example, was crucial to Marx's study of the dynamics of reproduction of capital involving a capacity of extracting surplus value by deadening human labour. Capital is a homeostatic system. It incorporates and discharges energy-flows outside its semi-open cycle so as to ensure constant reproduction. By sucking in all useful flows capital deprives the vital lymph of the forces of production distorting the equal relationship between life and death: the more wealth or balance the more death. In a similar way, this entropic death is fundamental to the psychoanalytical and anatomical study of the reproductive forces of the body. Death becomes the principle of finitude of life spreading across the pathology of sexual reproduction.

The biocultural overcodification of the organic entanglement between sex, reproduction and death partakes of the dynamics of stratification. The last is not a textual organization of signifiers, but maps the differential degrees of organization of matter (body–sex). This new level of stratification marks the intensification of the organic order of sex, meiotic sex. In particular, the organic bifurcation between content or phenotype and expression or genotype in the meiotic order of multicellular reproduction undergoes an unprecedented transformation in disciplinary society when entropy substitutes inert matter with a ceaseless movement (variation) of energy-forces.

The notion of entropy singularly demarcates the entanglement between sex and death, reproduction and collapse, catching the inorganic flows of life invading the forces of life beyond life. In particular, Freud's entropic study of the cycle of pleasure defines the tendency of life towards the inorganic (entropy): the repetition of death that confirms the homeostatic control of life through sexual reproduction. The Freudian biophysical study of the thermodynamics of pleasure, exposing the entanglement between sex, reproduction and death, are neither to be considered from the standpoint of psychoanalytical discourses nor from the psychoanalytical view of the subject. Rather, the relevance of this study indicates the virtual impact of the organic stratification of sex (meiotic sex) on the biocultural levels of organization. Here the *translation* of the biophysical dynamics of energy-forces (the germline and the somaline) unleashes an anonymous force of reproduction over the economy of filiation. This overcodification of the (nucleic and cytoplasmic) entanglement between sex, reproduction and death introduces a new bifurcation of the machines of sex on the biocultural stratum. This bifurcation is not of the sexes (masculine and feminine, man and woman) but of the assemblages of desire-power between the sadist erotics of filiation and the masochist desire of parthenogenesis.

The cycle of pleasure

In *Beyond the Pleasure Principle* (1920), Freud discusses the emergence of 'organic life', which binds pleasure and pain, life and death. He uses the example of a living vesicle, suspended in the middle of an external world charged with the most powerful energies from external stimuli, equipped with a receptive cortical layer and a protective shield. In order not to be killed by external energy, the exterior layers of the living vesicle have to become to some degree inorganic so as to function as a special envelope that protects from stimuli while incorporating their intensive energy. By reaching death, these exterior surfaces are able to protect the inner layer from being shocked by the intensive amount of external energy. According to Freud, in multicellular organisms, this shield against stimuli has imploded inside to become the function of the sense organs. This shield or sensorium can filter external stimuli. Conversely, the excitations touching the deeper layers of the organism extend and lead to feelings of pleasure and unpleasure.

The protective shield also operates as a receptive apparatus of the senses that links instinctual forces to the inorganic: the need of a suicidal death in order to incorporate intensive energy from outside. In this sense, the living substance demonstrates a compulsion to repeat death, a regressive rush towards the primordial stage of inorganic matter. *'It seems, then, that an instinct is an urge inherent in organic life to restore an earlier state of things* which the living entity has been obliged to abandon under the pressure of external disturbing forces' (Freud 1920: 36). These conservative instincts 'which impel towards repetition' of the inorganic, are complemented by instincts which 'provide them [elementary organisms] with a safe shelter while they are defenceless against the stimuli of the external world'. These instincts constitute the sexual instincts, which are conservative because resistant to external influences by means of which they preserve life itself: '[t]hey are the true life instincts' (40). This resistance and preservation of life, however, only succeeds if sexual instincts can feed off the intensive fluids of the outside. Between these instincts of death and life there is not opposition. Their action is regulated by negative feedback loops that restore the pleasure principle.

The homeostasis of the pleasure principle 'follows from the principle of constancy' that defines how the quantity of excitation present in the receptive cortex is kept as low as possible. This dynamics interrupts the accumulation of tension that would otherwise lead to unpleasure, the *limit* that deviates pleasure from its stability.[8] In order to block the tendency towards dissipation, the pleasure principle is substituted by the *reality principle*, only serving to postpone satisfaction through a temporary toleration of unpleasure as a step on the long indirect road to pleasure. The postponement of satisfaction only occurs by discharging accumulated tension. Here, inorganic stimuli far from dissipating turn into a function, sexual reproduction. In this sense, pleasure does not aim for reproduction but to channel the inorganic intensity that links pleasure and death. By introducing death into the world, pleasure becomes entangled with sexual reproduction.

Freud's theory of libido as the manifestation of sexual instincts, or the libidinal character of self-preservative instincts (libidinal life), is resolved in sexual reproduction: the discharge of inorganic tension, which re-affirms the pleasure principle. The pleasure principle, therefore, as a 'tendency of a function' aiming at liberating the cerebral cortex from excitation is confirmed by the return to inorganic life, 'associated with a momentary extinction of a highly intensified excitation. The binding of an instinctual impulse would be a preliminary function designed to prepare the excitation for its final elimination in the pleasure of discharge' (Freud 1920: 62). Through the principle of constancy, the threat of inorganic fluid is eluded by the discharge of a tension that would otherwise drag the organism towards its own dissipation. As Grosz argues:

> The pleasure principle provides a way in which the death drive can express itself through the processes of gratification, in this 'unwinding' or diminution of physical energies; and the death drive provides, as it were, the medium, the material – accumulation of tension – through which the pleasure principle gains its satisfaction. (1995: 201).

According to Freud, the drive towards the inorganic is balanced by a canalization of the flows into the womb as a machine able to transform death into life: a feminine machine annexed to the human body in order to maintain the constant reproduction of life. For sexual reproduction provides a mode of conserving this energy, capitalizing on energy-forces through filiation. As Irigaray argues, by discharging the fluid in a 'matrix, womb, earth, factory, bank', the seed capital is entrusted so that it may germinate and grow again anew without contamination with the inorganic (1985b: 18). Sexual reproduction corresponds to the postponement of unpleasure, the channelling of too intense inorganic fluids through the discharge of excessive energy – ejaculating flows to secure energy reproduction.

For Freud, the pleasure principle is so organized that it avoids unpleasure at all costs and aims at the primary search of satisfaction (discharge). Yet, the prevailing of pleasure rests on the compulsion to repeat the binding action of Eros, the energetic that binds excitation, and the biological that binds the cells. This libidinal repetition of energy – and unicellular life – is at the core of the pleasure principle. Although this repetition holds together the emergence and development of life, it also conveys the sense of repeating the inorganic, what was before such an instant moment of life: '[b]efore excitation disturbed the indifference of the inexcitable and life stirred the inanimate from its sleep' (Deleuze 1989a: 114). The sense of this repetition is not linear regression towards inert death. Rather, repetition becomes twofold: on the one hand it binds the excitation and on the other eliminates it. According to Deleuze, there is a qualitative difference between these processes that is marked by rhythms, amplitudes and time scales. Freud's synthesis of repetition marks the synthesis of time as the simultaneous constitution of a linear past, present and future. For Deleuze, the repetitions that bind and erase the cycle of life and death are traversed by another time of repetition, which involves a change, the opening up of a new dimension added to the past and the present (the virtual time of *before* and *during*). Beneath the binding repetition of Eros and Thanatos, repetition emerges with its own forces, deploying the primacy of death as the primacy of *becoming*, leaking outside the constant cycle of pleasure – the homeostasis of life and death.

The autonomy of desire from libido

The Freudian cycle of pleasure entails a transcendent law of sex and reproduction splitting the organic (nucleic) from the inorganic (cytoplasmic) through the negative principle of destruction, finitude and entropic collapse. Libido prevails over death through a discharge of tension, tunnelling dissipative forces of death towards sexual reproduction, the hereditary transmission of the germline. The pleasure principle ensures the (nucleic) reproduction of life. The tendency towards dissipation exposes the (cytoplasmic) deviations from life and pleasure that Freud ascribes to the *dark continent* of feminine sex. The non-functional bind between sex, reproduction and death marks the masochist desire for punishment or death. According to Freud, this dis-functionality of feminine sex rests upon a direct search for pain, the search 'to be beaten', to re-experience the pain of pleasure, the regress towards the inorganic. Masochism is a distorted perversion from sadism. Masochism is a form of sadism turned around upon the self, plunged into a sea of guilt. For sadism is a projected form of masochism: the sadistic infliction of pain only takes pleasure from having experienced the masochistic pleasure of pain.[9] Masochism is only a derivative of sadism governed by the law of the father or the phallus that directs the entropic bind between pain and pleasure. The Freudian reversal correspondence of 'sadomasochism' is a perversion that confirms the primacy of the pleasure principle (climax or discharge).

As Deleuze argues, the bind between pleasure and pain is never directly produced. 'Both sadism and masochism imply that a particular quantity of libidinal energy be neutralized, desexualized, displaced and put at the service of Thanatos' (1989a: 110). This process of defusion, far from a direct transformation, entails the displacement of 'cathectic energy', suggesting the autonomy of repetition from the cycle of life and death – the pleasure principle. As Deleuze glosses:

> In sadism and masochism there is no mysterious link between pain and pleasure; the mystery lies in the desexualization process which consolidates repetition at the opposite pole of pleasure, and in the subsequent resexualization which makes the pleasure of repetition seemingly proceed from pain. (121)

The autonomy of repetition lays out a new connection between sex, death and reproduction that implies a bifurcation not of the sexes but of the assemblages of desire-power in the disciplinary formation. These assemblages generate new machines of sex (collective modifications of reproduction) introducing a bifurcation between the sadist and masochist dynamics of death, reproduction and sex. Masochism is not the inverted tendency of sadism. Masochism – as the *repetition* of death beneath Eros and Thanatos – corresponds to the intensified autonomy of desire from the libido of sexual genitality, sexual reproduction and pleasure. In the masochist assemblage of reproduction and sex, death exposes the potential of a body to become rather than the finitude of the organism.

Disciplinary biopower responds to the virtual repetition of death in all dynamics of reproduction (from the reproductive body to reproductive capitalism, from the reproduction of the species to organs of reproduction) able to reproduce without filiation and libidinal pleasure. In disciplinary society, sadism corresponds to the erotics of the entropic order of biopower, the desire to eliminate all the spilling and leaking liquids, to channel runaway flows of reproduction by institutionalizing the meeting of violence and sexuality (Deleuze 1989a: 189). As Deleuze explains, sadism exposes the desire of a superior power, the authority of the instituted power corresponding to the despotic law of the father. Desire flows inside towards self-control and possession, unleashing an absolute force to negate life through the finitude of death, the intensity of apathic pleasure. In sadism, the victim sizes up to the torturer and speaks the language of the authority to actively negate the power of the Oedipal mother. In strong contrast with masochism, sadism rests on the determinant image of the father, the patriarchal order that incites the murder of the Oedipal mother. The sadist negation of feeling operates through the father—daughter negation of the mother, where the daughter is led to blow up the alliance with the mother by abolishing femininity.

The sadist assemblage of desire-power only partially defines the biocultural stratification of the organic machines of sex. This new stratum exposes a parallel level of order or nuclear filiation compared to the cytoplasmic pattern of reproduction, detaching from organic death through an autonomous assemblage of desire-power of reproduction. According to Deleuze, masochism presents an entirely autonomous set of elements and compounds of desire that, I argue, indicates a new mutation of the machines of sex on the disciplinary stratum. The masochist assemblage is not determined by the binarism of the sexes. Rather, it emerges and proliferates in all spheres of reproduction (from the reproductive body to capitalist reproduction, from social reproduction to technical reproduction) generating a biocultural perception of sex irreducible to the erotics of biopower.

The emphasis on this assemblage of sex does not aim to reiterate the identity of sexual difference and femininity in the disciplinary formation. As Deleuze affirms, in masochism masculine and feminine impulses do not equate to male and female instincts, dictated by the principle of pleasure (1989a). The distribution of cytoplasmic reproduction indicates the autonomy of sex and reproduction from the nucleic law of filiation and pleasure. This autonomy exposes the emergence of a masochist assemblage of desire-power where femininity lacks nothing. Deleuze shows that in masochism, femininity is placed alongside a suspended virility, in disavowal, where the absence or presence of the penis no longer indicates the lack or possession of the phallus.

This conception of masochism unpacks what lies beneath representation, where the penis-phallus acts as the signifier of sex, reproduction and death. Masochism conveys a feminine intensive desire that is irreducible to the patriarchal order of nucleic reproduction and the sadist erotics of pleasure. This desire-power is composed of two tendencies of deterritorialization and reterritorialization indicated by two mothers or feminine figures out of which or in the middle of which an intermediate figure silently emerges from the repetition of death. Deleuze draws on Bachofen's study of human evolution, indicated by three main feminine figures, to define the masochist poles of deterritorialization and reterritorialization of desire.[10]

At one extreme of the spectrum, the first epoch is characterized by the figure of the hetaeric or Aphroditic era of lustful chaos, when the feminine principle was dominant on the father figure. This is the era of the pagan, Grecian Aphrodite of lust, love and beauty. At the other extreme, there is the third Apollonian epoch, defining the triumph of patriarchy and the emergence of the Oedipal mother, a feminine figure acting for men and enslaved to men – the law of the father. The phase space between these two attractors or epochs, marking and synthesizing the two poles of continuity of femininity, constitutes the Demetrian era, the era of the Amazons. This era is ruled by a strict gynocratic and agricultural order, where the father acquires a new status directed by the woman. This is the era of the oral mother, 'the mother of the steppe' who nurtures by diffusing death in every birth. According to Deleuze, Masoch's three feminine types map on these figures, especially worshipping the triumph of the intermediate oral mother, ' "an Indian woman, a tartar from the Mongolian desert"; she has "the tender heart of a dove together with the cruel instincts of the feline race" '. The passage from lustful chaos to the Oedipal order involves an intermediate glacial epoch when sensuality was repressed in favour of the rise of severity (50–3).

The ideal of Masoch is indeed a cold and cruel femininity where sensuality is replaced by a supercarnal sentimentality, a *supersensuous* desire: an intensification of desire through the disavowal of sexuality. This is not a negation of desire, but only an intensification, a suspension, a waiting from satisfaction. Masochism does not deliver desire to the authority of the father (pleasure). Desire presupposes a contractual alliance between the victim and the torturer where the latter needs to be educated and persuaded by the victim. This alliance requires a reversal of the scene, a reduplication of positions, a transfer of power. It is not a matter of the victims' consent, but of their ability to persuade, to discipline and train the torturer.

The torturer-victim contract is not governed by the authority of the phallus or by the misconceived sadomasochism of the master/slave relationship. As already observed, sadomasochism always already rests upon the figure of the father, the presence or absence of the penis-phallus. Here, the victim projects authority on the torturer that inflicts a pleasurable pain on the victim as the torturer is only a projection of the victim. The pain of the masochist gives pleasure to the sadist torturer that was once a slave but now possesses the penis-phallus, the authority to inflict the pain.

Contrary to sadomasochism, Deleuze states that in masochism the contract between the master and the slave requires the building up of alliances, a symbiotic reversal of the respective contractual status between the master and the slave, the parasite and its host. In the patriarchal economy, the contractual relationship defines the woman as the object of exchange between men. In masochism, the slave/woman becomes the party with whom the contract is entered into. She initiates the contract by reversing the contractual status with the man. In this sense, the mother or the feminine oral woman from the steppe allies with the son and becomes the torturer, producing a new set of laws that expel the father from the symbolic, genital sex from the son, and pleasure from sex. [11]

The masochist contractual alliance involves a conversion of desire without identification between the masochist and the mother, femininity and the woman. This conversion implies the nullification of the authority of identity through a process of becoming: the waiting for a re-birth without law of the father. This waiting is not a pre-Oedipal regression where the father or the castrating mother beat the child. Rather, waiting follows the punishment directed to the father and its likeliness in the son. 'Masochist fantasy is about a father not a child to be beaten' (93). In Freud, castration is linked to the figure of the father preventing the son from accomplishing incest with the mother. In Masoch, castration becomes the very condition of a successful incest. Incest becomes a second birth, the interruption of genital sexuality that ultimately neutralizes the father's role. The suspension of sexual love in masochism conveys a state of transmutation where the disavowal of the father, expelled from the symbolic order, also leads to the disavowal of the mother (Oedipal mother and uterine mother).

This transmutation of desire is manifested through the autonomy of reproduction, a feminine parthenogenesis that disentangles repetition (death) from the cycle of pleasure. The parthenogenic link between sex, reproduction and death suspends the pleasure of discharge distributing a mutant desire on the biocultural stratum.

The emergence of sex in the disciplinary formation does not exclusively introduce the homoerotic economy of the two sexes – male and female. The disciplinary regime of sexual difference – anatomical and psychological – stemming from the construction of the two sexes, as argued by Laqueur (1990), extends and intensifies the law of the phallus through the overcodification of meiotic sex. Yet, the biopower of the two sexes only corresponds to the disciplinary institution of the patriarchal economy – the organization of desire according to the entropic cycle of pleasure. The regime of the two sexes defines the capture of a new kind of desire under the law of Sex, entropic pleasure. The regime of biopower acts to ward off the proliferation of the virtual or real mutations of the body–sex: the assemblage of the forces of reproduction of the body with those of technical machines.[12] This assemblage introduces a new time of reproduction that diverges from organic pleasure and the sadist liquidation of femininity.

ORGANIC CAPITAL

From this point on, every act of lovemaking, every industrial process entitled a modicum of self-destruction. Working and making love became exercises in dying; only to a limited extent were they still creative, life-affirming processes. Every single commodity a worker produced was a piece of his own death. Every act of lovemaking carries the bodies deeper into a debt of guilt that accumulated toward death.

Theweleit (1987: 420)

This means that *the very possibility of a sociocultural order requires homosexuality as its organizing principle.* Heterosexuality is nothing but the assignment of economic roles: there are producer subjects and agents of exchange (male) on the one hand, productive earth and commodities (female) on the other.

Irigaray (1985b: 192)

At the end of the eighteenth century – the beginning of disciplinary formation – life and death were no longer attached to the body of the King, but became subjected to the industrial apparatus of capitalist reproduction (Foucault 1991). This shift introduces a different system of capitalization of forces on the biocultural stratum, where the feudal regime of enslavement reaches a critical threshold of change through the emergence of the modern regime of docile subjection. As Deleuze and Guattari explain:

> The human being is no longer a component of the machine but a worker, a user. He or she is subjected to the machine and no longer enslaved by the machine. [. . .] It would appear, then, that the modern State, through technological development, has substituted an increasingly powerful docial subjection for machinic enslavement.' (1987: 457)

With industrial capitalism, reproducibility becomes abstracted from the socio-organic strata through a new organization of biophysical forms of content and expression aiming to subject and regulate masses of decoded bodies (substances of content and expression). Industrial capitalism involves a reterritorialization of decodified socio-organic modes of reproduction (nucleic and cytoplasmic) binding their sparse codes to the rhythms of mechanical reproduction. Yet, the technical machine of industrial capitalism is not to be considered as the driving force of this new level of reproduction. Rather, this machine indicates the singular variation of a 'technical social machine', a pre-individual machinic environment that pre-exists the formation of industrialism: the bio-social, bio-economic and bio-political virtual modes of reproduction. The collective engineering of these modes involves an unprecedented level of reproduction where the technical capacity to capitalize on social and natural forces marks the event of industrial capitalism, unleashing *another time* no longer defined by the classical physics of linearity – the Newtonian law of inertia. This time, absorbed and diffused by the technical machine of reproduction, deterritorializes and decodifies organic and social reproduction through a mutation of trajectory – from the reversibility of forms to the irreversibility of energy-forces.

This mutation cannot be explained by the genealogical conception of capitalism that exclusively links modes of capitalization to the progressive evolution of industrial capitalism. As Deleuze and Guattari affirm, capitalist flows define different phases of social organizations where markets precede the formation of industrial capitalism.[13] The genealogical conception of capitalism relies on the linearity of time where variations are treated as pure actualities, accumulated and ordered by a blind selection.[14] This conception, inspired by Darwinian natural selection, defines evolutionary changes through the elimination of ill-adapted variations gradually accumulated in populations. This evolutionary model constitutes industrial capitalism as a progressive social force of development directly selecting organic variations while eliminating deviations.[15] It is adopted to explain the transformations of modes of reproduction leading to the economical and social changes bound to *Das Kapital*. As a driving force of development, capitalism acts like the invisible hand of order that selects the most successful mode of reproduction originating from the individual struggle for survival. This conservative conception of natural selection preserving already actualized variations imposes transcendence on the immanent dynamics of composition and decomposition of bio-social, bio-technical, bio-economical, bio-political bodies. Here evolution is a passage from actual to actual variations minus the pre-individual or virtual forces of transformation of assemblages, the differential of actual realities. Transformations are reduced to the linear movement of possibilities from possibilities where reproduction corresponds to the homeostatic return to balance and homogeneity.

Capitalism, far from determining social progress, is an anti-productive body that subjectivizes and enslaves forces of reproduction. Yet it does not exhaust the potential for invention and transformation that characterizes the socio-technical collective machine of heterogeneous production (Guattari 1995). The transformation of capitalist reproduction is not determined by Darwinian natural selection. Rather, it exposes the endosymbiotic merging of heterogeneous machines of connection parasiting onto each other, generating hierarchical and horizontal relationship between hosts and guests. As DeLanda comments, from meshworks hierarchies emerge and conversely hierarchies drift towards meshworks (1997). From this standpoint, it can be argued that the industrial capitalization of reproduction involves a virtual mutation of all assembled forces unleashing a modification of time that escapes the self-valorization of capital. These auto-assembling forces are not reducible to the transcendent value of constant repetition: filiative reproduction and circulation.

In the *Grundrisse*, Marx addresses the question of the self-valorization of capital as defined by the law of reproduction of fixed capital and circulating capital. Fixed capital determines the organization of surplus value where the time of production of variable labour (human labour) is absorbed in constant labour (technical machine). The technical machine incorporates living labour, extorts surplus value by saving and increasing its value of production. The law of reproduction of fixed capital relies on capital's organic composition where variable labour remains its primary source for auto-valorization. The reproduction of fixed capital is dependent on variable capital as that which gives money-value to the product. Marx argues that the accumulation of value in the means of production (technical machines) turns variable labour into zombies and indicates the compulsion of capital to repeat or double the time of production of variable capital. By feeding off variable labour, capital preserves its forces of reproduction in technical machines (constant capital). By saving the value of variable labour, technical machines work out the tendency of capital towards dissipation, re-balancing its cycle of reproduction through the repetition of the variable time of labour. Thus, the time of production is simultaneously preserved and created as new value (exchange value) through means of production. According to Marx, this time is formally subsumed by capital[16] as it is able to increase value by transforming it into an object of exchange, a thing, a commodity. From this standpoint, the reproduction of profit can only remain constant or increase if surplus value is extorted from variable or concrete labour accumulated in the technical machine in the form of dead labour. The organic composition of capital distinguishes the *value composition* from its *technical composition* and attributes growth to its variable constituent (human labour).[17] The formal distinction between variable and constant capital takes the subjection of human beings to a new point. It 'exhibit[s] a singular cruelty, yet still be justified in its humanist cry: No, human beings are not machines, we don't treat them like machines, we certainly don't confuse variable capital with constant capital' (Deleuze and Guattari 1987: 457).

The reproduction of fixed capital echoes the Freudian hypothesis of the dynamics of reproduction of life, relying on the distinctive yet mutual function of death and life drives, Thanatos and Eros. This function is mediated by the transcendence of the pleasure principle governed by the primary tendency towards the compulsive repetition of death, involving a regression towards the inorganic stage of matter, opposed to life drives: the progressive development towards the organic.[18] In order to overcome the primary tendency of matter towards the inorganic, the compulsion to repeat death – defining the accumulation of flows in the system – needs to be counterbalanced by the libidinal impulse of life that discharges useless flows from the system and re-establishes balance. This thermodynamics of pleasure based on the constancy of reproduction – accumulation and discharge of inorganic flows – defines a linear repetition of the time of death and life (before and after) on the virtual conditions of real time, the intensive duration of the past and the future in the present: Bergson's conception of virtual time.[19] In a similar way, it can be argued that the concept of fixed capital in Marx deploys an entropic conception of reproduction. The latter rests on the organic composition of capital: variable labour (the organic) constitutes the source of value saved and repeated in the technical machine (constant labour or the inorganic) that enables the reproduction of capital value. The capitalist tendency towards the inorganic – the automation of the time of production – is counterbalanced by the constant reproduction of capital value.

The capitalist cycle of reproduction feeds on human labour in order to gain eternal rejuvenation, increasing its value through the zombification of the time of production. This cycle involves a compulsion to repeat death: the regression of capital towards the inorganic (the technical machine) that defines its tendency towards dissolution. The increasing automation of labour, where human and technical machines are plugged into the repetitive rhythms of capitalist reproduction, ensures the increasing of value and the prevention of chaos. Industrial capitalism formally subsumes the natural, social and technical body to its entropic body.[20] This subsumption is regulated by the law of exchange that capitalizes on existing forces of production through mechanisms of subjection – the subjection of a decoded corporeality to the regime of wages. In particular, money marks the equivalence between all values that deterritorializes all socio-political specificities. During its industrial phase, the law of equivalence is regulated by the capitalist libidinal incorporation of useful flows that feeds on and wards off the inorganic.

The Marxian entropic conception of the auto-valorization of fixed capital introduces the law of transcendent value in the process of reproduction that involves a double rather than linear repetition of time. This repetition exposes the virtual or potential transformations of actual productions rather than the constant subjection of all forces to the law of equivalence and value.[21] In this sense, the tendency of capital to automate labour through the technical machine – by investing in inorganic repetition – does not define its limit point, the tendency towards its own dissolution.[22] Rather, the limit of fixed capital is defined by the virtual time of repetition proliferating through technical machines of reproduction able to crystallize *inorganic time*, the virtual or potential time of actual forces of production (Deleuze

1989b). This crystallization exposes a singular connection between heterogeneous bodies of transmission of information (substances of content and expression) whose potential distributes a kind of parasitism of assembled bacteria attached from the outside onto the nucleic body of capital.

The circulation of commodities also defines, according to Marx, the function of capital reproduction, the way it is diffused and realized along and across strata formations. The repetition of circulating capital unfolds the proliferation of heterogeneous modes of reproduction assembling all forces of production and relinquishing all pretences of exteriority between economy and society. According to Marx, the process of commodification hides the real inequalities of capitalism between wage and profit money. The commodity is a fetish that displaces the real value of labour into a system of equivalence regulated by money. The organic composition of capital subjects variable labour to the cycle of filiative reproduction where the labour of the proletariat is substituted by the value of the commodity. Commodities circulate in the system of exchange spreading the seed of capital, its symbolic law of subsumption. For the value of commodities is dependent on the value of labour, where the law of equivalence hides the real value of the commodity. The commodity is a fetish that displaces the true unequal relationship between salary and profit, between subsistence and exploitation. The fetish or the commodity only has value in the reproductive cycle of capital, where exchange rests on the exploitation of organic labour. The fetish hides the inequality of the law of exchange in the capital cycle of circulation and reproduction.

In the Freudian study of sexuality, the fetish is the image or substitute of the female phallus, the mean by which it is possible to deny that the woman lacks a penis. The fetishist selects a fetish according to the last object he saw before becoming aware of the absence of the phallus in the woman. The constant return to this object aims to confer value to the missing organ. Yet such value, according to Deleuze, is not symbolic (1989a). The fetish is not a symbol that represents the socio-cultural value of the phallus, but a frozen two-dimensional image. This arrested image ceaselessly comes back to repeat the anti-climax of suspense, the disavowal of the law of the phallus. In this sense, the commodity as a fetish does not confirm the principle of exchange, where the commodity hides the relations of power between labour and profit. Rather the fetish-commodity deploys a process of disavowal and suspension of the climactic reproduction of genital sexuality. The circulation of the commodity-fetish suggests the proliferation of autonomous values that do not represent a penis – the use value – but unfold a potential variation of reproduction through the repetition of death (the interruption of pleasure). The parallel use of the entropic model of reproduction (the meiotic order of sex) by both Marxian and Freudian theories of bio-social and bio-economic energy-forces of reproduction does not imply an identity of their concepts. More importantly, it points at the relevance of the entropic dynamics to define the biocultural overcodification and decodification of the organic entanglement between sex, reproduction and death in disciplinary society. The overcodification of these dynamics imposes the transcendence of value and pleasure on the virtual time of techno-social machines of modification. The emphasis on the constancy of exchange for satisfaction or profit deploys the bio-disciplinary overcodification of the organic entanglement between sex, reproduction and death, where the circulation of commodities (energy-forces) is subordinated to the valorization of fixed capital or filiative reproduction. In Freud as in Marx, the fetish is mainly a projection or representation of the already actualized force of use value or the phallus.

On the contrary, Deleuze's study of masochism reveals that the fetish is proper to the contractual relationship between the tortured and the torturer that rules masochism. Fetishism is singular to the masochist system of disavowal and suspension of belief and value. As opposed to the Freudian indistinct association of the fetish with the masochist and the sadist, Deleuze points out that the fetish is appropriated by the sadist only in a secondary moment. The fetish is detached by its primal relationship to suspension to pass into the totally different economy of sadist pleasure. In masochism, the fetish serves neither to replace something missing nor to destroy what it represents. The fetish demarcates the suspension of the phallic symbolic and the waiting for the emergence of an autonomous sex stripped of genitality. The masochist process of disavowal is so extensive that it affects sexual pleasure itself; pleasure is postponed as long as possible and it is thus disavowed. The masochist is therefore able to deny the reality of pleasure at every point of experiencing it, in order to construct a 'new sexless man', naked of the phallus-value (Deleuze 1989b: 33). The contractual nature of the masochist perversion, the reversal agreement between the tortured and the torturer demands the refutation of the law of sexual reproduction and filiation. It requires a timeless waiting in order to become genital-less: an intensification of desire that defines the autonomy of reproduction or the emergence of parthenogenesis.

The commodity-fetish does not represent the law of value — phallus — regulated by exchange value that substitutes the lack of a penis with another penis. The circulation of commodities does not only increase the value of capital filiative reproduction but marks the proliferation of parthenogenic energy-forces (cytoplasmic substances of content and expression) marking the virtual transformation of the machines of sex on the biocultural stratum. In masochism, the fetish is part of a contractual, reversible mode of exchange; a trade that is independent of the law of the phallus — the symbolic organization of values determined by the patriarchal economy of representation. The commodity is not just a product of the cycle of pleasure of capital that incorporates labour into the machine, life into death, in order to endlessly rejuvenate. The circulation of the commodity-fetish rather defines the autonomy of the time of repetition from linear time (pleasure): the virtual time of reproduction crystallized in the technical machine through the novel assemblages of reproductive bodies.

Masochism practises the suspension and refutation of the law of the father without professing mere negation or destruction — organic death. Quite the contrary, the masochist's contract relies on alliance: a fluctuating agreement between the torturer and the tortured to destratify the law of filiation, to beat the figure of the father in order to be born again as a sexless — non-genital — body. The autonomy of circulation (invention and transformation) from filiation, the autonomy of collective alliances from linear heredity exposes the distribution of a supersensual mode of reproduction, a parthenogenic desire leaking out of the organic cycle of value.

From this standpoint, the industrial capitalization of reproduction introduces a bifurcation between two parallel assemblages: (nucleic) filiation — fixed capital — and (cytoplasmic) alliance — circulating capital — on the biocultural stratum. These assemblages emerge from a process of repetition or doubling of the time of production (organic and inorganic) whose potential, crystallized in the technical machine, remains autonomous from the self-valorization of capital. The differential variations between filiative and parthenogenic reproduction point to a decodification of the substances of content and expression (cytoplasm and phenotype) from the forms of content and expression (chromosomal heredity and genotype) entangling sex, reproduction and death on the organic strata. Although it has been argued that the economy of patriarchy and capitalism are both entangled with the law of the phallus, linear reproduction and pleasure, the disciplinary formation lays out a strange attraction between the proliferation of

109

commodities and masochist (or cytoplasmic) parthenogenesis.[23] This attraction is deployed by the crystallization of the virtual time of reproduction in the technical machine distributing inorganic energy-forces beneath and above the sadist erotics of biopower.

SEX AND DEATH: THE MEDIA OF FLUID REPRODUCTION

[. . .] life with its real duration and disease as a possibility of deviation find their origin in the deeply buried point of death; it commands their existence from below. Death, which, in the anatomical gaze, spoke retroactively the truth of disease, makes possible its real form by anticipation.

Foucault (1994: 158)

[. . .] this formidable power of death [. . .] now presents itself as the counterpart of a power that exerts a positive influence on life, that endeavors to administer, optimize, and multiply it, subjecting it to precise controls and comprehensive regulations.

Foucault (1990: 137)

When Foucault discusses biopower, he emphasizes the immanent models of realization of decoded biological and social organizations through disciplinary practices. The disciplinary formation capitalizes on the forces of reproduction of qualified integrities (mothers, patients, workers, perverts) assembled through technologies of power (health, education, army, factories) (Foucault 1990: 140). This capitalization of forces converges with a wider transformation of reversible death into an irreversible tendency towards entropy that introduces a new perception of the body–sex on the biocultural stratum. Foucault's study of the reformation of death in the *Birth of the Clinic* (1973; 1994) depicts the universal reaction against putrefaction and decadence that blurs the forces of life and death. The irreversibility of death is a crack on the unity of the biocultural stratification of sex. The relation between life and death is no longer defined by a difference of degree presupposing an equivalence of forces. It now involves a thermodynamic looping of energy-information through irreversibility, a constant balance of the flows of equilibrium.

With the study of epidemics and diseases, abnormalities and pathologies, disciplines such as bacteriology and anatomy, gynaecology and psychology diffuse throughout the social body the irreversibility of death. Similarly, technologies of power such as schools, hospitals, prisons present a new focus 'on the species body, the body imbued with the mechanics of life and serving as the basis of biological processes' (Foucault 1990: 139). In contrast with the regime of reversible death and life, the disciplinary formation plunges into the inorganic forces of reproduction and their utilization for the preservation of life. In particular, singular to the disciplinary formation is the over-codification of meiotic sex or sexual mating – the exchange of sexed chromosomes and genetic heredity. This overcoding is not unrelated to the industrial capitalist dynamics of filiation and exchange: the preservation of the germline as value of reproduction becomes entangled with the financial evolution of the species. Not only the preservation of the germline, but also the constancy of pleasure, stopping the dissipation towards the inorganic, deploys the disciplinary link between sex and death of the organic composition of capital and human body. This link also exposes the proliferation of another (cytoplasmic) time of reproduction unleashing the inorganic forces preceding and exceeding the cycle of (nucleic) pleasure. Inorganic flows spill in and out of the female body integrated 'into the sphere of medical practices, by reason of a pathology intrinsic to it' (Foucault 1990: 104). As Irigaray argues, 'both by her and for her, the invisible work of death goes on. Relentlessly, woman reconnects the end to the beginning, though the end and the beginning are not *hers*. (Re)calling death in utero' (1985a: 146). Sex becomes the *medium* of preservation of life folding the inorganic soma, capitalizing on the surplus energy of pathological reproduction.

Death is grasped everywhere in the anatomy of diseases, where the morbid 'authorizes a subtle perception of the way in which life finds in death its most differentiated figure. The morbid is the rarefied form of life, exhausted working itself into the void of death' (Foucault 1994: 171). The morbid unfolds the secrets of life through a topology of forces that ceaselessly change, rather than being opposed. Drawing on the anatomist Bichat, Foucault announces that '[i]t is when death became the concrete a priori of medical experience that death could detach itself from counter-nature and become *embodied* in the *living bodies* of individuals' (196). In particular, death 'offer[s] modern man the obstinate, yet reassuring face of his finitude' without ceasing to constitute a menace, a subtle threat for something coming 'from elsewhere' that has to be 'exorcized' (198).

Death remains the obscure compulsion to be warded off by the pleasure principle that functions to contain the diffusion of the pathologically morbid, the inorganic (cytoplasmic death). For far from being finalized to reproduction, pleasure aims to repress the flow of death, the mutations of sex. As a semi-open cycle or loop apt to maintain equilibrium, the cycle of pleasure sucks in inorganic flows, imparting a deviance, a transfer that channels fluids towards the inside. In the 'Mechanics of Fluids' (1985b), Irigaray argues against the Freudian thermodynamic conception of constancy, holding onto an inside that regulates fluids' inflows and outflows. For Freud, feminine sex is itself the full manifestation of an inorganic to be warded off.

The anatomical perception of sex and death

[. . .] since sexuality was a medical and medicalizable object, one has to try and detect it – as a lesion, a dysfunction, or a symptom – in depths of the organism, or on the surface of the skin, or among all the signs of behaviour.

Foucault (1990: 44)

There's nothing the matter with the instrument, it's the body, the woman's body was all wrong.

Beverly in Cronenberg's Dead Ringers (1988)

In fact, it ought to be apparent to any unprejudiced observer that what man who fear vagina must really be afraid of is the vagina's ability to take the male member into itself (devour it, swallow it up). For whatever it can take in, it can easily keep for itself.

Theweleit (1987: 201)

In David Cronenberg's film Dead Ringers, the abstract line between reproduction, sex and death connects the anatomo-pathologies of feminine sex with inorganic flows. The menace of death expands from within sexual organs and alongside its enveloping tissues. In particular, the vagina, the clitoris, the uterus become the places of intervention of forms of expression (i.e. gynaecology, psychology, anatomy) and forms of content (Woman's Hospital) producing a new space of perception of sex and death. In Dead Ringers, the Mantle Siamese twin brothers' encounter with the three-cervix sterile woman Claire Niveau, activates the 'line of abolition' of the BwO, the pure drive towards death, a 'cancerous, mad, proliferation' of destruction.[24] The morphological 'unorganization' of Claire's womb turns reproducibility into a black hole of dissipation.

Beverly and Elliot, twin brothers and famous gynaecologists specialized in the surgical cure of sterility are consulted by Claire in a desperate bid to fight her sterility ascribed to her trifurcated uterus whose cervixes lead to three separate chambers in her womb. This anatomical disturbance defines her pathological body–sex, the irreversible tendency towards the inorganic. The detection of Claire's anatomo-pathology is entangled with the disciplinary overcodification of sex that synthesizes the organic order of meiotic sex (heterosexual mating) through the production of the bio-social category of gender.

Before the disciplinary formation, sexual anatomy corresponded to the system of cosmic analogies, which formed the 'classical' historical formation of 'the world of infinite representation' (Deleuze 1988b: 125). As Laqueur emphasizes, classical medical knowledge was dominated by Galen, the second century AD anatomist, whose conception of the 'structural, though not spatial, identity of the male and female reproductive organs' (1990: 4), still characterized the anatomy of the Renaissance. This anatomy of dead bodies follows the principle of analogy: the mirroring of female anatomy in the male, where the vagina appeared as a folded penis.

What Vesalius and his followers continued to see was a one-sex body in which the configuration of organs might be different, but in which structure and form, and indeed names given to apparently corresponding male and female parts, was the same.

Shildrick (1997: 28)

Nevertheless, as Foucault points out, the post-mortem examinations by Renaissance anatomists already contained the germs of a new science of perception of sex. The detached gaze of classical formation turned into an affected clinical glance. As in *Dead Ringers,* Beverly and Elliot's anatomical gaze is overwhelmed by the dens, tubes and vessels of the body that deploy the morbid traits of reproducibility. Their clinical gaze is part of a new science of perception inaugurated by Bichat's anatomo-pathology. According to Foucault, this anatomo-pathology was no longer looking for the general symptoms corresponding to a general disease, but was rather exposing the 'seats', the 'analogies', the 'frequencies' of diseases disclosing the body to the synthetic environment of functions, rhythms and structures. In this space 'organs appear as simple functional folds, entirely relative, both in their role and in their disorders, to the elements of which they are made up and to the groups to which they belong' (1994: 128). Tissual spaces rather than organs define the coordinates of pathology; the analysis of this mutable tissual surface substitutes the previous regime of analogy and symmetry between organs. While the play of symmetry focused on the eternal correspondences of the same organic structure, now the clinical perception of tissual space detects and classifies what was obscure before. The tissual space of the visible becomes the space where 'the human body finds the concrete forms of its unity' (128). The pathological state of organs manifests itself through morbid tissual surfaces that 'envelop them, divide them, compose and decompose them' (129).

With Bichat, the contemplative gaze of classical medicine is deterritorialized from the bio-social and cultural fields to become a clinical 'glance' which 'goes straight to its object'. Unlike the gaze, still operating within a general field (the world of language), the 'glance is of non-verbal order of contact, a purely ideal contact perhaps, but in fact a more striking contact, since it traverses more easily, and goes further beneath things' (122). The glance operates as 'a sort of sensorial triangulation' where the senses of touch and hearing are integrated to the sight under a new organization of the corporeal space. The glance produces a 'sovereign unity that [. . .] belongs to a lower level of the eye, the ear, and the sense of touch' (165). Thus, what was once invisible becomes duplicated by this abstract or incorporeal[25] space of perception involving a new assemblage of the senses where the eye becomes acoustic and the ears become ocular.[26] This space exhibits no centre of vision, but an assemblage of the senses that constitutes the 'zones of indetermination' in perception.[27] The glance no longer contemplates and interprets the effects of symptoms. It no longer determines the cause hiding behind the effects.

The object is not merely seen but also heard, touched, smelled. The gaze is not transcendent to the object. Quite the contrary, the glance – the assembling network of the senses – is immanent to the mutating surfaces of the body. The glance assembles the indeterminate zones of sensory perception where the eye manifests its tactility. The glance follows the motions of the tissual surface through a 'distracted perception'.[28]

The medical glance of the Mantle twins is not another example of the objectifying gaze, the voyeurist gaze enacting a sado-masochistic exercise of pain and control, attraction and repulsion, pleasure and fear of a pathological body. The clinical glance does not correspond to an empirical enforcement of the Cartesian mental gaze, locating perception in the mind, the site of the cyclopean eye.[29] Such a glance is not governed by the reality principle that channels pleasure by controlling unpleasure. The singular constitution of the biomedical glance is part of the disciplinary formation where the body becomes a mutant object marked by irreversible dynamics. This object is an incorporeal artefact linked to a supersensorious eye that feels and hears. The capacity to assemble all deviances of the body under the mobile tower of perception – the Panopticon – involves the emergence of a new tactile, visceral vision of the body impacting on the biocultural perception of the body–sex.

The shift in the perception of diseases is intertwined with the shift in the perception of sexual organs that defines the passage from the 'one-sex model' to the 'two-sex model' (Laqueur 1990). The establishment of this model does not simply deploy a binary classification of sex through negative oppositions, the closed system of norm and deviance. This model corresponds to an overcodification of the body – of its mutating surfaces – that reduces the unknown to abnormality and subjects the unknown to the signifier (norm), the primary referent of reality. Yet, this overcodification defines only one face of the bio-disciplinary assemblages of desire–power enfolding a virtual or real perception of a mutant body–sex. More like a mould than a model, the anatomical production of the two sexes is entangled with the anatomo-pathological perception of sex (the folding of inorganic flows into organic forms). The anatomical eye does not primarily construct the binary system of sexual difference. Its audio-visual sensorium is rather modified by the impact of the autonomy of reproduction on the bio-medical and biocultural apparatus of perception. The disciplinary piercing into the morbid secrets of the body – the tissual surface enveloping sexual organs – pushes on the surface another time of reproduction and sex moving outside the constancy of sexual functions.

MUTANT SEX

She does not set herself up as *one*, a single female unit. She is not closed up or around one single truth or essence. The essence of a truth remains foreign to her. She neither has nor is a being. And she does not oppose a feminine truth to the masculine truth. Because this would once again amount to playing the – man's – game of castration.

Irigaray (1993: 86)

The biomedical perception of sex defines the pathology of reproduction through the study of the morbid tissues enveloping the womb, the ovary, the fallopian tube, the vagina, the cervix and the clitoris. The disciplinary formation saw an increasing investment in surgical operations of sterility associated with the pathologies of sexuality and sexual organs.

In 1852, the 'Father of Modern Gynaecology' J. Marion Sims (1813–83) invented a surgical instrument, the vagina speculum, in order to cure one of the pathologies of sterility, the vesico-vaginal fistula.[30] This instrument was also used to uncover the pathologies of infertile women either diagnosed as inflammatory states of ovaries, uterus, cervix, or as structural defects, such as the obstruction of fallopian tubes, the reversed position of the uterus, dysmenorrhoea, the 'imperforation of the hymen'.[31] The medical glance extends itself to the instrument. Hence, the location of female pathologies also becomes a place of mutilating interventions. In Dead Ringers, Beverly and Elliot invent the 'Mantle retractor', able to descend in the obscure cavities of the womb. This vicelike device allows the enlargement of the cavities of the vagina, disclosing the pack of dark tissues to light. This instrument can only be used in post-mortem operations. Beverly, however, uses it on one of his patients. He is obsessed by the pleasure of mutilating the womb – femininity – in order to stop the inorganic flow from spilling out of sexual organs. At this point in the film, Beverly's escalation towards total abjection lays out a tendency towards entropic death localized in the anonymous space of the female body.

It has been argued that Claire's trifurcate womb recalls the pathological symptoms of hysteria, marking an exceeding sexuality that disturbs the masculine economy of the gynaecologists. For example, in her reading of Dead Ringers, Kapsalis associates Claire's sexuality with a phallic abundance, suggested by the sixteenth-century conception of female gonads drawn as an upside-down penis (1997). For this abundance involves the presence of a third term which threatens the phallic economy and exceeds the 'twin's doubleness' (146). Kapsalis places femininity on the exterior yet still inside the value of symbolic, the entropic economy of regulation and excess, possession and lack, governing the Oedipal law of sex and reproduction (filiation). Her arguments rely on the model of pleasure excluding the virtual or real time of sex and reproduction that are autonomous from organic death.

Claire's trifurcated body exposes the incorporeal desire of reproduction without constancy, without organs, no vagina, no pelvis, no clitoris, without principle of death and life, defying all sense of organic unity. Claire's sterility marks the failure of the pleasure principle, the autonomy of reproduction of the twin brothers from the symbolic (the law of filiation). Her sterility does not represent the tendency towards the inorganic, the regression towards a state of disequilibrium that confirms the pleasure principle. Her sterility lays out another time of reproducibility requiring the castration of the phallus and the unlocking of (parthenogenic) desire from (entropic) pleasure. Castration, rather than a return to the Oedipal womb, leads to a new sense of doubleness unfinalized to pleasure. Like the Siamese twins Chang and Eng, merged in an intensive repetition without distinction of the one from the other, castration exhibits the schizo-duplicity of reproduction without identity. Beverly's constant nightmare in which Claire eats the fleshy tie between him and his twin brother Elliot indicates the splitting of their endosymbiotic doubleness where the host and the guest compose a mutant body–sex.

The encounter between the twins and Claire above all displays a duplication of sex – the autonomy of inorganic repetition from organic pleasure. Death coincides with sterility only to expose non-climactic (non-discharging) flows of desire proliferating before and during sexual reproduction. It is not sexual reproduction that interrupts death. Rather, death pours out of sexual reproduction without ceasing to increase the intensity of desire. For Claire's three cervixes' 'anatomical beauty' marks the twins' masochist desire to become genital-less, to be castrated in order to reproduce outside the economy of pleasure.

Beverly designs uncanny surgical tools to operate on mutant women. These instruments are disproportionate compared to the size of a womb: their shape is spiny and abominable. The anatomy of these weapon-instruments is indicative of the sadist desire of the disciplinary formation to adjust the monstrosity of the body–sex, when 'the concrete form of the struggle against the flowing-machinic productive force of the unconscious [was] and (still is) a battle against women, against female sexuality' (Theweleit 1987: 258). The invention of surgical instruments to adjust abnormal, dysfunctional and diseased sexual organs started in the middle of the nineteenth century. 'Récamier's curette and the Sims speculum, the uterotome, uterine guillotine, and uterine injector provided new opportunities for seeing, and for reconfiguring, the interior of women's bodies' (Marsh and Ronner 1996: 442). These surgical instruments expose a continuum between the animate and the inanimate defining the reproducibility of matter outside the organic–inorganic dichotomy.[32] Ovariotomy, amputation of the cervix, and hysterectomy (the removal of the womb) involve a moulding of surgical instruments to the size and depth of the infection or disease, sharpening the efficacy of amputation.

The uterus, which was previously thought to be wandering within the body and to provoke *suffucatio matricis* or hysteria,[33] acquires a proper location, whose 'malposition', retroversion or anteversion, is adjusted through a manual rectification of the womb, or through the use of a flexible stick. The invention of pessaries introduces a new method to re-position the uterus: these 'u-shaped' instruments, placed inside the womb, re-position the uterus during sexual intercourse so as to facilitate impregnation.[34] The passage from the wandering womb, as a mark of hysteria, to the dislocated womb, as a mark of sterility, defines the disciplinary organization of sex, the adjustment of patholo-gical reproducibility and sterility. By the end of the nineteenth century, Sims also invented the use of the 'impregnating syringe', the precursor of NRTs (new reproductive technologies). This syringe, for uterine and vaginal insemination, enabled the transfer of sperm into the uterus.[35]

The line of connection between gynaecological and surgical instru-ments and sexual organs exposes the surfacing of another time of reproducibility in the disciplinary formation. In *Dead Ringers*, this reproducibility pushes Elliot to share Beverly's 'obsession', following his desire of abolition. In the final scenes, Beverly finds his monstrous tools displayed in an art gallery, classified as 'Instruments for Operating on Mutant Women', with which he can finally actualize his desire of reproduction without sexual organs. He starts to dissect Elliot's abdomen as a womb, which becomes the place of separation from his Siamese twin as well as the place of their rebirth, their death in becoming. In the end, both twins lie on the floor, one upon the other, in a flood of blood.

Beverly's attempt to enact reproduction does not suggest his delusion for the dissipation of the twins' germline, unable to reproduce without regressing towards the inorganic dens of the female body and feminine sex. This act rather exposes a masochistic ritual of reproduction demanding the visceral dissection – castration – of the sexed body. Beverly and Elliot's double act of mortification coincides with a desire to reproduce reproduction beyond the bio-social order of filiation.

The strange attraction between industrial reproduction and feminine parthenogenesis

What we see in the crystal is therefore a dividing in two that the crystal itself constantly causes to turn on itself, that it prevents from reaching completion, because it is a perpetual self-distinguishing, a distinction in the process of being produced; which always resumes the distinct terms in itself, in order to constantly relaunch them.

Deleuze (1989b: 81–2)

But what if these 'commodities' refused to go to 'market'? What if they maintained 'another' kind of commerce, among themselves? Exchanges without identifiable terms, without accounts, without end . . . Without additions and accumulations, one plus one, woman after woman . . . Without sequence or number. Without standard or yardstick.

Irigaray (1985b: 196)

Masochism unlocks desire from its stratified organic channels (meiotic sex), or the repressing activity of pleasure, to expose the power of a body to be affected that is not reducible to direct pain. As Deleuze points out, neither sadism nor masochism has a direct relationship to pain, which like suffering, is rather linked to desire and enjoyment (1989a). This misunderstanding of pain is part of the psychoanalytic interpretation of masochism as deriving from sadism, constituting the complementary entity of sadomasochism. Deleuze demonstrates that masochism, contrary to sadism, distinctively disavows the superego, abolishes the father and rejects sexuality.[36]

Masochism favours the mutating oral mother, absorbing both the uterine and the Oedipal mother. The father is excluded and castration becomes a prerequisite for the success of incest, allowing the son-daughter to be born again without phallus. Masochism aims to dismember the organism from the law of the two sexes, from the organic bond of sex with sexual mating and somatic death constituting the functions of heredity transmission, socio-economic and sexual reproduction. As a mode of desexualization singular to masochism, the disavowal (abolition and rejection) of the paternal invents reproducibility without nucleic heredity (filiation).

The industrial capitalist investment in the technical machine exposes the double side of reproducibility bifurcating between the order of filiation and the order of parthenogenesis. The entropic loop of capitalist filiation divides the space of the organic from the inorganic, maintaining balance inside through the accumulation and discharge of forces. Yet this loop can only operate by suspending the urge to let energy go, incorporating forces that in spite of dying dissipate within to produce a new composition of energy-forces. The cycle of linear reproduction based on commodity exchange is interrupted. The commodity serves no longer to camouflage the industrial law of money-equivalence. The commodity is a fetish that stands not for filiation and reproduction but for an intensive interruption of satisfaction, stretching the capacity of desire to desire. The circulation of commodities does not repeat the linear cycle of accumulation and realization, but repeats the suspension of sexual reproduction, the ultimate pleasure or satisfaction for profit. Escaping the law of filiation, the commodity interrupts energy-forces from being channelled towards genital reproduction, intensifying reproducibility without discharge: feminine parthenogenesis (cytoplasmic sex).

In masochism, the contractual ritual of the commodity-fetish regulates parthenogenic reproducibility, not to hide the Oedipal fear/pleasure of punishment and castration, but to intensify the collective desire to interrupt filiative reproduction and the symbolic value of the phallus. This interruption precludes capital from discharging in order to accumulate again and exposes a (bio-socio-technical) capacity to reproduce reproduction beneath the law of sexual exchange. The parthenogenic reproduction of industrial capitalism exposes the capillary diffusion of a masochist repetition of death without pleasure. Here reproductive desire precedes and exceeds pleasure.

Signs of death, surfacing out of the morbid tissues and obscure cavities of sexual organs, also affect the disciplinary perception of the body–sex. This perception does not primarily involve the voyeurism of the reflected image of identity and difference or the technoscientific representation of the body–sex. Rather, it marks the emergence of a new apparatus of sensory perception, the Foucauldian glance or the Benjaminian tactile eye, an audible-tactile distribution of death on the body–sex. This distribution desexualizes pleasure but resexualizes the repetition of death blending inorganic dissipation into the potential time of reproduction. Here 'repetition runs wild and becomes independent of all previous pleasure' (Deleuze 1989: 120).

By unlocking death from pleasure, reproducibility becomes parthenogenesis, involving a rebirth of feminine sex, a second yet initial becoming independent both of the father and of the uterine and Oedipal mother. In masochism, 'femininity is positioned as lacking nothing and placed alongside a virility suspended in disavowal' (68). In a sense, Claire's masochist demand expressed by her 'need for humiliation' strongly resonates with the masochism of Beverly and Elliot, the parthenogenetic desire to be born again without organs, independent of pleasure, sexual reproduction and semen discharge. Rebirth is not an experience of pleasure, but a becoming where castration ceases to be a punishment of incest. Rather, castration prepares the body for real mutation: a threshold towards supersensual desire, disclosing the organism to the body of the earth.

When the torture is inflicted upon Elliot, who is at the same time Beverly himself, his brother, and son (that they cannot have), what is sacrificed and ritually expiated from the organic body is the genital sexuality inherited from their father, from sexual reproduction, Eros and Thanatos. This organic apostasy leads to a second birth, where the twins are reborn from the woman alone, in this case the sexually sterile Claire, who can only afford a parthenogenetic rebirth (inorganic repetition of desire). Beverly and Elliot are encompassed by a feminine desire to be affected, frozen, immobilized in a virtual time of reproduction: parthenogenetic reproduction without pivotal climax.

The biocultural entanglement of sex, reproduction and death introduces another time on the anthropomorphic strata, the virtual time of reproducibility, the crystal of time.[37] Industrial reproducibility, as Benjamin argues, involves a technological process of duplication that characterizes both the mass-produced commodity and the technically produced image – from the photograph to the moving image – defining the mutations of reproducibility.[38] What Benjamin considers historically new in the nineteenth century is the technical acceleration of the reproductive process delineating the velocity of reproduction itself, an intensification of repetition. Here it is not the technique that returns, the mechanical copy or reproduction of an original object. What returns is the kinematics of reproducibility, the doubling of time, the centrifugal mixing of particle-forces unleashing the virtual time of perception: a new time of death (cytoplasmic reproduction). According to Benjamin, the reproduction of images exposes the freezing of the image, the suspension and intensification of its reproducibility that define socio-historical transformations as shocks or impacts of colliding atoms. The stoppage of the image interrupts the time of contemplation to lay out an intensive duration: a continuum between past and future. The momentum of a click marks a disavowal of constant time, the cycle of charge and discharge, pleasure and organic death. It is a momentum that suspends linear time through a kinematic reproduction (parthenogenesis).[39]

The frozen image – as the fetish commodity – does not mark the return to regressive (organic) death, but distributes a cytoplasmic reproducibility of the body, masses, nature and capital, an intensive continuum of time. In particular, the emergence of media technologies involves an accelerated reproducibility that subtracts sex from sexual reproduction, the masses from identity, nature from the organic, capital from the unity of organic value. The death of the aura marks the proliferation of a process of repetition: a parthenogenesis that disposes of the Eden of creation through the rejection of life and death, pleasure and unpleasure. This deterritorialization of the forces of reproduction (substances of content and expression, the cytoplasmic and somatic multiplicities of bodies) is counteracted by a fascistic reterritorialization of forces, masses and flows. The capacity of media technologies to crytallize irreversible time (exposing the variations of reproduction) also provokes the diffusion of a despotic desire of identity (the nucleic and genotypic forms of expression and content). The sadist homo-erotics wards off the liquidification of genital sexuality, through an active negation of femininity.[40] This regulated reterritorialization of parthenogenic desire corresponds to the sadist law of paternal reproduction that distributes organic death beyond itself through the disciplinary regime of surveillance and obedience (Foucault 1991).

The technological autonomy of repetition – investing the biotechnical, socio-cultural and economic fields – from the drives of death and life, filiation and profit, deploys a double assemblage of desire-power in the disciplinary formation: masochism and sadism. This bifurcation rests upon the entanglement of violence and sexuality, death and reproduction and produces a singular micropolitical alliance between industrial reproduction, the technical machine and the female body. The deterritorializing forces of reproducibility expose the emergence of a parthenogenetic desire that requires the abolition of genital sex, pleasure and death. The reterritorializing forces of Oedipal reproduction reintroduce genitality everywhere through the biopower of sex. Yet, these movements do not exclude each other through negative oppositions because they are not engendered by the same system of signification. The coexistence of singular assemblages of desire-power on the biocultural stratum suggests the primary process of transformation of the organic entanglement between sex, reproduction and death that precedes and exceeds structures of signification and representation.

The disciplinary environment of industrial capitalism, thermodynamic techno-science and anatomical death exposes the capillary expansion of a new assemblage of desire (parthenogenic reproduction) linking circulating commodities to the circulating flows of sex. This parthenogenic autonomy from filiative pleasure indicates a new variation of machines of sex on the biocultural stratum mapping the incorporeal rather than biological or discursive mutations of a body–sex.

Notes

1 See M. Foucault 1990. On the concept of the disciplinary formation, see Deleuze 1988b: 124.

2 Deleuze and Guattari argue that the third major group of strata is defined less by human essence than by a new distribution of forms and substances of content and expression on the strata. See 1987: 60; 64; 302; 395.

3 As Félix Guattari argues, genetic encodings function independently of the constitution of a semiotic substance. See 1984: 149.

4 Deleuze and Guattari specify the difference between the genetic code and language, which also explains the difference between the organic and anthropomorphic strata. See 1987: 62.

5 This assemblage points to the primacy of desire or productive lines of flight over power or biopower: a stratified dimension of assemblages. Lines of flight are not lines of resistances or counter-attacks, but cutting edges of creation and deterritorialization. See Deleuze and Guattari 1987: 530, note 39. On the relation of power and desire, see also M. Foucault 1989: 186–9; 207–13; 382–90.

6 See I. Prigogine 1997: 36–7.

7 See W. Benjamin 1968: 211–44; M. McLuhan 1964.

8 Freud derives the dynamics of the death drive from Fechner's constancy principle to demonstrate that the organism keeps the quantity of energy or excitation as low as possible by never approaching death, and keeping it low enough not to overstimulate the organism, which will release the excessive energy otherwise accumulated. This marks the entropic tendency that internally directs the organism, gradually forcing it towards death. See E. Grosz 1995: 200–1.

9 See S. Freud 1955–64.

10 See T. Reik 1949.

11 Masochism and sadism subvert the law in very different ways. For sadism the very regime of the law allows the tyrant to exist. The law of sex – sexual reproduction and linear filiation – allows the tyrant to impose authority on sexes. The anarchic spirit of sadism is in net contrast with the contractual nature of law in masochism. Here, the authority of the law of the father, prohibiting the satisfaction of desire through the threat of punishment (castration), is converted in a law that requires punishment first, and then waits for release to follow punishment. The law is disentangled from the signifier penis-phallus-father to become intramaternal, where the mother – rather than the father – stands for the law. The contractual alliance between the mother and the son does not correspond to the female–male Oedipal tie. See Deleuze 1989a: 74.

12 Walter Benjamin discusses the relationship between reproducibility and technology by linking the shock produced by the assembly line of industrial capitalism to the shock produced in the chain of assembled images in cinematographic production. He links collective perception and memory to the collective socialization and development of capitalism (1968). Lazzarato criticizes Benjamin's conception of reproduction as it reintroduces a mechanical understanding of

image technologies. Lazzarato argues for the innovative capacity of technologies of reproduction – media – to reproduce and crystallize time and not things. The capitalist reproduction of time is primarily related to the virtual time of matter in perception, memory and subjectivity. See M. Lazzarato 1996: 191.

13 See Deleuze and Guattari 1983: 222–61; Deleuze and Guattari 1987: 424–73. Arguing against the genealogical conception of capitalism, Manuel DeLanda draws on Fernand Braudel to explain the mutual relationship between markets and anti-markets, meshworks and hierarchical structures. See DeLanda 1997: 25–56. See also F. Braudel 1986: 28–47, 1973.

14 Philip Mirowsky's work on the physical study of economics explains how the concept of the 'invisible hand' was formalized in the nineteenth century by simply copying the form of equilibrium thermodynamics. See 1991: 238–41.

15 This model subjects all forces of association and inventions, belief and desire to the law of auto-valorization of capital and use-exchange value. Gabriel Tarde argues that the Darwinian natural selection acts by excluding potential. It acts after invention has actualized the conditional reality of forces and their relations. This natural selection has a conservative and not an innovative function. It operates as an agent of stability and not of transformation. See M. Lazzarato 2002: 63–75. See also Deleuze and Guattari 1987: 218–19.

16 Marx clearly points out that industrial capitalism does not obtain its valorization through the profit on the quantity of living labour employed in the process of production (exchange value). Rather, the auto-valorization of capital stems from the application of technoscientific knowledge on production. Nevertheless, capitalism remains cynical as it reduces the quantity of variable (human) labour while, on the other hand, maintaining the time of labour as the unique measure of valorization of capital. See Karl Marx 1973: 673–95. See also Marx 1954: 351–72.

17 See Marx 1954: 574.

18 On the libidinal dynamics of capital, see J. F. Lyotard 1993.

19 See H. Bergson 1991: 5, 304, 370.

20 As M. Hardt explains, Marx defined the passage from formal to real subsumption of labour under capitalism in nineteenth-century society as a tendency. According to Marx, in the formal subsumption, social labour processes are subsumed, they are enveloped within the capitalist relations of production in such a manner that capital intervenes as the director or manager. In this arrangement capital subsumes labour the way it finds it. It takes over existing labour processes that were developed previously or at any rate outside of capitalist production. This subsumption is formal insofar as the labour process exists within capital subordinated to its command as an imported foreign force, born outside capital's domain. See Hardt 1998: 23–39.

21 Deleuze and Guattari argue that the production of surplus value involves the differential relations between the time of labour and the wages. Financial money circulating in the structures of credit is not the same money that is employed to pay wages. Salary money is only a mean to pay the reproduction of labour force

that cannot determine the real transformations of society. According to Deleuze and Guattari, money cannot be equated with labour as it defines a destructive creation of difference: a potential of deterritorialization (1983: 222–40). In Tarde, contrary to Marx, economic flows presuppose flows of another nature: currents of desire and beliefs that generate inventions eventually captured in hierarchical organizations. Tarde's economical psychology aims to disconnect forces of reproduction from capital's law of equivalence, and connect them to invention. See Lazzarato 2002: 52–3.

22 See Marx 1973: 142.

23 Irigaray's question 'What if commodities could speak?', provocatively directed to Marxian and Marxists' analysis of capital's reproduction, suggests an alternative conception of reproduction in terms of becoming rather than filiation. See Irigaray 1985b.

24 On the line of abolition as fascistic desire, see Deleuze and Guattari 1987: 229; 163.

25 The incorporeal indicates the virtual power of corporeality, which precedes and exceeds embodiment: the pre-individual for Simondon, the virtual for Bergson and the Substance or the Thing for Spinoza, the Body without Organs for Deleuze and Guattari. See M. Foucault 1977: 165–99.

26 McLuhan discusses the emergence of the acoustic sensory perception in relation to electronic media. It could be argued that this new audio-visual space, increasingly less dominated by the visual perspective of Renaissance, already emerged through this disciplinary biomedical perception. See M. McLuhan and B. R. Powers 1989: 35–47. On the dominance of vision, see M. Jay 1993.

27 For Bergson, pure perception defines an isomorphism between image and matter, where image is not perceived by the eye – the awareness of seeing – but is a mere centre of action that receives and transmits movement. Images have no centre, no direction and orientation. The reception and transmission is not realized by the visual organ, the eye, but by all elementary particles of images. Organs of perception are therefore zones of indetermination in the flow of matter-images that collide. This kind of perception is never subjected to a division of reality. Perception is not in us but in things. See Bergson 1991.

28 Benjamin suggests that the mechanical reproduction of images – photography and moving image – leads to a distracted perception. The latter exposes the sense of a perception that follows the motions of the object. This perception involves a tactile grasp of these motions rather than subjective or objective perspectives. See Benjamin 1968.

29 For a discussion of the Cartesian model of perception or mental gaze, see J. Crary 1998: 245–52.

30 The vesico-vaginal fistula is an abnormal passage or connection between the vagina and the bladder, caused by prolonged labour failing to progress. See M. Marsh and W. Ronner 1996: 41–74; T. Kapsalis 1997: 31.

31 See J. Marion Sims 1873.

32 For a literary example of this continuum, see M. Shelley 1993. See also D. Musselwhite 1987.

33 See M. Shildrick 1997: 42.

34 See J. Marion Sims 1873.

35 M. Marsh and W. Ronner 1996. See also N. Pfeffer 1993.

36 In sadism, paternal and patriarchal themes predominate. Man is the spectator and presiding genius to whom all the activities are dedicated. Sade's androgynous creations are the product of an incestuous union of father and daughter. The mother is equated with secondary nature and subjected to the laws of creations, conservation and sexual reproduction. The father pertains to primary nature but only through social conservatism. The sadistic fantasy relies on the destruction of the family on behalf of the father, by inciting the daughter to murder the mother. According to Deleuze, the Oedipal image of the mother is the true victim of sadism, actively negating the mother and exalting the father who is beyond the law. See Deleuze 1989a: 59-60.

37 On the crystal of time and the virtual actual twinning of images, see Deleuze 1989b: 68-97.

38 Benjamin identifies this process of transformation with technologies that have 'subjected the human sensorium to a complex kind of training'. He singles out photography and film as media that – in their techniques of rapid cutting, multiple cutting, multiple camera angles, instantaneous shifts in time and place – raise the experience of shock to collective perception. See Benjamin 1968: 211-44. See also E. Cadava 1997: 102.

39 Benjamin's conception of reproduction was influenced by Bergson's concepts of duration, memory and perception. Yet, for Bergson, the photographic image only tells us that perception must be thought in relation to what is no longer present, in relation to the structure of memory. Perception begins only at the moment when it begins to withdraw, when what is seen can no longer be seen. Bergson 1991: 208; Cadava 1997: 87-97.

40 See K. Theweleit 1987: 3-204.

CHAPTER 4

Biodigital Sex

Growing from other turbulences, in the erasure of contour, turbulence ends only in watery path or in a flowing manner. Inflection
itself becomes vortical, and at the same time its variation opens up
onto fluctuation, it becomes fluctuations.

Deleuze (1993: 17)

INTRODUCTION

In disciplinary society, then, biopower overcodifies the organic mode
of sexual reproduction – meiotic sex – and actualizes the *formal
subsumption* of value through industrial capitalism. This subsumption
acts as a trigger for the release of new forces of connection and transmission crystallized in the technical machine of reproduction.

This chapter argues that the disciplinary logic of industrial capitalism
reaches a critical threshold in the second half of the twentieth
century. The double tendency of entropy (organic death and death as
becoming) culminating with the Second World War pushes the process
of subsumption towards a new portal of transformation. The investment in the entropic dynamics of energy-information undergoes an
irreversible crisis when thermodynamic modes of reproduction no
longer match the capacity of energy and information to change without
collapse. Rather, collapse comes to demarcate the unexpected mutations of any system of information (biophysical, organic, cultural, technical and economic). No longer based on the inverted relation between
energy and information – i.e. more energy less information and vice
versa – that characterized thermodynamic systems of communication
and reproduction, the new focus on differential variability within rates
of energy-information deploys the productivity of turbulent information. The threshold towards far-from-equilibrium modes of communication and reproduction defines the *real subsumption* of all machines of
sex actualized through biodigital modes of information transmission.

Turbulence rather than entropy deploys the cultural logic of bio-informatic capitalism; biodigital rather than thermodynamic machines define the strategy of abstraction and distribution of all energy-forces of transmission.

Real subsumption has been attributed to the postmodern cultural logic of capitalism dominated by techno-scientific knowledge and information technologies constructing the history of posthumanity.[1] In particular, it has been argued that this logic involves the waning of affect (Jameson 1984), the triumph of simulation (Baudrillard 1994b), the end of social struggle (Robins 1996), the disintegration of the organic body or cybernetic hybridization (Haraway 1985), the emergence of a global empire (Hardt and Negri 2000). Most of these debates refer to the dissolution of the metaphysical concepts of reality, body–sex, and politics.

This chapter questions this critical trajectory. Real subsumption defines the immanent selection of all contents and expressions of the biophysical and biocultural strata. This biodigital level of capitalization incorporates all machines of sex – from autocatalytic loops to bacterial cells, from the egg cell to meiotic sex, descending in the molecular layers of the body–sex, colonizing life before life. Yet it will be misleading to attribute to capitalism the traits of a closed self-organizing system engulfing all energy-information for its own sake. Real subsumption cannot be disjointed from the virtual–actual kinematics of energy-information feeding this new level of capitalization.

From this standpoint, the forces erupting out and rebelling against the disciplinary and industrial organization of the body–sex are not to be exclusively ascribed to the rises of marginal identities (the unitary categories of marginal class, gender and race). These forces precede and exceed the categories formed by modern biopower. The passage from formal to real subsumption involves indefinite declinations from the linear trajectory of filiative capitalism. These are lines of flight that do not exclusively match with the struggle advanced by disciplinary categories formed through the subjection of the body to the sadism of biopower. These struggles are rather themselves induced by the insurgencies of anonymous forces of inventions that are indifferent to the categories of representation. These are virtual forces emerging at the intersection, the molecular edges of the biophysical and biocultural imperatives of meiotic sex and filiative heredity. These pre-individual forces of communication-reproduction cut across organic reproduction, filiative capital and disciplinary sex.

The emergence of biodigital machines of information (genetic engineering and cybernetics) leads to the constitution of 'control societies' no longer imbued with the logic of organic sex or entropic reproduction (Deleuze 1995). The disciplinary assemblage of desire–power, sadist death and masochist parthenogenesis, reaches a critical point of change by releasing sex from sexual reproduction and reproduction from autopoietic filiation. This releasing marks a mutation of desire–power encompassing the biophysical and biocultural variables of content and expression of matter. Control societies are defined by the capacities of biodigital machines to capture all variables of reproduction through an immanent modulation (selection) of information potential. These machines introduce recombinant sex as a new assemblage of desire-power in the process of stratification. Recombinant sex delineates an undecidable proposition (i.e. an immanent condition) between the proliferation of decodified information and the capitalization of its potential through virtual control.

This chapter is divided into four sections. The first section explains that the passage from disciplinary societies to control societies is marked by a threshold that − as in far-from-equilibrium dynamics − defines a new level of order. The threshold from formal to real subsumption is catalysed by biodigital machines able to fold twice the information variables of biophysical and biocultural modes of reproduction. These machines map the bio-informatic phase of capitalism distributing a new assemblage of reproduction on the strata, recombinant sex.

In the second section, I question the teleological understanding of capitalism based upon the Darwinian and neo-Darwinian conception of blind selection, survival of the fittest and individual competition. The machinic composition of capitalism affords no dualistic distinction between recombinant trading and monopolistic filiation. Here, biodigital machines double fold − fold twice − cytoplasmic and nucleic variables of information involving a virtual control of their potential variations as suggested by genetic engineering and genetic mapping.

In the third section, I will discuss bio-technological and digital cloning that map the biodigital assemblage of the bio-informatic real subsumption of all machines of sex. Biodigital cloning points to the proliferation of molecular mutations of contents and expressions of matter impacting on the body–sex. It intensifies non-linear reproduction by tapping into the virtual-actual circuits of a matrix of potential mutations.

In the last section, I will briefly recapitulate the implications of the biodigital machines of sex. This new parasitic recombination exposes a bio-informatic war between all layers of stratification of sex. This war entails the colliding encounters of particles and compounds, the reversible qualities of poison, the emergence of novelty by contamination. It lays out the reversible parasitic line between absolute control and absolute destratification of all machines of sex in the bio-informatic phase of capitalism.

THE THRESHOLD

We can now posit a conceptual difference between the 'limit' and the 'threshold': the limit designates the penultimate marking a necessary rebeginning, and the threshold the ultimate marking an inevitable change.

Deleuze and Guattari (1987: 438)

The second half of the twentieth century demarcates a new threshold of change in modes of communication and reproduction. The entropic organization of energy-information that characterizes industrial disciplinary societies oscillates around a critical point after the Second World War. Yet, the formation of biopower has not vanished into a void. In the previous chapter, this formation was conceived as an abstract composition of forces and tendencies, perceptions, affections and disentanglements that are irreducible to epistemological paradigms. The actualization of biopower is inseparable from the release of a potential, a virtual power that is not localizable in chronological time.

The diffusion of biopower also involves the virtual expansion of the biophysical machines of sex (the sex of molecules and compounds), triggering the decodification of organic and disciplinary forms and substances of expression (genotype and regimes of signs) and content (phenotype and technologies of power) across the biocultural stratum. As previously explained, biopower entails a practice of subsumption of the forces of reproduction and communication through the law of sex and entropy. Yet this subsumption exposes a bifurcation between two parallel processes. On the one hand, the disciplinary overcodification of sexual reproduction and genital sex wards off inorganic forces of repetition. On the other, the decodification of reproduction and sex anticipates the emergence of a new tendency of forces. This bifurcation demarcates 'a function of *a threshold or degree*, beyond which what is anticipated takes on consistency or fails to, and what is conjured away ceases to be so and arrives' (Deleuze and Guattari 1987: 432). In warding off inorganic sex, disciplinary biopower intervenes in time, where changes are anticipated rather than avoided. This intervention is defined by the tendency of a threshold, which coexists with what is crossing and with what has yet to cross. In other words, a tendency marks a continual line of variation whose arrows of time are neither progressive nor regressive.

The notion of tendency is often ascribed to evolutionary development, linear and gradual progression of time localized in the Euclidean grid of space. Nevertheless, as the diagrams of venture capitalists show, the tendency towards change will more likely designate a curve, a declination from linear development. As Bergson argues, a tendency delineates the split between virtual and actual lines of intensive and extensive differences (1991). Far from deriving from an actual point, the tendency of evolution entails the clashing of multidirectional lines of time, unfolding a non-linear virtual-actual circuit of emergence. The tendency emerges in the coalescence of the past and the present that is passing and that is yet to cross it. This coalescence maps the smallest feedback loop between the actual present and the virtual past. In this sense, a tendency does not have a starting point, a source of emission. It can only loop the lines of time passing in a non-linear fashion from the past into the present and from the present into the past.[2]

This understanding questions Newton's conception of time-symmetric trajectories where the space-time of initial conditions does not diverge from linearity. For example, if an arrow is launched twice, and the second time with slightly more force or in a slightly different direction, it is assumed that its trajectory will only change slightly, and in a predictable way. In assuming a principle of identity and unity as constantly maintained through motion, this conception defines a tendency as a predictable line without potential. In moving beyond linearity and equilibrium, the theorists of chaos, Ilya Prigogine and Isabelle Stengers emphasize the singular potential of a system to change through critical points of becoming. Becoming is not to be considered as a fixed point in which potential exists, but as a process involving the emergence of one of the dimensions of a turbulent or 'far-from-equilibrium' system.[3] This theory provides a new understanding of the dynamics of transformation. No longer determined by formal qualities and development towards irreversible change (entropic death and ultimate collapse), physical, biological, social and economic systems expose the patterns of far-from-equilibrium dynamics crossing the micro and macro scales of order. According to Prigogine and Stengers, bifurcation defines a continuum between micro and macro scales of order as the momentum between rigid and chaotic phases: a vortex of creation and destruction. This bifurcation is turbulence: a declining arrow of time conjugating the past and the future through the actions of a passing present immersed in a multidirectional flow of time beyond chronological accumulation and entropic collapse. Prigogine defines the momentum of bifurcation as a 'declination' from the trajectory of the atom. He draws on Lucretius's theorization of the *clinamen* that highlights the slightest movement in the angle of declination of a laminar flow initiating turbulence:[4]

> *When the atoms are travelling straight down through empty space by their own weight, at quite indeterminate times and places they swerve ever so little from their course,* just so much that you can call it a change of direction. (Lucretius, *On the Nature of the Universe*, Book II, par. 220)

As Deleuze explains, the *clinamen* is the original determination of the direction of the movement of the atom (1990a: 269). It is a differential. The *clinamen* designates neither contingency nor indetermination. On the contrary, it indicates the *lex atomi*, the irreducible multiplicities of causes, serial causes or quasi-causes, the impossibility to gather causes into one whole. Challenging the laws of inertia and entropic irreversibility regulating the dynamics of nature, turbulence defines the assemblage of micro-causes leading to an unpredictable series of effects. Turbulence marks the double bifurcation between a time falling in the past and a time falling in the present, the asymmetrical relation between pre-individual and individuated multiplicities composing all assemblages of energy-forces. According to Prigogine and Stengers, turbulent or unstable systems constitute the norm rather than the exception of the biophysical universe, defined no longer by individual trajectory of time-symmetry but by differential arrows of time. In far-from-equilibrium systems, the slightest change in initial conditions can stir up a hurricane of unpredictable effects, as the infamous flap of a butterfly's wings demonstrates.

The disciplinary overcodification and decodification of the organic entanglement between sex, reproduction and death anticipates the tendency towards an intensified decodification of the biophysical strata. The threshold towards a new level of stratification of sex announces the passage towards the real subsumption of the body–sex involving an immanent selection and modulation of all variables of matter.

The Superfold

Attention has recently been focused on the fact that modern power is not at all reducible to the classical alternative 'repression or ideology' but implies processes of normalization, modulation, modelling, and information that bear on language, perception, desire, movement, etc., and which proceed by way of microassemblages. This aggregate includes both subjection and enslavement taken to extremes, as two simultaneous parts that constantly reinforce and nourish each other.

Deleuze and Guattari (1987: 458)

In the Foucauldian study of biopower, the fold designates the abstract diagram of disciplinary society (Deleuze 1988b). By folding energy-forces of reproduction, the regime of social subjection of the body organizes the transmission of information through new technologies of individuation (e.g. the factory, the school, the hospital, the prison etc.). The entropic organization of bio-social forces of reproduction constitutes the disciplinary archipelago of power. Invariable mouldings or variations arranged the biomass of populations into a hierarchical pyramid of individuated bodies (e.g. the worker, the pupil, the patient, etc.) marking a new bifurcation of content and expressions on the strata of sex. This irreversible folding lays out a striated space of order where regimes of signs (words-things: variables of expression) and technologies of power (socio-technical machines: variables of content) define the disciplinary duplication of the time of reproduction preserved and distributed through the industrial technical machine.

Far from defining an eternal form of organization, the disciplinary organization of the forces of reproduction constitutes a temporary assemblage in the wider dynamics of transformation.[5] The crossing of the threshold towards a new level of order marks the emergence and formation of 'control societies'. Deleuze defines the passage from disciplinary to control societies as a breakdown of all technologies of confinement and interiority, where individuals and signatures are decomposed on a micro scale of assembled information generating the data banks of 'dividuals' and passwords (1995: 80). Rather than confining forces of reproduction to fixed forms and stable functions, control follows their variations by modulating all divergences of information. Control exposes the ceaseless modulation of information that follows the auto-transmutation of matter by changing its activity of selection from one moment to the next. As opposed to deterrence (the realm of pre-programmed simulation), modulation captures the interval between states: differential virtuals without actuality. In other words, its operational continuum is entangled with the turbulent emergence of variations whose selection catalyses (accelerates) their potential tendencies. Control becomes immanent to virtual variables. This control is inseparable from the proliferation of automated machines of communication studied by cybernetics.[6] No longer does control operate by imposing homeostasis and balance to the flows of information transmission, but by following the metastable equilibrium of parallel networks of communication incorporating all variables of connection. Cybernetic control spreads through the positive feedback loops of data-processing between human and machine. As Deleuze and Guattari argue:

> If motorized machines constituted the second age of the technical machine, cybernetic and informational machines form a third age that reconstructs a generalized regime of subjection: recurrent and reversible 'human–machines systems' replace the old non-recurrent and nonreversible relations of subjection between the two elements; the relation between human and machine is based on internal, mutual communication, and no longer on usage or action. (1987: 458)

Third generation machines involve a symbiotic assemblage of non-analogous modes of information that multiply the lines of transmission – stimuli and receptions – between all modes of communication: a virus, a human being, an animal, a computer. This new control expands on the Panoptical striated space of surveillance through a decentralized network of open nodes of connection modelled on the algorithmic behaviour of genetic information. The pyramidal model of management of energy-forces is replaced by a smooth (uninterrupted) space of undetermined flows through which capitalism reaches 'absolute speed' (Deleuze and Guattari 1987: 492).

The disciplinary fold has trans-mutated – mutated across strata – into a Superfold 'borne out by the foldings proper to the chains of the genetic code, and the potential of silicon in third-generation machines' (Deleuze 1988b: 131). This new diagram of power involves a double folding of energy-forces where turbulent or far-from-equilibrium biodigital machines no longer reproduce but recombine the micro-variations of all modes of information through a human–machine symbiotic merging. Rather than reducing variables to identities, this double folding (recombination) defines the continual modulation of variations, the capture and optimization of their potential tendencies. Modulation operates through an immanent selection of microvariations entailing the emergence (and not the elimination) of new molecular assemblages. This immanent selection of biophysical and biocultural potentials of reproduction defines the bio-informatic phase of capitalism.

Bio-informatics: the modulation of information flows

[. . .] modulating is a molding in a continuous and variable fashion.
Deleuze (1993: 19)

It is difficult to discuss the bio-informatic phase of capitalism without considering the techno-scientific relationship between molecular biology and cybernetics upon which the immanent modulation of molecular variations depends. Donna Haraway points to the convergence between cybernetics and molecular biology in the 'Cyborg Manifesto', when she discusses the shift towards post-disciplinary modes of power involving communication networks, where '[b]iological organisms have become bionic systems, communication devices like others' (1991: 177–8). As Eugene Thacker also explains, bio-informatics maps the confluence of genetic engineering and bio-technology stemming from developments in molecular biology (including genetics, immunology, endocrinology), applied research and clinical technologies (genomic mapping, gene therapy, PCR, DNA chips) and cybernetics.[7] Lab-based computing technologies, the growth of the Internet and the Web, have also contributed to a new set of techniques aimed at organizing amounts of genetic information through software programming.

In the second half of the twentieth century, in the mid-1950s, the first merging between cybernetics and molecular biology occurred on the level of the code, conceived as a transmissible unit of information. After the double helix was X-rayed by Rosalind Franklin,[8] Francis Crick and James Watson adopted it as evidence to define the behaviour of genetic transmission patterns, the linear translation of information from DNA to RNA to protein. Franklin's X-rayed photograph showed DNA (deoxyribonucleic acid) in its spiral figure consisting of four genetic-paired bases, Adenine-Thymine, Guanine-Cytosine. As a result of the discovery of this genetic structure, in the late 1960s, molecular biologist Jacques Monod questioned the distinctions among living organisms based on taxonomic classification.[9] Influenced by homeostatic cybernetics and entropic thermodynamics, the structure of DNA was in a first moment considered to be a stable unit of life. In linearly replicating itself, DNA was thought to determine RNA and influence amino acid sequences in the polypeptide chain composing protein (Shostak 1999: 33). Shröndinger defined the activity of DNA as the commanding operations of a 'master molecule', hierarchically providing the secret information of life to the cell.[10]

Nevertheless, the composition of nucleic DNA has revealed itself to be regulated by non-linear patterns, characterized by mutational 'hot spots' in the nucleus, more prone to changes than other portions of DNA, and by recombinant 'hot spots', more prone to insert sequences of foreign DNA. Even the size of DNA suggests that, far from being isolated, nucleic DNA is immediately in contact with the body of the cell, whose activity is influenced by the amount of DNA in the nucleus (Shostak 1999: 37). Similarly, retroviruses and pararetroviruses, operating through transverse transcriptase (RNA>DNA) and characterizing, among other diseases, HIV (Human Immunodeficiency retrovirus), also have displayed the non-linearity of the DNA unit in transferring information. The turbulent dynamics of nucleic DNA, therefore, have been demonstrated by the retroaffects that RNA and protein have on nucleic base pairs. Far from defining a hierarchy, the genome complex lays out parallel networks of information transmission regulated by metastable feedbacks. As Michel Serres observes:

> The cybernetic model temporarily allows us to imagine certain links between these levels, from molecular activity to the organization of the cell, tissues, organs, and so forth. In relatively simple cases it would even be possible to write a mathematical model, a system of differential equations representing cellular activity. The conditions at the limits of that activity would describe the state of the boundaries, the limits of the level under consideration, and hence the nature of the proximity of one level to the next, the manner in which one level is submerged in the next. (1982: 77)

By providing a model of communication that involves different layers of connection in a body or between bodies, cybernetics, theorized by Norbert Wiener, is based on feedbacks: 'the property of being able to adjust future conduct by past performance' (1989: 33). The input/output loops of transmission define cybernetics as the study of control and communication regulating information patterns. This control is not exercised from the outside. Rather, it emerges from the dynamics of

regulation of parallel activities of transmission that increase and
decrease the passage of energy-information through feedback loops.
The machine corrects itself by receiving information through the feedback exchange between input – internal information – and output –
external information. This process can be proven to operate within a
machine, but also in a human/living organism. In particular, Wiener
distinguishes two types of feedback relations, the negative feedback,
which tends to maintain stability in a system (e.g. gadgets such as
thermostats), and positive feedback, that is the tendency of the system
to run out of control – to change.

Wiener's major intuition develops from Gibb's probabilistic hypothesis of the universe to study the regulation of information in animals,
humans and machines. Cybernetics draws on the convergence between
biological and mechanical behaviours according to which 'the body is
very far from a conservative system, [. . .] its component parts work in
an environment where the available power is much less limited than
we have taken it to be' (Wiener 1961: 42). The body is no longer
determined by individual qualities constituting the difference between
animal, human and machine. Although the first and second waves of
cybernetics are entangled with the thermodynamic view of a universe
tending towards collapse or fighting against the sprawling of noise, the
third cybernetic wave points out the productive force of turbulent
transformations and the autonomy of emergent properties.[11] The study
of retroviruses, viral transmission and bacterial recombination
converges onto the study of far-from-equilibrium and chaotic systems
of information mapping the movement of the threshold towards the
third wave of cybernetics at the core of artificial life and genetic
engineering.[12]

The bio-informatic capitalization of information relies on this turbulent equilibrium, the potential of the trajectory of transmission to
produce new connections through a network of parallel communication
and reproduction. This biodigital capitalization accelerates the schizophrenic recombination of all information flows conjugating discon-
nected variables of expression and content from the strata formations
previously analysed. In particular, the decodification of the organic
strata with genetic engineering and biotechnology increases the mutations of molecular variations distributing non-genital sex through a
new assemblage of desire-power on the strata. In contrast with the
Freudian libido, this assemblage operates through parallel networks of
positive feedbacks between organic and inorganic reproduction. The
bio-informatic phase of capital no longer wards off but feeds on the

proliferation of turbulent recombinations by modulating (i.e. capturing, producing and multiplying) rather than repressing (i.e. excluding) the emergent variations. It marks the real subsumption of the body–sex unfolding the autonomy of the variables of recombination from organic sex and entropic pleasure.

MACHINIC CAPITAL

According to Deleuze and Guattari, capital operates through a conjunction of deterritorialized and decoded flows. It abstracts codes and territories (forms and substances of expression and content) from all strata and reassembles them on a new abstract plane channelling their potential of differentiation in multiple directions. As Guattari affirms, abstraction has also to be understood in terms of extraction and composition, like the dynamics of a cinematographic montage whose consistent motion embraces a correlative multiplicity of different levels and their relations (1995: 40). Abstraction operates by processes of codes drifting and side-communication. As the Deleuze–Guattarian example of the wasp and the orchid suggests, these processes involve the formation of a rhizome – a zigzagging line – assembling codes from different systems of reproduction. By pollinating the orchid, the wasp becomes a piece in the orchid's reproductive apparatus, which at the same time becomes a piece of the wasp. This '*aparallel evolution* of two beings that have absolutely nothing to do with each other' involves the capture of a code, an extraction that induces becoming by contamination (Deleuze and Guattari 1987: 10). As François Jacob puts it: '[N]ature operates to create diversity by endlessly combining bits and pieces'(1974: 39). There is no intrinsic or primordial organic quality that defines nature and life as opposed to the artificial and death. The process of abstraction accelerated by the bio-informatic capitalization of all modes of reproduction entails an immanent capture of the biochemical, socio-cultural and techno-economic partial codes by connecting all forms of value through a machinic surplus value of information.

Bio-informatic capital decodifies all established codes substituting them with sets of axioms. Axioms can be conceived as a set of equations indifferently determining and immediately combining variables and coefficients without assigning them a specific value. Axioms operate through a regulating conjunction of decoded flows – of money, labour capacity, raw materials, skills and technology, consumer tastes and so forth – in the production of machinic surplus value (Holland 1997:

528). Deleuze and Guattari have individuated two orders that suppress molecular differences in the process of capture and valorization: codes – the qualitative order of resemblances – and axioms – the quantitative order of equivalencies. Nevertheless, the bio-informatic process of decodification and axiomatization simultaneously captures and unfolds molecular variables of behaviour, desire, production and consumption of information spreading across all levels of control societies.

In order to define the dynamics of the real subsumption of the body–sex, it is important to challenge the model of evolution based on the Darwinian and neo-Darwinian notions of natural selection, competition and survival.[13] In particular, at the core of neo-Darwinian theories lies the assumption of a blind mechanism of natural selection operating upon specific values that replicate themselves according to the rule of the survival of the fittest.[14] Far from explaining processes of transformation, these theories reduce molecular variations to isolated and individuated values. On the immanent plane of relations, transformations entail the auto-assemblage of variations introducing unexpected novelties on the strata. The transformation of the means of production (from thermodynamic to cybernetic machines) involves the decodification of biophysical and biocultural modifications of reproduction marking the emergence of a differential time crystallized and distributed by biodigital machines.

Instead of being engendered by structures (monopolies and hierarchies), novelties and inventions emerge from the symbiotic composition of the most indifferent bodies generating nuclear structures. The dynamics of capitalization is not governed by an external mechanism of selection that preserves the fittest order of information determined by a blind law of value. This conservative conception of selection dismisses the anonymous capacities of auto-organization favoured by an immanent selection whose primary function is not to eliminate but to unleash potential.

According to Manuel DeLanda, the confusion over the notion of capitalism arbitrarily used to refer to 'free enterprise', 'industrial mode of production', and 'world-economy', is usefully resolved by Fernard Braudel's concept of 'anti-market' (1997: 49).[15] A freedom of movement and organization of profit made possible by extensive credit characterize anti-markets. These are apparatuses of capture that convert grassroots trading into monopoly: molar assemblages regulating the flow of money by channelling potentials in short-term investments and profits. According to Braudel, the difference between anti-markets and markets already came to the fore with the coexistence of world trading and monopoly in the thirteenth century. For a long time there has been a coexistence of heterogeneous institutions, some ruled by demand and supply, properly called markets, and others operating through the manipulation of market forces, anti-markets, where centralization dominates and command replaces the fluctuation of prices as a coordinating mechanism of human activity. Real markets emerge from the unintended aggregations of independent trades defining synergistic compositions of forces. Markets are autonomous and constituted by interacting heterogeneous components, ecosystems whose parts always exceed the whole, transforming itself through the interaction of its components.

Instead of postulating a teleological whole, a capitalist system, supposed to function according to the transcendent model of selection and survival, DeLanda argues that capitalism is a complex environment of heterogeneous forces of production, populations of institutions, markets, corporations and bureaucratic agencies. Capitalism is not a general source of free enterprise and exploitation – a homogeneous and stable body always already reproducing itself. Rather, its composition changes through the fluctuating interactions of institutions and markets, nucleic and trading organizations. In this sense, capitalism is not a closed system of exchange engendering and subjecting all forces of reproduction. Even the individuation of monopolies and economic institutions should not be limited to a mere identification or representation of capitalism, but rather exposed to the wider microphysical environment of which they are part. For example, economic institutions are always part of larger institutional organizations, such as the military complex, but also wider ecosystems of desire-power that make their purpose redundant.[16]

Thus, it can be argued that the threshold towards bio-informatic capitalism does not just entail a new kind of subjection to increasingly flexible and supple hierarchies of reproduction. Rather, it primarily highlights that the proliferation of decoded modes of reproduction involves an immanent selection of emerging micro-variations (molecular mutations). This immanence defines an undecidable proposition between absolute control and absolute deterritorialization of the molecular variables of matter.

Unnatural body v organic autopoiesis

I argue that the 'artificial' ecosystems – containing humans, technology and the requisite elements for long-term recycling in materially closed environments – are not at all artificial but, rather, the first in a batch of planetary propagules whose proliferation is in keeping with prior epochal evolutionary developments (for example, bacterial spores, animal bodies, plant seeds and so on).

Sagan (1992: 374–5)

The endosymbiotic assemblage between bacteria, animals, plants, humans and technology constitutes a heterogeneous biosphere of evolution that challenges the neo-Darwinian emphasis on individuated units of selection. Although Sagan's definition of biosphere defies the traditional distinction between organic and inorganic, wholes and parts, the Deleuze–Guattarian notion of *Mechanosphere* is more adequate to discuss the immanent capitalization conjugating biophysical and biodigital information. When describing the isomorphism of stratification, the continuum and reversibility between organic, anthropomorphic and technical strata, Deleuze and Guattari prefer to avoid any confusion with cosmic and spiritual evolution. They use the notion of Mechanosphere that neutralizes the differences in kinds and degrees among strata determining hierarchies of qualification and quantification. 'The apparent order can be reversed, with cultural or technical phenomena providing a fertile soil, a good soup, for the development of insects, bacteria, germs, or even particles. The industrial age defined as the age of insects' (1987: 69). Deleuze and Guattari's mechanosphere also questions the vitalist and mechanist dualism that reduces to teleological causes the assembling processes of transformation. This mechanosphere is composed of abstract machines – symbiotic compositions of molecular bodies whose differences are ceaselessly engineered.[17] The abstract machine lays out the activities of pre-individual anonymous forces unleashing the unpredictable potential of every actual assemblage. There is no internal will or external determination.[18] The machinic assemblage of forces exposes the virtual-actual multiplicities of differentiation that mark a continuum between the inside and the outside according to differential degrees of variation, depending on kinetic velocities and anonymous capacities of affection. The abstract machine privileges neither biological nor social systems, organic or social structures. It is not a question of whether the biological comes before the social and the economical or the other way around. The abstract machine maps the engineering capacities of a body to compose, decompose and differentiate beyond individuated differences (static identity). What comes first is not unity and form but intensive velocities: micro-durations

141

cutting across organic and social stratifications, unfolding a heterogeneous mechanosphere of information.

The bio-informatic capitalization of information exposes the immanent relations between the biophysical and biodigital machines of sex accelerating the decodification of the organic and biocultural orders of reproduction. According to DeLanda, the dynamics of capitalization are linked to the capacities of mesh-works or markets to auto-organize. He argues that mesh-works behave like auto-catalytic loops that explain the autopoietic capacities of biochemical systems to reproduce without the external intervention of natural selection. Humberto Maturana and Francisco Varela inspire his analysis of the auto-sustaining dynamics of mesh-works or markets.[19] Their hypothesis distinguishes two general characteristics of autocatalytic or semi-closed circuits. On the one hand, these circuits are defined as: 'dynamical systems that endogenously generate their own *stable states* (called "attractors" or "eigenstates")', on the other, 'they grow and evolve by *drift*' (DeLanda 1997: 63). The former characteristic of autocatalytic loops involves an accumulation of chemical reactions that alternate at perfectly regular intervals. The latter marks the emergence of new catalytic nodes from a basic two-node network formed by two chemical reactions in a simple catalytic loop. Maturana and Varela attribute the notion of autopoiesis (self-organization) only to living systems, and allopoiesis to self-organizing machines that produce something different from themselves, for example social systems, technological systems and so on (Guattari 1995: 44). Although DeLanda relates the process of autocatalytic loops to the study of geological, biological and human generating structures, in Maturana and Varela autopoiesis is exclusively referred to the autonomous self-organization of living entities, as primarily individuated and closed.

The emphasis on closed self-sustaining loops at the core of cybernetics, molecular biology and evolutionary theories rests on entropic dynamics regulated by internal and external relations of exchange (e.g. the nucleus from the rest of the cell, a cell from other cells, a human being from the environment, a natural being from a machine). Yet, the machinic or symbiotic conception of capital neither relies on the closed nature of autocatalytic loops of living structures or on allopoietic socio-economic and technological structures. As Deleuze and Guattari put it: 'consistency, far from being restricted to complex life forms, fully pertains even to the most elementary atoms and particles' (1987: 335). Instead of indicating the external property of technological and social structures, the notion of mechanosphere exposes the molecular assemblages composing individuated systems, bypassing their ends or purposes, functions and structures. This notion entails a 'domain of nondifference between the microphysical and the biological, there being as many living beings in the machine as there are machines in the living' (Deleuze and Guattari 1983: 287). Not only is capitalism part of the mechanosphere, but also the capitalization of information can be analysed across different layers of stratification that do not exclusively relate to the emergence of technical machines of communication and reproduction.

This capitalization also encompasses the biophysical strata where the emergence of new parasiting assemblages involves the incorporation of all information-energies of their host bodies. For example, the biophysical stratification of sex maps the emergence of meiotic sex through the merging of microbes (distinct forms and substances of content), forming eukaryotic cells and the genotype (new forms and substances of expression) that are able to detach from the phenotype and the cytoplasm (content). This detachment introduces the eukaryotic and nucleic capitalization of bacterial and cytoplasmic modes of information transmission. Nevertheless, the emergence of this hierarchical capitalization does not substitute the micro-organizations of bacterial and cytoplasmic machines with the macro-order of nucleic transmission. The process of stratification points to the molecular constitution of hierarchical organizations, the continual flow of variation that runs beneath molar aggregations. The nucleic and eukaryotic apparatuses of information-capture run parallel to the mesh-works or autocatalytic loops of bacterial reproduction ceaselessly declining from stationary states.

In a recent theorization of the dynamics of global capitalism and transnational state apparatuses, Negri and Hardt define the new phase of capitalist power as an a-central apparatus of rules constituting what they call the *Empire* (2000). This is a matrix of power without limits distributing command through the inclusive, differential and managerial modes of abstraction of surplus value. In the elaboration of the dynamics of growth and expansion of global capitalism, they contrast the conception of capital's cycles and return, which defines a dominant model for the evolutionary study of the history of capital. In their view, the emphasis on the reproductive cycles of capital does not account for the rise of events, immanent forces disturbing the linear repetition of capitalism (2000: 239). In presupposing isolated and closed strategies of reproduction, the cyclic hypothesis, relying on autopoiesis, adopts a transcendent conception of power dynamics, which is insufficient to map the heterogeneous productions of multiplicities (cultural, social, political and economical) emerging out of different capital's formations. Nevertheless, in Negri and Hardt's theorization of immanence, it is still assumed that the new communicative organization of the world order carried from communication industries relies on a self-validating, autopoietic machine (34). This machine is able to self-reproduce through the abstraction of surplus value rising from the conjunction of brains and bodies, which develops ways of cooperation that are not necessarily provided or incorporated by capitalism. The apparatus of capital reproduction is opposed to the creative events engendered by the *multitude*. The latter drives the changes of capitalism forced to become an immanent apparatus of command and control, rather than a transcendent system closed in itself. As they point out, the multitude constitutes 'the networked real productive force of our social world, whereas Empire is a mere apparatus of capture that lives off the vitality of the multitude' (62). In net contrast with the autopoietic machine of capitalism, Negri and Hardt emphasize the creative, communicative, networked relations of virtualized production (i.e. immaterial labour), based on decentralized, innovative and 'abstract cooperation' of bodies constituting global capitalism.[20]

By considering Empire a parasitical web of bodies living off the creative vitality of the multitude characterized by the networked intelligence of humans and machines, Negri and Hardt still assume a formal distinction of death and life, inorganic and organic. Although they often refer to open systems and immanent ruling procedures of command and relations, their systematic conception of capital does not grasp the critical point of far-from-equilibrium dynamics able to auto-constitute differential degrees of order through turbulence. These dynamics do not presuppose a distinction between global and flexible capital on the one hand and resistance and autonomous power of the multitude on the other. As a far-from-equilibrium system, capital is defined by many levels of order – meshworks and hierarchies – emerging from unnatural assemblages that amplify their effects through an *internal resonance* expanding through dynamics of capture and deterritorialization across strata formations. Far from drawing a line between Empire and the multitude, the endosymbiotic conception of capital exposes a machinic composition of molecular bodies involving continual and differential degrees of variation between bodies that capture and bodies that are captured. These degrees of variation are non-linear and involve a reversibility of positions that is not ruled by resistances and oppositions but by viral intrusions and convertible infections.

The limit of capital no longer designates the contours of a closed system that sees the rest as its outside, but marks a threshold of change – an amplification of the molecular – crossing the animate and inanimate spheres of production-consumption, creation-destruction of all contents and expressions. Hardt and Negri's critique of the Empire – the informatic structure of transnational capitalism – as a parasitic organism sucking and neutralizing the vital energies of the multitude – problematically recalls the Freudian thermodynamic cycle of death and life drives. Rather than engaging with molecular mutations, Negri and Hardt characterize capitalism through the negative qualities of destruction and parasitism as opposed to the striving living qualities of the multitude. Empire misses the fluctuating coexistence of information trading and monopoly, markets and antimarkets. It re-imposes the binarism between organic and inorganic, life and death, closed and open systems on multifaceted compositions.

By highlighting the auto-consistency of the multitude, Negri and Hardt interestingly refer to Spinoza's plane of immanence as delineating the conceptual bifurcation in human history between the Renaissance autonomous subject versus the Modern heritage of Enlightenment and its disciplinary social orders. Nevertheless, by relying on human forms of subjectivity and agency their intervention excludes capital from the consistent plane of nature, and as a consequence redefines the dialectic between the natural and the artificial rejected by the Spinozist anti-genealogy and anti-naturalism.[21] As Deleuze and Guattari point out, the plane of nature is a *Body without Organs* and the autonomy of reproduction does not imply the auto-constitution of an individual body but the composition of a collective *conatus* (desire) that expands its infinite potential through encounters. Monopolistic capital is not the sole form of capitalization. The latter is not external but consistent with the multiplicity of orders and scales of a plane of nature that constitutes the biophysical, biocultural and techno-economic layers of organization. In order to map the turbo-dynamics of capitalization, it is necessary to engage with non-linear dynamics of evolution depending on contagions and epidemics rather than homeostatic reproduction and linear transmission.

The biodigital sex of capital

Your people will change. Your young will be more like us and ours more like you. Your hierarchical tendencies will be modified and if we learn to regenerate limbs and reshape our bodies, we'll share those abilities with you. That's part of the trade. We're overdue for it.

(Butler 1987: 40)

Thus, the bio-informatic capitalization of information is immanent to the microcellular variables of reproduction and communication defined by endosymbiotic evolution.[22] Lynn Margulis argued that cytoplasmic genes (mitochondria, plastids and cilia residing in the soma of the cell), far from being sterile, deploy a bacterial-like mode of reproduction. Information transmission does not exclusively involve the eukaryotic imperative of chromosomal or nucleic exchange and filiation. Rather, it also includes the recombination of bacterial-like organelles entrapped in the eukaryotic cell. Information is not exclusively transmissible through the germline (nucleic DNA), but also through the somaline, the bacterial-like recombination of cytoplasmic genes. Chromosomal heredity ensured by sexual reproduction or meiotic sex no longer is determinant of all genetic variations and modes of transmission. Meiotic sex also involves the transfer of cytoplasmic material or mitochondrial DNA passed through the egg cell from mother to daughter. Indeed mitochondrial DNA constitutes the supplementary inherited genome that marks the feminine line of bacterial recombination or *Mitochondrial Eve*.[23]

Drawing on this hypothesis of microbial evolution, it could be argued that capitalism lays out a parallel coexistence of nucleic dynamics of capitalization – monopoly and hierarchies – and cytoplasmic bacterial-like trading or recombination of information, defining continual variations in modes of reproduction. Chromosomal reproduction at the core of sexual filiation does not determine all orders of capitalization. Rather, nucleic reproduction is affected by bacterial and mitochondrial recombinations. The transmission of nucleic DNA is open to genetic reversibility responsible for retroviruses and pararetroviruses, operating through transverse transcriptase (RNA > DNA). In this sense, although nucleic transmission presents a more sequential organization of information, its forms and substances of expression (genotype and chromosomes) are continuously affected by forms and substances of content (phenotype and cytoplasmic material) able to reverse chromosomal trajectory.

From the standpoint of endosymbiosis, it becomes problematic to distinguish nucleic apparatuses of capitalization of information (anti-markets) from bacterial trading of information (markets). Monopolistic organizations of information, such as nuclear genes, could feed on the most virulent trades that would expand despite aggregating monopolies. Similarly the most subverting bacterial trades could give way to the most hierarchical and rigid corporations. The question of the host and the guest in endosymbiotic dynamics remains unsolved as it deploys the expansion of molecular sexes (bacterial, viral, mitochondrial) preceding and exceeding nucleic exchange and filiation – meiotic sex. The overcodification and decodification of meiotic sex demarcates the parallel process of reproduction adopted by disciplinary biopower and industrial capitalism. The unpredictable and differential potential of molecular information defines the bio-informatic stratification of sex. In particular, the decodification of the biophysical variables of expression and content introduces a new assemblage of desire-power on the strata: biodigital sex.

This biodigital recombination entails dynamics of immanent control: a continual modulation (i.e. the capture of emerging variations) of chemical particles, genetic substances and cellular forms. Modulation delineates the biodigital conjunction of all modes of reproduction and communication (from cellular phones to computer viruses, from cellular symbiosis to genetic engineering and artificial life) on a smooth space of potential variations. Biodigital machines enable a virtual control of information (i.e. capturing the present-futurity of variations), tapping into the potentials of reproduction. Following Bergson, Deleuze explains that the virtual is neither the ideal nor the imaginary. It is neither possible nor given (1988a). The virtual defines the *real* potential of all actual modes of existence unleashing continual capacities of variation. The biodigital recombination of all machines of sex exposes a virtualization (acceleration of potential tendencies) of molecular reproduction deploying an immanent selection (positive differentiation) and modulation of their capacities to transmit anew.

Virtualizing the genomic pool

What is virtual is the connect*ibility*: potential (the reality of change). It cannot be overemphasized that the virtual is less the connection itself than its *-ibility*.

Massumi (2001: 1080–1)

The real surprise had come when he tested his altered microbes. The computing capacity of even bacterial DNA was enormous compared to man-made electronics. All Vergil had to do was take advantage of what was already there – just give it a nudge, as it were. [. . .] Once he started the process and switched on the genetic sequences which could compound and duplicate the biological segments, the cell began to function as autonomous units. [. . .] the bacteria – lowly prokaryotes – were doing better than multicellular eukaryotes! And within months, he had them running more complex mazes at rates – allowing for scale adjustments – comparable to those of mice.

Bear (1985: 22)

The virtualization of cellular and genetic variations is linked to the rise of the biotech industry in the late 1970s and early 1980s which invested in recombinant DNA (cloning or transgenesis) through PCR (polymerase chain reaction) techniques for decrypting, ordering and eventually recombining genetic material. As a result of the real subsumption of genetic information, this investment involves a variable and immanent channelling of codes' potential through 'a sieve whose mesh varies from one point to another' (Deleuze 1995: 188). The mapping of the genome or genetic sequences constitutes the most literal examples of the new virtualization of profit. The latter refers neither to a possible profit nor to its simulation. Rather, it defines a real event: the actual differentiation of virtual potential or the actual emergence of genetic potential modulated through biodigital machines of information.

As Margulis and Sagan point out, genetic engineering as a cellular process was invented by bacteria billions of eras ago. '[T]he biotechnology revolution exploits the tendency of bacteria to donate and receive each other's genes: genetic engineering is based on the ancient sexual propensities of bacteria' (1997: 50). Bacteria invented genetic trading as a way to repair strings of DNA burned by intense solar radiations. The biotechnological virtualization of bacterial sex involves an immanent investment in its potential to recombine through the bio-commercial apparatus of patenting. Haraway argues that the bio-informatic modulation of bacterial recombination entails the patenting of new bio-technological devices exploiting the unnatural merging of information systems. She compares the onco mouse, a 'rat implanted with a cyber-control device', to Margulis and Sagan's discovery of *Mixotricha paradoxa* (1995). This modern South Australian termite presents a symbiotic assemblage of 'multiple heterologous genomes' (five distinct kinds of internal and external prokaryotic symbionts). This heterogeneous molecular composition of a cell engenders new cells with a mutated genetic package. Similarly, this bionic onco mouse defines the bio-informatic virtualization of symbionts that modulates their potential recombination to test the development of cancerous cells. This bionic oncomouse crystallizes molecular variations, which will be selected and distributed in the new patenting and pharmaceutical markets.

Recombinant DNA or bacterial sex is at the core of virtual control. Genetic cloning or transgenesis exploits the ability of bacteria to take up and replicate any piece of DNA without treating it as foreign and rejecting it. As commonly known, bacteria do not have immune systems and are therefore highly compatible and conductible to replicate any gene. It is not by chance that media communication corporations, such as British Telecom, are also looking at bacterial recombination to smooth information traffic and connect varied information packets. In a recent report on how to solve the problem of adaptability of the Internet network and Internet traffic, BT's research centre in Suffolk has proposed a new software design.[24] Rather than having software that oversees the entire network, the junctions of a network could be designed so that each could be run by a piece of autonomous software. This software design modulates the replicating and reproductive behaviour of bacteria able to process information without the need of hierarchical structures such as those involved in eukaryotic mitosis and meiosis.[25] Without centralized knowledge and overall control of the network, and with software packages able to imitate the capacity of bacteria to process information by recombination, this report argues that information traffic would speed up.

The BT research centre already adopts programs of transmission based on genetic algorithms as an artificial model of replicating information. Genetic algorithms are modelled on the behaviour of singular strings of genes, which are treated as strings of data. These strings can be combined and mutated to produce offspring yet only the fittest ones are bred to produce more offspring and the best design. Compared to bacterial sex (trading), genetic algorithms are considered too slow for *real-time* applications, as they constantly require evaluation of the fittest pattern of information. The plasmid migrations performed by bacterial sex induce a faster reproduction-replication of genetic material spreading through bacterial colonies more rapidly as they adapt the length of information while passing it. In a network, bacterial sex will allow 'buffer' memory, discrete packets of information, to move faster without losing data. The capitalization of recombinant information on bacterial sex unites the platforms of financial investments in the virtual tendencies of transmission for both biotechnological and digital corporations. Yet this converging capitalization could not have occurred without the late 1970s' and 1980s' boom in bio-technological experiments.

In 1973, the first modulation of recombinant DNA molecules required the use of viruses as vectors or vehicles to insert a foreign DNA fragment into the genome of a host cell, a plasmid (bacteria), so as to recombine it. The American geneticists Herbert Boyer and Stanley Cohen used restriction enzymes – to cut particular sequences of DNA – and ligase enzymes – to stitch DNA molecules. In isolating a gene for antibiotic resistance, they found out that besides the cleavage, restriction enzymes synthesized the sticky ends required for the ligase procedure. After combining these fragments into the first recombinant bacteria, these bacterial cells were used to reproduce-replicate this recombinant gene. As Rabinow argues:

> The discovery of 'restriction enzymes' provided a major advance in mapping capabilities. These proteins serve to cut DNA into chunks at specific sites. The chunk of DNA can be cloned and its makeup chemically analyzed and then reconstructed in its original order in the genome. (1996: 238)

As a technique of genetic identification, genetic cloning aims to locate physical chunks of DNA on a larger chromosomal map. Not only does cloning speed up the replication and individuation of DNA strings, but also allows the emergence of a bacterial cell with new mutated genes. The new cell will express the inserted gene, which can be once again isolated and re-processed through the technique of gene splicing or recombinant DNA, patented in 1980 by Stanley-Boyer.[26] This virtualization of bacterial sex through cloning involves an intensification of genes' transmission, which smooths the space of speciation between populations (animals and humans).

In the mid-1980s, a group of researchers, based at the bio-technological company Cetus, invented a procedure able to analyse and replicate DNA sequences on a large scale. As one of the many technical hybrids contributing to the biotechnology boom of the 1980s, PCR (Polymerase Chain Reaction) accelerated the copying procedures of desired regions of DNA with a much higher precision compared to genetic recombination via enzymes. PCR enabled the time-consuming procedures such as cloning and physical maps, which used restriction enzymes, to be avoided. As a machine of cleavage and replication, PCR only requires a small piece of DNA, called primer or oligonucleotide, which can be recombined ad infinitum. As Rabinow observes:

Two primers are targeted to attach themselves to the DNA at specific sites called 'sequence-tagged-sites' (sts's). These primers then simply 'instruct' the single strand of DNA to reproduce itself without having to be inserted into another organism – this is the polymerase chain reaction (PCR). (1992: 239)

PCR and sequence-tagged-sites' techniques yield information as if directly collecting it in a database. Just by knowing which primers to construct, it is possible to replicate the required bit of DNA that can then be sequenced and entered into a database. The accelerated functions of replication and sequencing have facilitated the transnational project of mapping the human genome. The latter is an example of the bio-informatic virtualization (i.e. the acceleration of potential tendencies) of the biophysical strata involving the commercialization of information through patenting.

The Human Genome Project

From the very beginning, Vergil had known his ideas were neither far-out nor useless. His first three months at Genetron, helping establish the silicon–protein interface for the biochips, had convinced him the project designers had missed something very obvious and extremely interesting. Why limit oneself to silicon and protein and biochips a hundredth of a millimeter wide, when in almost every living cell there was already a functioning computer with a huge memory? A mammalian cell had a DNA complement of several billion base pairs, each acting as a piece of information. What was reproduction, after all, but a computerized biological process of enormous complexity and reliability?

Bear (1985: 21).

The Human Genome Project provides another example of virtual control relying on the automized technical social machine of researching, sequencing, classifying and marketing genetic material and its potential usability.[27] Multibillion state-financed projects, such as the Human Genome Project, and genetic databasing projects of corporations such as GenBank, and The Institute for Genomic Research (TIGR – a not-for-profit genetic analysis organization) are the most discussed examples in the bio-informatic field of virtual profit (Thacker 2000a; Mae-Wan Ho 2001).

It is relevant to specify that the genome includes the entire complement of genetic material in the set of chromosomes of a cellular and multicellular body. Although the genome defines four genetic pair bases of the double helix (Adenine–Thymine, Guanine–Cytosine), the human genome is composed of three billion base pairs. It has been estimated that the functions of 90 per cent of the human genome, commonly defined as junk DNA, are unknown and yet considered crucial for the study of past and future evolutionary mutations. Only the remaining 10 per cent of the genome are acknowledged genes, segments of the DNA coding for proteins, and are defined by specific compositions and functions:

> [Genes] are regions of DNA made up of spans called 'exons' interspersed by regions called 'introns'. When a gene is activated – and little is known about this process – the segment of DNA is transcribed to a type of RNA. The itrons are spliced out, and the exons are joined together to form messenger RNA. This segment is then translated to code for protein (Rabinow 1992: 237).

Of the one hundred and fifty thousand genes, most remain unidentified genetic regions on the chromosome. The Human Genome and affiliated projects of genetic research aim to individuate and order DNA fragments and genetic sequences on the chromosome. Their system of classification has relied on the development of computer software programmes (such as genetic algorithms), techniques and procedures for analysing DNA sequences (cloning, PCR, physical maps), for mapping chromosomes (Genome DataBase, The Visual Human Project), and producing protein sequences and structures (Protein Information Resources). At the core of the bio-informatic phase of capitalism, genomic mapping entails the selection of the potential tendencies of genetic regions on a body.

Rather than being specific, the search for the human genome loses all of its particular qualities in the procedures of classification where viruses and mice genomes have been utilized as genetic models for humans' pool of genes. As an example of real subsumption of molecular information under capital, the HGP processes genetic information without regard for its bifurcated substances of content and expression (unnucleated and nucleated DNA), decodifying the specificity of the human species. As Massumi points out:

> The singular-generic human genome lies at the point of capital indistinction between the biological and the chemical, where the

'human' is more closely akin to a sellable virus, neither dead nor
alive, than a reasonable animal standing at the pinnacle of earthly
life-forms, one step below the divine and on a ladder of perfection. (1998: 60).

Since 1994, the capitalization of recombinant information through
patenting has been intensively accelerated. The pharmaceutical giant
Merck & Co, in conjunction with Washington University, set up
GenBank. As an archive for ESTs ('expressed sequence tags'), GenBank
aimed to offer public access to the database and to sell clones for
commercial sources (Shostak 1999: 56). GenBank marks a new capitalization of information: from international government-supported
research (Human Genome Project and Human Genome Diversity
Project) to a commercial or corporate financed research in the gene
business. In May 2000, the Perkin-Elmer Corporation (a leading
supplier of 'life systems' technologies for pharmaceutical, biotechnological, environmental and agricultural industries) and The Institute for
Genomic Research (TIGR) announced the formation of a new company
aiming to complete the human genome map in less time and for less
money than the government-supported Human Genome Project
(Shostak 1999).

Nevertheless, the virtualization of the genome through databasing is
not exclusively animated by the business of genetic research and
patenting (led by the Human Genome Sciences), the business of
genome sequencing (led by Celera Inc.) or technology providers
(Perkin-Elmer). As Deleuze underlines (1995), if business is the soul
of control society then service providers are the linking nodes between
the modulation of information and the realization of surplus value. The
ultimate virtualization of control depends on statistical optimizations,
approximate calculations of the micro order and position of genes,
eventually providing clues for genetic deficiency, protein coding and so
on. As Shostak argues, the method of evaluation of genetic sequence
consists of 'metricizing' the genome, preserving more information
while setting up a typology based on individual positions (1999).

The geometrical figure describing this space becomes progressively
complex depending on the number of sequences compared and the
classes of monomers. Distance categories are then compared through
the methods of statistical geometry, requiring the computer to handle
all possible combinations of substitution in every position (Shostak
1999: 73–4). The use of computerized techniques to organize data
entails a virtualization of molecular structures and their relationships.

This immersion in the micro rates of genetic information, involving an approximate study of their frequencies, determines the organization of genomic sequences represented in the Visible Human Project (Waldby 2000, Thacker 2000b). In a similar way, small bio-informatic companies, such as Double Twist, an 'applications service provider' (ASP), use existing genetic information in order to develop statistical models to make potential tendencies as profitable as possible. Through the use of software, Double Twist has produced the first overall analysis of the human genome months before the Human Genome Project and Celera Inc. In partnership with Sun Microsystems, Double Twist has estimated potential gene targets in new and previously characterized genes, identified splice variants, exons, introns, promoter regions, and developed predictable models of protein structures. Bio-informatic companies such as Double Twist modulate the virtual-actual circuit of genetic differentiation by selecting information divergence at the moment of its emergence and providing a statistical estimation of genomic functions. Whereas this phase of evaluation usually constitutes a final step in the process of genomic mapping, the service provided by Double Twist starts with the potential estimation of genetic information, sequencing, classification and so on, deploying the present-futurity of virtual control.

The HGP and Celera Inc. mainly aim to sequence genetic letters, according to which the order of nucleotides – base sequences – in a DNA or RNA molecule or the order of amino acids in a protein come to be determined. Double Twist, instead, has concentrated on modulating variations by optimizing the function and application of genetic information already mapped in cyberspace. In other words, Double Twist virtualizes – immanently selects the potential application of – genetic maps that identify genetic polymorphisms and order the sequences of a genetic assembly. Relying upon the ability of computers to reproduce information or data from scratch while diminishing information redundancies, Double Twist aims to forecast potential alignments of pair sequences by modulating the variables of genetic transmissions. This modulating evaluation allows Double Twist to channel the tendencies of genetic information within the fields of pharmaconogenomics, gene therapy, proteomics (the study of proteins).

This virtual control involves an immanent modulation of the molecular rates of variation between genetic sequences by using software that selects the micro-variations of genetic transmission and translation. Nevertheless, to some extent, the information that comprises

154

genetic sequences is still considered to be linear, moving from the DNA to RNA to protein. Genes, and especially those constituting nucleic DNA, are the main sources of reference to map the molecular variations of a body. The analysis of genomic sequences is processed by software database management, gene assembly algorithms, protein prediction software, molecular modelling, genetic screening software that mainly modulate the central structure of nucleic or chromosomal DNA. These cybernetic genes are grouped in gene families and classes that trace new arborescences by re-striating the smooth space of the biodigital decodification of the genome.

This complex agglomeration of genes does not consist of mere nucleic or chromosomal parts. It cannot be isolated from RNA and protein retroviruses, mitochondrial and cytoplasmic DNA, intra and extra-cellular elements, environmental pressures and biochemical reactions. As DeLanda underlines, 'The more self-organizing processes scientists discover, the smaller the domain of DNA's control appears to be' (1992: 148). The virtualization of the genome (i.e. the acceleration of its tendencies of variation) through service providers mainly operates on the differential rates of nucleic genes that only partially explain the new dynamics of desire–power in the biodigital phase of capitalization. The modulation of the virtual tendencies of molecular reproduction also operates on the relation between biophysical and biodigital machines deployed by the new centrality of the egg cell in genetic engineering. From the standpoint of this cell, nucleic DNA appears relatively inert, archival (it constitutes a kind of structural reference point for molecular processes), and partial (it is not an autonomous agent but is interwoven with the molecular makeup of the organism). In particular, the egg cell unfolds the feedback relations between nucleic and cytoplasmic genes, where mitochondrial recombination precedes and exceeds the chromosomal hierarchies of genetic filiation.

THE SCHIZOPHRENIC EGG

We're not hierarchical, you see. We never were. But we are powerfully acquisitive. We acquire life – seek it, manipulate it, sort it, use it. We carry the drive to do this in a miniscule cell within a cell – a tiny organelle within every cell of our bodies. Do you understand me?

Butler (1987: 39)

'We are witnessing a different kind of pregnancy. It isn't new – it's happened many times before. It's evolution, but it's directed, short term, immediate, not gradual, and I have no idea what kind of children will be produced,' she went on. 'but they will not be monsters.'

Bear (1999: 230)

Another example of immanent capitalization of biophysical sex will be drawn from technologies of reproduction. Biomedical practices such as IVF, sperm and egg retrieval, embryo transfer and hibernation,[28] are part of the bio-technological apparatus of decodification of cellular and molecular potentials. Although bio-technologies already suggest the process of disentanglement of reproduction from mating and sex from pleasure, mammal cloning more clearly indicates the transformation of the meiotic machine of sex on the biodigital stratum.

Mammal cloning suggests that the molecular variations of the egg cell are only secondarily captured by the functions of sexed chromosomes (haploids X and Y). The meiotic programme of reproduction and heredity is not isolated from a parthenogenic reprogramming – double repetition – of the molecular variables of transmission in the egg cell. Instead of providing an embryological model of evolution determined by genetic structures (nucleic DNA), the molecular dynamics of the egg cell unfold the schizophrenic coexistence of singular orders of transmission – nucleic and cytoplasmic – where turbulence (the cytoplasmic swerve) declines from laminar flows (layers of nucleic segments). Mammal cloning does not exclusively constitute another example of virtual control involving the patenting and monopoly of information potentials. It also lays out the intensive conjunction of biophysical and biodigital molecular sexes: the bio-informatic reversibility of capitalization. The recombination of cytoplasmic material maps a mutation of sex and reproduction, the proliferation of micro-feminine particles as inheritable yet autonomous from the nucleic order of filiation (chromosomal exchange).

Mammal cloning is a technique of genetic and cellular reproduction requiring various levels of extraction and fusion of genetic particles and cellular bodies. In 1997, the first successful report on mammal cloning announced the birth of the first female clone, Dolly the sheep. This technique involves the re-programming of an adult diploid cell inserted in the cytoplasmic body of an a-nucleated egg cell. For example, Dolly was cloned by re-programming the diploid nucleus of her udder cell in an egg cell. In order to be cloned, Dolly's udder cell was brought back to a virtual stage of growth also defined as zero degree of development. As some scientists argued, this cellular *regression* demonstrates that the biological development of cells is neither irreversible nor highly specific. Rather, the ageing time of adult cells can be reversed and reprogrammed for new functions.[29]

This molecular time is not chronological. It is not defined by regressive and progressive linearity where a return to zero is a return to the inorganic, to a ground zero out of which life grows. On the contrary, the reversibility of cellular time marks the non-linear relationship between causes and effects: a positive feedback where effects act back on their causes – the future on the present, the present on the past, unfolding a declination from the trajectory of time. This is turbulence, the virtual-actual vortex of time. For this reason, for example, stem or totipotent cells can be re-programmed as heart cells, blood cells or islets used for transplant therapies.[30] Yet this re-programming is not to be confused with the realization of an already defined potential that determines the possibility of stem cells to grow as blood cells. The virtual-actual circuit of differentiation does not cease to happen without unleashing unprecedented mutations. The reversible time of cells indicates the proliferation of unpredictable differentiation, the actual becoming of cells whose implications are yet to be realized. Hence, the cloning of the diploid udder cell triggers an unexpected cellular becoming rather than engendering a mere copy of an original Dolly as wished by the tradition of representation, analogy and resemblance.

While turning back the clock of growth of Dolly's udder cell, from another female 'sheep X' the egg cell was retrieved, and its haploid nucleus – containing XX chromosomes – extracted (only the body of the egg is used to accomplish the cloning). Finally, Dolly's diploid cell and the egg cell without nucleus were fused through an electric current.[31] After fusion, the egg cell showed a full complement of new DNA (Dolly's DNA), which at some 'non-defined point' started to divide and grow into an embryo. This parthenogenic procedure is still quite obscure for scientists. They do not yet know how nucleated DNA is activated and reprogrammed by the egg cell. This activation has also been called 'reprogramming magic'.[32]

This reprogramming magic indicates a double folding of the molecular time of reproduction exposing parallel relations between nucleic and cytoplasmic rates of variations. On the one hand, by reversing the time of the diploid cell to be cloned, bio-technological machines modulate the virtual potential (i.e. capture the interval between states) of actual cellular differentiations through molecular clonings. On the other, the electric symbiosis between the mitochondrial genetic material from the udder's cell and the egg cell deploys a machinic acceleration of molecular variables leading to an unprecedented mutation of the biophysical machines of sex. No longer entangled with chromosomal transmission and sexual reproduction, mammal cloning exposes the proliferation of somatic symbiosis (the fusion between the udder cell and the egg cell) and mitochondrial recombination (the genetic recombination between cytoplasmic material from the udder and egg cells).

As some scientists observe, although the nucleus of a human cell contains about 100,000 genes, while each mitochondrion has only 37, mitochondria define many of the crucial dimensions of cellular bodies. For example, they act as probe heads selecting which of a mother's germ cells can mature into the egg (from which an embryo will grow) and deciding the living duration of a body (Cohen 2000: 30–1). Mitochondrial DNA supplies energy to the cell and performs the core reactions of aerobic respiration, burning nutrients and realizing energy that is then stored in molecules called ATP (adeninetriphosphate). For this special function, mitochondrial DNA is considered to mutate 10 times as fast as nuclear DNA and is proved responsible for age-related diseases such as Alzheimer's and Parkinson's (Cohen 2000: 32–5). The recombination of cytoplasmic genes coming from the donor and the recipient's cells (the udder cell and the egg cell) introduces a double merger of a-segmented genetic material (mitochondrial DNA), which does not characterize sexual reproduction or biotechnological reproduction such as IVF. Mammal cloning involves a highly turbulent process of mitochondrial and cellular symbiosis irreducible to the scissiparity of the Identical. It taps into the virtual-actual circuit of genetic differentiation catalysing the emergence of molecular variations between nucleic and somatic information patterns in embryological development.

Although traditional embryology attributes to nucleic DNA a central role for the development of the embryo, recent research on mitochondrial genes confirms their crucial relevance for embryogenesis. Mammal cloning echoes the debates on the emergence of multicellular life deployed between epigenesis and ontogenesis, as well as Aristotle's belief that 'man is the source of life' and the Preformationist theory (the animalcule inhabiting the human spermatozoon and the ovist preformationism).[33] These theories exclude from the process of development the asymmetric relations between pre-individual energy-forces of difference and individuating differentiation. They ascribe novelties and transformations to the genealogy of forms and functions and the teleology of origin.

Instead of nucleic structures, the egg cell is composed of molecular agents, base pairs, chromosomes and cytoplasm, which are 'governed by attractors and bifurcations, thus constrained but not created by genetic information' (DeLanda 1992: 145). As already explained, the egg cell is constituted by nucleic DNA and cytoplasmic material, which consists of mitochondrial DNA transmitted by/through the egg – by the mother – which, unlike nucleic DNA, recombine like bacteria. Not only is mitochondrial DNA inheritable, but this genetic material has also been 'found to constitute a fundamental source of asymmetry guiding the development of the first few stages in embryo-genesis' (DeLanda 1992: 146). The egg cell displays an intensive *spatium* of relational forces, where the nucleic DNA of a sperm instead of being the 'organizer' of the egg cell, reveals itself to be a 'mere inductor'.[34] As a Mobius strip of variations, cytoplasmic and nucleic membranes mark an immanent relation among independent yet coexistent orders of reproduction and communication of information, forms and substances of expression (germline or genotype) and content (phenotype or somaline). These coexistent orders define the autonomy of potential recombination from linear reproduction.

As a diagram of bio-informatic capitalization, mammal cloning maps the immanent conjunction between the biophysical and bio-technological molecular rates of variation. Bio-technologies double fold the molecular differences of biophysical machines of sex stretching their unpredictable potential to differentiate beyond expectation. In particular, mammal cloning exposes the emergence of a new kind of sex and reproduction defined by the intensification of mitochondrial recombination. In this sense, the new level of bio-informatic capitalization introduces a new mitochondrial symbiosis on the stratification of sex. This new parasiting assemblage defines a reversible relation between absolute control or virtual subsumption (the capture of the interval between states) and absolute deterritorialization or molecular recombination of all machines of sex and reproduction (biophysical, biocultural and bio-technical machines).

Digital cloning

The philosophy of representation – of the original, the first time, resemblance, imitation, faithfulness – is dissolving; and the arrow of the simulacrum released by the Epicurean is headed in our direction. It gives birth—rebirth – to a 'phantasmaphysics'.

Foucault (1977: 309)

Bio-technological machines double fold the molecular time of reproduction and recombination by stretching the potential of non-linear mutations. Digital machines also double fold the molecular flow of energy-forces captured in the ceaseless replication of images: the replication/recombination of information processed through computer imaging, rendering and animating, CD-ROMs, CT scannings. Yet debates about the proliferation of digital images—information attribute digital cloning or image replications to sterile repetition, copies or simulacra, mimicry of eternal forms, reality, being.

For example, in his cultural history of simulation, Jean Baudrillard associates cloning to the fourth order of simulacra that defines the age of 'soft technologies, of genetic and mental software'. The triumph of replication, mimesis and copies ruling the economic, socio-cultural and popular scenes produces an anaesthetized space denuded of conflicts with the other. 'This is our clone-ideal today: a subject purged of the other, deprived of its divided character and doomed to self-metastasis, to pure repetition. No longer the hell of other people, but the hell of the same' (1993: 122). Cloning negates both the subject and the object, leaving us suspended in an ocean of data, surfing digital waves in a deserted matrix of the real. For Baudrillard, cloning bypasses 'the sexual function of the father and the mother, through an operational mode from which all chance sexual elements have been expunged [. . .] as well as the otherness of the twin in the reiteration of the same' (1993: 115). As a mere repetition of codes, a cancerous metastasis, cloning implies the realization of the death drive, unbinding sex from reproduction, inducing regression towards inorganic replication.

What, if not death drive, would push sexed beings to regress to a form of reproduction prior to sexuation, [. . .] and that, at the same time, would push them metaphysically to deny all alterity, all alternation of the Same in order to aim solely for the perpetuation of an identity, a transparency of the genetic inscription no longer even subject to the vicissitudes of procreation?

(1994b: 96).

By identifying sexual reproduction with the realm of exchange and variation, Baudrillard argues that biodigital sex marks a regressive divergence from life instincts, diversity and procreation. Cloning inherits the burden of the metaphysics of representation, ante-posing the ideal to the material, the real to the copy, the organic to the inorganic. Here, biodigital capitalism has absorbed all forces and particles, engulfed all varieties and diversifications under its logic of replicating commodification. This Baudrillardian scenario re-affirms the negative relativism of the fallacious model of the principle of reality (pleasure) and signification outside which nothing is believed to happen.

Following this tradition, the digitalization of the body in virtual reality, computer imaging, rendering and animating, CD-ROMs, photography and video has been mainly considered as a process of disembodiment that dismisses the physical reality of the body-identity (the bio-categories of sex, gender, race, ethnicity, class and so on). As previously argued, these insights share a common conception of matter-materiality that reiterates the schism in Western culture between the line of incorporeal materialism versus the metaphysics of representation.[35]

This metaphysics imparts a split between essence—appearance, model—copy, defining images as mere imitations, mimicry of the real or model. In *Philebus*, Plato points to the autonomy of simulacra – huge dimensions, depths and distances out of sight from the observer – only to repress them, to accuse them of sterile effects compared to the reality of the cause defined by sight, the noblest of the senses. Sight is conceived as the inner eye of the mind able to select reality through eternal given ideas. In reversing Platonism, Luce Irigaray unravels the conjectures of the 'myth of the cave' through which the world of pure representations – eternal ideas – speculates on the material—maternal shadows of the cave (1985a). Far from being reducible to eternal lights, the shadows of the cave are real and not mere projections of the gaze, proliferating through a perpetual matter-mater-matrix metamorphosis. The wet tunnels of the cave mirror the uterine environment where the philosopher is imprisoned and from where he has to depart, reaching the reality enlightened by the sun outside the cave. This uterine space has recently been reconstructed in the 1999 blockbuster *The Matrix* (the Latin for womb and the Greek for hysteria) as a network of simulations echoing the Baudrillardian 'desert of the real': the world where images have taken over reality. This cave of parthenogenic simulations imprisons humans in a matrix of copies, image replications or clonings that are metamorphic shadows, projections of the real. The liberation from the world of replications involves the liberation from the seduction of copies, hiding the real behind superficial disguise. This illusion is at the core of all economies of representation detaching sight from the senses, mind from the body, the real from simulacrum, the ideal from the material. The illusion of reaching the real behind simulations is only attainable through the (illusion) of organic unity-origin dismissing the fact that 'behind each cave another opens still more deeply, and beyond each surface a subterranean world yet more vast, more strange. Richer still ... and under all foundations, under every ground, a subsoil still more profound' (Deleuze 1991: 263). Simulacra are not copies of ideas and forms but are bodies flying from objects and impacting on our sensory organs. As Lucretius explains: 'the existence of what we call images of things [is] a sort of outer skin perpetually peeled off the surface of objects and flying about this way and that through the air' (Book IV, 24). Atoms leave the surface of objects as complete coherent images or films, which preserve both the shape and the appearance of the object. When a film of something enters our eyes, it touches our organs of sight, stimulating perception and making us see the object. Objects emit particles that strike the eyes and provoke sight. Touch and sight are brought forth by the same stimulus as the stream of matter spreads out in all directions and without intermission. The simulacrum is an image without resemblance, an incorporeal image composed of particles moving through air, rather than an image engendered by ideas.

In the tradition of representation, the Platonic and Cartesian distrust of images and bodily senses are adopted as dominant models in the analysis of the impact of technologies of vision on the strategies of mastering, surveillance and subjection (Martin Jay 1993). The anti-ocular tradition in Western culture and critical thought relies on this very specific understanding of vision rooted in the representational schism between the world of the material and ideal separating the visual from the audible and tangible, and the mind from the kinetics of particle-forces. Such a schism perpetuates a representational understanding of perception based on the central perspective of the subject.

The matter-image-body assemblage

Seeing is never separate from other sense modalities. It is by nature synaesthetic, and synaesthesia is by nature kinaesthetic. Every look reactivates a many-dimensioned, shifting surface of experience from which cognitive functions habitually emerge but which is not reducible to them. It is on that abstract surface of movement that we 'live' and locate.

Massumi (2001: 1076)

Overturning the Platonic tradition of representation where matter and images are always depositories of something else – the self, the real, the ideal – the bio-informatic proliferation of simulacra exposes a virtualization (an intensified differentiation) of a matter-image-body continuum crystallized and diffused through digital technologies of replication. In order to map the traits of this process, it is necessary to give some clues about matter-image-body assemblage first as conceived by Henri Bergson.

> Matter, in our view, is an aggregate of 'images'. And by 'image' we mean a certain existence which is more than that which the idealist calls a representation, but less that that which the realist calls a thing – an existence placed half-way between the 'thing' and 'the representation' [. . .] the object exists in itself, and, on the other hand, the object is, in itself, pictorial, as we perceive it: the image it is, but a self-existing image. (1991: 9–10)

Arguing against the phenomenological tradition based on a centralized, subjective and organic vision, Bergson moves away from natural perception. All consciousness is always consciousness of something else that comes before and after our awareness of things. Before consciousness, there is movement of light and energy that exposes the incessant flow of matter stripped of stable form and purposeful function. As composed of light-energy flows, matter is an agglomeration of images whereas perception and memory, as attributes of the mind, are modes of accessing to the present and the past movement of flows. Rather than the hidden force lying behind the body and the image, according to Bergson, matter is composed of moving particle-lights acting as forces of contraction and extension, where my body, my eyes, my brain are images; they do not represent or contain anything. By defining the independence of matter from subjective perception, Bergson's materialism also defies metaphysical idealism.

The perception of moving images involves neither contemplation nor observation of objects. In the aggregate of images, there are indeterminate centres of action, such as the body. The body is, in the composition of the material world, an image, which acts like other images, receiving and giving back movements. As a compound of light-energy, a body exists in the middle of universal moving images, where the brain, as a zone of indetermination, neither reflects nor produces images. Rather, the function of a brain is 'to put images directed from elsewhere into the context of action' governed by a gap between stimulus and response that marks the indeterminable relations between what a body receives (in terms of perception or affection) and how it acts. '[T]he brain is no more than a kind of central telephone exchange: its office is to allow communication or to delay it. It adds nothing to what it receives' (1991: 30).

Perception, according to Bergson, is not a representation of something, but conveys action through the zones of indetermination of a body. Perception measures the action of the body upon things and the action of things on the body. This action is a virtual, hence real action as it exposes the capacity of objects to impinge upon the body 'abandon[ing] something of their real action in order to manifest their virtual influence of the living being upon them' (37). The movement of light-energy-matter renders the border between body and objects an elastic membrane of transmission, the reversible transfer of a virtual potential in an actual process of action. The body, constituted by receiving and active zones of indetermination, *transduces* the impact of images crowding the universe through a virtual action. Transduction involves the transfer of particle-forces from one region of intensity to another, the expansion of information through internal resonances between and across zones of perception unleashing a virtual action that remains on the body. These zones 'play in some sort the part of the screen [. . .] add[ing] nothing to what is there. They effect merely this: that the real action passes through, the virtual remains' (39).

Being different from memory – the past as duration and virtual time – perception cannot be reduced to the phenomenology of the lived experience, only dependent on actualized realities observed, represented and then stored in the distant past. Perception is always an action that links the action in the past to action in the future. Hence, an image is not mainly there to be seen, its duration can be heard, felt, touched. For example, an image is produced each time we listen or feel something not simply because it reminds us of something that we have seen. Matter as an agglomeration of images-bodies defines a continuum between perception and memory that mixes what we have seen with what we are about to see. The movement from matter (repetition of images) to memory (individuating zone of perception) displays the activities of perception: arresting the real actions of external things on the body in order to retain that which is virtual.

'[T]his virtual action of things upon our body and of our own body upon things is our perception itself' (232). Perception does not serve to shed more light on things but to arrest the incessant flows of images-things impacting on the body.

Rather than defining the disappearance of material variations, the digital replication of images crystallizes the kinetic movements of particle-lights, the virtual action of images-bodies. The impact of digital simulacra on the body's zones of perception enlarges the leap – the interval – between stimuli and response by intensifying the delay between affect and action, the virtual action of things upon the body and the body upon things to an unprecedented extent. Digital cloning is linked to the proliferation not of copies of the original but of virtual actions of images-things increasing and decreasing the capacities of a body to be affected and to act.[36] Here perception is neither subjective nor objective, but maps portals of immersion in the swerving flows of matter (pure duration). Digital perception blends in the tendencies of recombinant information. It entails a virtual action on the body's capacities of reception and action, unleashing the emergence of unpredictable sensory mutations.

The smooth storm of molecular information

The metaphysical assertion that our body and matter itself is constituted by light interacting infinitely with itself as its own hyperabstract surface, feeling absolutely its own variations, has little or no importance in itself. It can however act as a reminder: to bring it all back to perception. To perception, understood positively, as actually productive of existence, or as virtually preceding existing separations of form. To perception, in continuity with the world (unform).

Massumi (2001: 1084)

Electrochemical stimulation of certain nerves, certain parts of your brain ... What happened was real. Your body knows how real it was. Your interpretations were illusion. The sensations were entirely real. You can have them again or you can have others.

Butler (1987: 189)

The virtualization (i.e. acceleration of potential tendencies) of the biophysical, biocultural and biodigital modes of communication and reproduction blends perception in a smooth space (uninterrupted matrix) of recombinant variations. The smooth space of digital cloning

165

shrinks optical distances through a close vision, an intensified loop between reception and action amplifying the virtual impact of things upon the body and the body upon things. This smooth space deterritorializes the disciplinary glance into a matrix of digital mapping. The Panoptical glance and industrial machines of reproduction already exposed an intensification of tactile perception compared to distant vision. Electronic and digital machines become portals towards a matrix of particle-lights.

As Deleuze and Guattari argue, smooth space 'is both object of close vision and the element of a haptic space (which may be as much visual or auditory space)' (1987: 493). For example, time coding permits the synchronization of images with sounds, and the replication or editing of images without the linear time-consuming editing practices of backwarding and forwarding. As Peter Weibel points out, the ability to store and manipulate time has transformed the cinematic or photographic images into abstract mathematics. In operating with codes units, computer editing has become analogous to working with musical scores (1999: 46). When translating the continuous phenomena of the analogue world into discrete digital units, digital video as compared, for example, to the photographic image, displays not only the frame but each of the 1000 scanlines, and each of the 1000 pixels that will comprise each line (45). The grid has become transparently crowded with algorithmic patterns mapping the analogue sound-image through digit pairs or series of digits. This digital sound-image undergoes micro spatial and temporal transformations that increase the pace of the virtual impact (i.e. the present-futurity) of energy-particles on the body.

As an element of a haptic space, digital mapping defines new modes of orientation, the linkages and landmarks conveying a sense of immersive vision. This is an audible and touchable space immersing the body in a grid of recombined information where the eye itself acquires haptic or nonoptical functions. The eye no longer separates objects, but becomes rather part of a fractional, flat heterogeneity participating in the same substance or matrix of information (virtual matter). In this space points of reference are interchangeable and recombinant, they are "monadological" points of view [that] can be interlinked only on a nomad space' (Deleuze and Guattari 1987: 494). This is the ultra and multi sensuous space of electronic and digitized time-based media defining the immersion of the body in the virtual flows of matter-images (i.e. the participation in the present-future loop of mutant perception).

Far from defining the end of the body–sex and reality, digital cloning marks the emergence of a hypersensorial perception unleashing new capacities of a body to be affected and to act. Digital cloning double folds the incessant flow of light-energy-matter increasing some channels of affection-action rather than others, selecting the potential of some stimuli-receptions rather than others. This liquid perception indicates the mutations of the capacities of transmission of a body–sex in bio-informatic capitalism impacting on the biophysical and biocultural modes of communication and reproduction.

INCORPOREAL TRANSFORMATIONS

> [. . .] we add that incorporeal transformations, incorporeal attri-butes, apply to bodies and only to bodies.
>
> Deleuze and Guattari (1987: 86)

Biodigital machines introduce a new level of order in the process of stratification of sex: a turbulent recombination of all machines of reproduction unleashing unprecendented mutations of the body. Genetic engineering intensifies the decodification of the organic entan-glement between sex, reproduction and death by double folding the molecular variables of content and expression (mitochondrial splitting, bacterial replications and retroviruses). It exposes the immanent capi-talization (i.e. the capture of the interval between states) of the rela-tionship between cytoplasmic and nucleic reproduction by accelerating their potential to recombine and mutate.

Digital cloning marks a molecular deterritorialization of the field of perception submerging the body in the flows of energy-light, capturing virtual matter through the emergence of hypersensorial perception. By increasing the virtual action of the body on things-images and vice versa, digital cloning accelerates the potential of a body to be affected and to act. It exposes the body to the virtual matrix of molecular mutations unfolding its differential capacities of reception and action. The biodigital process of subsumption does not absorb all forces of reproduction. Rather, it captures the new interval between states of reproduction and communication by recombining the virtual tenden-cies of all machines of sex (from bacteria to cybersex).

Biodigital sex deprives pleasure from its immediate release, demanding that flows never reach a climax by prolonging virtual action as long and as much as possible. Biodigital cloning intensifies the recom-binant desire of continual transmission: the reversibility of potentials.

Biodigital cloning points to the virtual tendencies of sex that feed neither back nor forward in time. Rather they are indexes of a transition – an intensive variation between phases, such as the biophysical and the biodigital levels of symbiotic matter. This transition defines transductive time: a present or current futurity (i.e. the action of the present on the future – the immanence between the past and the future in virtual time). In this sense, the emergent properties of bio-digital cloning act as catalysers of the virtual tendencies of this unprecedented variation of sex.

The immanent conjunction of all variables of communication and reproduction fuels the turbulent relationship between minimal causes and unpredictable effects, tiny changes in transmission and massive effects in modes of communication. In this sense, biodigital recombination precedes and exceeds the model of evolution based on binary sexes, heredity and filiation, death and life drives, pleasure and discharge that reduces the body–sex to a given essence, a biological, socio-cultural and bio-technological identity. The emergence of these machines of recombination involves another kind of sex and reproduction that goes beyond human and posthuman sex (organic sex and technological pleasure). In this sense, biodigital machines unfold the incorporeal mutations of molecular bodies–sexes irreducible to the law of sexual reproduction and sexual identification. These mutations expose the symbiotic assemblage of biophysical, biocultural and biotechnical bodies of particle-forces, microbes, multicells, signs and techniques. Biodigital cloning impacts on all levels of stratification generating a new assemblage of desire.

This recombinant assemblage marks the expansion of a bio-informatic warfare: the immanent collision between the strata of sex unleashing aimless modifications. The collision defines a reversible parasitism (i.e. present-futurity) between biodigital machines of absolute control and absolute destratification (intensive mutation) of matter. The reversible line between hosts and guests discloses the symbiotic coexistence of nucleic and bacterial organizations. This immanent relation implies a continual modification of transmission: bacterial sex anticipates, speeds up and slows down nucleic reproduction. Bio-informatic warfare displays the virtual mutations of a body–sex. As discussed in the following chapter, these mutations lay out a hypernature of bodies–sexes cutting across all layers of stratification of matter.

Notes

1 On the concept of the posthuman in postmodernity see K. N. Hayles 1999: 283–92.
2 On the coalescence of the past and the present, see G. Deleuze 1989b: 78–83.
3 See I. Prigogine and I. Stengers 1984; I. Prigogine 1997.
4 On the clinamen, see G. Deleuze and F. Guattari 1987: 489. See also M. Serres 1982: 98–124; 2000: 27–66; Lucretius 1994, Book 2.
5 On the transformation of the disciplinary formation, see B. Massumi 1988: 23–76.
6 On cybernetics, see C. Wiener 1961, 1989. See also K. N. Hayles 1999.
7 See E. Thacker 2000a, 2000b.
8 On the story of Rosalind Franklin, see E. F. Keller 1992; B. Maddox 2002.
9 Monod's famous affirmation that there is no genetic distinction between the elephant and the bacteria *Escherichia Coli* is based on the unidimensional genetic line of transmission and expression: DNA>RNA>protein. Monod also defined DNA as a self-regulating cybernetic machine. See J. Monod 1972.
10 See E. Shröndinger 1944: 60–1.
11 On a historical explanation of the three waves of cybernetics, see K. N. Hayles, 1999: 50–83, 131–59.
12 See L. Parisi and T. Terranova 2000.
13 For a recent account of market dynamics linked to the neo-Darwinian model, see K. Kelly 1994.
14 On this conception of evolution, see R. Dawkins 1989, 1991.
15 See F. Braudel 1973.
16 For example, as DeLanda points out, despite its origins in the hands of military planners, the Internet itself is an entity emerging from the assemblage of synergistic agents, whose interaction has acted as a motor of complexification, as the example of computer service providers and clients demonstrates. See DeLanda 1997: 71–99.
17 On the abstract machine, see Deleuze and Guattari 1987: 63; 69–74.
18 The vitalist conception of capitalism presupposes economic (cultural and sociopolitical) transformations for capital's sake, a self-sufficient organism. The mechanical conception rather defines capital as a system subjected to technological developments and therefore constructed by an external power of selection.
19 In particular, see H. R. Maturana and F. J. Varela 1980. See also DeLanda 1997.
20 On the concept of immaterial labour, see M. Lazzarato 1996. See also T. Terranova 2000: 33–58.
21 For the definition of the plane of nature, see Deleuze 1988c; Spinoza 1992, Books I and V.
22 See L. Margulis, 1981: 1–14. On the history of endosymbiosis, see J. Sapp 1994.
23 On the 'Mitochondrial Eve', see R. Dawkins 1995. See also D. C. Dennett 1995.
24 On the use of bacterial sex to accelerate information transmission, see D. Graham-Rowe 2000.

25 In molecular biology, replication corresponds to strings of DNA able to replicate exponentially by mutations. For example, viruses replicate exponentially in a host body and are able to mutate the genetic code. Reproduction involves an exchange of information between cells. This exchange occurs in different ways. It may involve the chromosomal fusion and reduction of genetic information involving two eukaryotic cells but also the splitting of bacterial cells in more cells. In the case of bacteria, replication and reproduction operate simultaneously.

26 For a historical account of genetic engineering, see S. Aldridge 1996.

27 On the Human Genome Project, see K. J. Daniel and L. Hood 1992. See also R. C. Lewontin 2000.

28 For a historical insight on IVF and reproductive technologies, see G. Corea 1985; L. Birke *et al.* 1990; D. Farquhar 1997.

29 For a more detailed explanation of this process, see A. Coghlan 1997: 4; P. Cohen 1998, 26–37.

30 Human embryonic stem cells, and other cells derived from the inner cell mass of the pre-implantation embryo, are totipotent: they are capable of forming any cell or tissue in the human body.

31 The reduction of the DNA of the donor cell occurs by starving the cell into a dormant (G0 or G1) stage of the cell cycle. See E. Pennisi and N. Williams 1997: 1415–16; A. Kahn 1997: 119; R. C. Lewontin 1997.

32 On this particular point, see E. Pennisi and N. Williams 1997: 1415–16.

33 On epigenesis and ontogenesis, see S. J. Gould 1977. On ovist preformationism, see N. Tuana 1989: 35–59.

34 On the schizophrenic egg, see Deleuze and Guattari 1983: 91.

35 On the thought of the incorporeal, see M. Foucault 1977: 165–96.

36 On the impact of digital images on perception, see Parisi and Terranova 2001: 121–8.

CHAPTER 5

Hypernature: A Diagram of Molecular Modifications

Physics and biology present us with reverse causalities that are *without finality* but testify nonetheless to an action of the future on the present, or of the present on the past, for example, the convergent wave and the anticipated potential, which imply an inversion of time. More than breaks or zigzags, it is these reverse causalities that shatter evolution.

Deleuze and Guattari (1987: 431)

INTRODUCTION

This chapter argues that machines of stratification of sex (meiotic sex, disciplinary sex, modulating sex) are immanent to a plane of consistency that is prior yet adjacent to the strata (biophysical, biocultural, biodigital). This plane defines the symbiotic modifications of sex and reproduction that unfold the potential tendencies of hypernature.

As Deleuze suggests, a plane in itself indicates neither a project nor a programme to install. A plane delineates a 'geometric section, an intersection, a diagram' moving in the *middle* of a modal plane (1988c: 199). Deleuze distinguishes two senses of the word 'plan' in relation to the double distinct composition and expression of the abstract machine (endosymbiosis). The plan of organization implies a transcendence, 'a theological plan: a design in the mind of god, but also an evolution in the supposed depths of nature, or a society's organization of power' (128). This is a structured and genetic plane including forms and their developments, the formation of subjects. This is a hidden plane that 'can only be divined, induced, inferred, from what it gives' (128). Conversely, on the plane of consistency the process of molecular composition is directly unfolded 'through that which it gives, in that which it gives'. Here, there are no forms, but only relations of speed and slowness among molecular flows and infinitesimal particles that connect bodies.

The plane of consistency is crowded with Spinozist memories of an immanent God (Substance or the Thing) engineering nature through kinetic combinations and dynamic affections among bodies.[1] This God consists of one substance per an infinity of attributes. But this God is not numbered One.[2] Challenging Cartesian metaphysics that separates minds from bodies, eternal forms from mutable nature, this Spinozist substance exposes a machinic unity of all bodies (a bacterium, an animal, a human being, a microchip): intensive mutant matter. For Spinoza, substance cannot be defined by an external cause (*Ethics* I, D. 3). All that exists in nature exists in God as an intensive network of bodies generating hypernature (plane of consistency) as 'peopled by anonymous matter, by infinite bits of impalpable matter entering into varying connections' (Deleuze and Guattari 1987: 255).

This Spinozist hypernature defines the abstract machine of destratification or immanent symbiosis of all modes of sex and reproduction cutting across all strata. It is only from this plane of consistency, prior to and coexistent with different organizations of sex (meiotic sex, sexual reproduction and genetic control), that processes of stratification can be mapped out. On this plane, organizations correspond to steady states (approximate aggregations of bodies around a point of equilibrium), which are always related to wider dynamics of motion in an ecosystem of bodies. As Deleuze and Guattari argue, the abstract machine of consistency is always immanent to the strata. They 'always coexist as two different states of intensities' (1987: 57).

The abstract machine of stratification (endosymbiosis) delineates the turbulent (far-from-equilibrium) organization of sex marked by bifurcation points between actualizations on a singular stratum (bacterial sex and meiotic sex) and between strata, a leap (intensive connection) from one level of organization (biophysical sex) to another (biocultural sex). This metastable auto-organization also involves a 'reverse causality or advanced determinism' between machines of sex. Deleuze and Guattari use this notion to define non-linear causality between different strata. Non-linear causality entails feedback loops, which are defined by mutually stabilizing causes or negative feedback (the negative balance of meiotic sex) or by mutually intensifying causes or positive feedback loops (the positive mutations of retroviruses). This is a circular causality where effects react back on their causes producing new levels of organization. Reverse causality eliminates linear (and universal) causes.[3] It explains the capacity of one level (bacterial sex) to affect and be affected by another level (biodigital sex) through feedback loops able to stabilize or intensify causalities (the disentanglement of sex or desire from sexual reproduction).

This quasi-deterministic process of organization does not constitute all dynamics of matter. As Deleuze and Guattari argue, there is another, non-deterministic, process that deploys a machinic continuum of bodies–sexes designating the auto-consistency of mutating matter. This machinic phylum is composed of abstract machines of consistency (a pack of symbiotic mixtures) that are not assimilated to the strata. These machines mark the strata's singular lines of inflection, 'bottle-necks, knots, foyers [. . .]; points of fusion, condensation, and boiling, points of tears and joy, sickness and health, hope and anxiety, "sensi-tive points" ' (Deleuze 1990a: 52).

Machines of consistency delineate a destratification (continual decli-nation) of bodies–sexes from stable forms. They compose a hyperna-ture of potential mutations (pure 'matter-function') independent of the contents and expressions that it will eventuate. These diagrammatic or abstract machines do not operate to represent a reality that is already there but to construct a real that is yet to come, a new type of reality (Deleuze and Guattari 1987: 142).

Abstract machines convene not persons or subjects but events with names and dates. This final chapter draws on *nomad or minor* sciences[4] to designate these events of destratification of sex and reproduction on hypernature. The first section expands on the theory of endosymbiosis to unfold the destratification of meiotic sex (which emerged 1500 millions of years ago, in the Proterozoic Aeon) through microbial machines of sex (bacterial sex, which emerged 3900 millions of years ago, in the Archean Aeon; mitochondrial sex, which emerged 2000 millions of years ago, in the Proterozoic Aeon). The second section draws on the theory of the aquatic ape to deploy the destratification of the hominid modes of sex, reproduction and communication (which emerged between 6–7 million years ago, in the Miocene era, and 3500 million years ago, in the Pliocene era). The third section discusses the biodigital mutations of sex and reproduction (late twentieth century up to now) impacting on the biophysical and biocultural orders of the body–sex. The last section defines hypernature as a plane of coexisting assemblages of desire composing an intensive essence of a body–sex through symbiotic mixtures.

MICROBIAL SEX

The human body, too, is an architectonic compilation of millions of agencies of chimerical cells. Each cell in the hand typing this sen-tence comes from two, maybe three kinds of bacteria. The cells

173

themselves appear to represent the latter-day result, the fearful symmetry, of microbial communities so consolidated, so tightly organized and histologically orchestrated, that they have been selected
together, one for all and all for one, as societies in the shape of
organisms.

Sagan (1992: 368)

Sex in bacteria crosses species boundaries and allows a flow of
genetic information that some consider the basis for a worldwide
gene pool composed of bacteria.

Margulis and Sagan (1986: 1)

According to Darwinian and neo-Darwinian evolutionism, eukaryotic
cells, meiotic sex and sexual mating are the result of the accumulation
of random mutations engendering more complex cellular organisms
directly favoured by natural selection. Conversely, Margulis's endosymbiotic theory hypothesizes that the eukaryotic cell and meiotic sex
emerge from a process of cellular incorporation, reversal parasitism
and bacterial hijacking. A far cry from progressive evolution, endosymbiosis maps a continuum among microbial modes of information
transfer generating a multiplicity of machines of sex on the biophysical
strata. The distance between the macro and the micro no longer
applies to this world of molecular sexes where evolution implies the
modifications of content and expression of information (genetic material and membranes, genetic and proteic sequences, cellular architectures) through contagion rather than filiation.

The cell with the nucleus is not an individual and independent body
favoured by natural selection and random mutation. Rather, it emerges
from an assemblage of singular bacterial bodies – swimming, oxygen-
respiring and photosynthetic bacteria – incorporating and eating each
other. Not only is the eukaryotic cell an uncanny assembly of microbes
but also meiotic sex – the doubling and reduction of chromosomes –
that eventually bounds up with sexual reproduction – is a divergence
from a sort of cannibalism between eukaryotic cells. As Margulis
explains, eukaryotic cells in the form of protocists – unicellular bodies
– learnt to swallow each other for feeding and respiring and then to
divide in order to reduce their doubled cellular body to a single stage.
This gulp provoked cellular and nucleic duplicity, a reversible twinning
where the attacker is abducted by the attacked. The return of this
duplicity to singularity defines the meiotic machine of sex. The passage
from the double or diploid (46) to the singular or haploid (23) set of

chromosomes is crowded with microbial memories and cellular parasitism between eukaryotes. Meiotic sex is not a newly selected form of sex and reproduction favouring the development of complex multicellular bodies. In animals and plants, this new machine of sex would never have emerged without the symbiotic cannibalism between unicellular eukaryotes.

The neo-Darwinian Red Queen hypothesis suggests that two-parent sex is a better strategy of reproduction selected to regenerate genetic variations. This hypothesis of sex selection rests upon the binary organization of the sexes (male and female) determined by the centrality of sexual mating.[5] Sex selection is supposed to accelerate evolution by transmitting the most varied traits to the next generation and driving sexed organisms to adapt faster to changing conditions. This hypothesis regards selection as a negative force that eliminates ill-fitted sexual traits. Here variations are defined by gradual differences between less and more complex populations (bacterial and eukaryotic) where sexual mating is the mode of reproduction best-adapted to external conditions. Endosymbiosis instead points to a microbial continuum of variations: bacterial sex and parthenogenesis present as many genetic variations as two-parent sex. Sex can neither be lost nor gained; it corresponds neither to genders nor to two-parent reproduction. Reproduction requires no filiation, and sex needs no mating. Sex is not directly selected, but selection relates to the potential capacities of microbodies to trigger new modes of transmission. There are as many sexes as there are terms in symbiosis constituting a molecular ecosystem of micro-mutations where information transfers proceed by contagion. Meiotic sex marks a critical point in symbiotic evolution, the microbial constitution of a new machine of sex introducing a modification in cellular and genetic reproduction.

Sex selection needs to be correlated to the micro-percepts of a microbial environment of association, where the response to direct stimuli leads to the expansion of the capacity of a body to act, invent and mutate. Percepts are not reducible to human cognition, but define a capacity of reception investing the whole bacterial, viral and unicellular population. Percepts neither involve a passive adaptation to external changes nor a subjective phenomenon of understanding. Bergson argues that we must follow the phylum of 'external perception' in monera – non-nucleated protoplasmic bodies – and higher invertebrates to move away from centred perception ascribed to the subjective mind. 'Tiny bacilli or longer filaments swim to align themselves along gradients of increased sugar concentration as they approach a perceived food source. Sensing they act on the basis of their sensation' (1991: 157). For Bergson, the necessity of prolonging a stimulus through a response implies a direct relation between perception and movement in protozoa. In multicellular bodies this relation involves a delay, an uncertainty between a perceptual reaction and a motor response. Yet, as Deleuze explains, there is not a difference in kind between unicellular and multicellular bodies, but an intensive degree of differentiation (1988a). This intensification emerges out of a delay between percepts and actions in multicellular bodies that generates an intermittence of chaos. This gap between stimulus and response unfolds a zone of affection that includes the active microperception of thousands of microbial bodies, intensifying their capacity of action-mutation in a multicellular body–sex. Sex selection does not select the fittest sperms to ensure successful filiation, but relies upon an ecosystem of molecular perceptions: a continual variation of microbial reception and action.

Bacterial recombination also re-emerges in the mutation of mitochondrial DNA, designating small-rate variations parallel to nucleic (chromosomal) transmission. Recent research on the cytoplasmic material of the egg cell affirms that mitochondria (organelles) have an independent genetic apparatus (DNA, messenger RNA and ribosomes) from nucleic genes. Like bacteria, mitochondria reproduce without systematic genetic transfer, assembling protein on ribosomes, reacting to similar antibiotics, and recombining at a similar speed as the bacterium-like division. The presence of mitochondria in every eukaryotic cell suggests that mitochondria were once autonomous respiring bacteria – purple bacteria – ingested by larger anaerobic archeabacteria during the oxygen revolution, 2000 million years ago (McMenamin 1994: 36–40).

The spreading of oxygen in the atmosphere was poisonous to most anaerobic bacteria. The latter ingested but failed to digest oxygen-respiring bacteria that grew inside their host keeping them alive. Our eukaryotic cells emerge from this ancient hypersexual merging where former infectors – mitochondria – are still trapped in our cells. Mitochondria are the hereditary guests of their anaerobic hosts, the descent of aerobic bacteria able to synthesize oxygen, produce carbon dioxide and ATP (adenosine triphosphate, storing energy for the metabolic functions of eukaryotic cells). From unicellular amoebas to plants and animals, cytoplasmic genes are broods of free-living bacteria captivated in the eukaryotic cell.

The microbial composition of the eukaryotic cell and mitochondrial recombination, rather than two-parent sexual mating, defines meiotic sex. Meiosis occurs in many protocists, plants and animals that bypass two-parent sex. This machine of stratification is not a unity of selection but a multiplicity of heterogeneous reproductions enveloping the schizo-coexistence of bacterial, mitochondrial and nucleic machines of information transmission. In particular, mitochondrial recombination, a unique matrilinear mode of information transfer, indicates further dynamics of mutations in meiotic sex. On the biophysical strata, mitochondrial transmission tracks the matrilineal lineage of the 'Mitochondrial Eve'. On the plane of consistency, this heritage unfolds the speed of microbial rates of variation distributed across multicellular bodies.

The hypothesis of the Mitochondrial Eve focuses on recent scientific claims suggesting that small rates of mitochondrial mutations evolve more rapidly than genes located in the cell nucleus. Nuclear genes are shuffled and recombined in every generation and obscure the small-scale features of parallel evolutionary lineages, such as the Mitochondrial Eve. This hypothesis explains that out of the many thousands of females who lived 200,000 years ago, only one of those who passed on to us their nuclear genes (X chromosomes) succeeded in passing on her mitochondria in an unbroken lineage up to the present. In all the other women's lineages, disaster struck at various times after 200,000 BCE, so that mitochondria ceased to be passed on – even though the women in question had chromosomal descendants in every generation existing between then and now. This disaster is attributed to a drastic reduction in population size or to the generation of only male children in various lineages forced to seek mates and acquire the mitochondria from other lineages.[6]

This matrilineal lineage defines a parallel machine of sex (mitochondrial recombination) compared to nucleic reproduction. On the plane of consistency, the small rate variations of mitochondrial DNA designate the dynamics of destratification (declination) from the nucleic transmission of the germline distributing microbial mutations through meiotic sex.

AQUATIC SEX

And we tend to forget, landlubbers that we are, that until comparatively recently an aquatic environment was the sole milieu for life on Earth. The planet has apparently hosted living organisms for an astonishing 3.8 billion years of its 4.6-billion year history, and yet the colonization of the land began only around 450 million years ago.

Ball (1999: 206)

Lakes and pools shrink or dry up; rivers change their courses; land sinks below sea level; estuaries silt up. The first land vertebrates, like mud skippers found in the tropics today, were creatures who found themselves stranded for at least part of the time by movements of the tide or by seasonal droughts. They did not move out of their natural habitat to advance upon the land and colonise it. They stayed where they had always been. It was the earth that moved.

Morgan (1990: 49)

The mutations of sex and reproduction emerge from a web of micro-relations that are localized neither inside nor outside the body. There is a series of interactions or resonances between intramolecular and extramolecular levels of perception of a body that deploys a reversible correspondence between genomes and environments unleashing the emergence of mutations. The jaguar's skin, for instance, which provides it with camouflage, is an expression of the jaguar's genetic composition, which in turn, constitutes the content of the patterns of light and dark in the forest. As an act of selection, perception entails a collision of bodies that unfolds the virtual action of the environment on the body, affecting the capacity of reception and action of a body in the environment. This collision continuously enables the body–sex to drift away from acquired forms and functions of reproduction. In this sense, environmental adaptation involves not a passive but a potential modification of the body's field of action, inventing new internal regions of reception that are resonances of an outside in which they are, as it were, in permanent metastable communication. Internal resonances do not represent a genuine interiority or internal will of the individual body. The invention of internal regions only deploys a process of transduction of information that takes place on the porous membranes of a body. As Simondon argues: 'The living being can be considered to be a node of information that is being transmitted inside itself – it is a system within a system, containing *within itself* a mediation between two different orders of magnitude' (1992: 306).

In particular, the movement from the ape-like to the hominid-like body's capacities of reception and action involves a series of communicative – audio-visual-phonetic sensorium – reproductive – concealed ovulation, lunar menstruation, ventro-ventral copulation – and morphological – bipedalism, hairlessness, breathing – modifications of the quadruped body. These are biophysical and biocultural changes that entail altering relations between variables of codes and milieus, populations and territories, interweaving different orders of stratification. The virtual impact of drifting milieus on the body marks the passage from the ape to the hominid mode of reproduction and communication: a critical point of emergence of unenvisageable variations of information transmission.

The dominant story in primate literature implies that the passage from the ape to the hominid was driven by the internal needs of the ape to adapt to new difficult environmental conditions.[7] These conditions gradually led the ape to change its mode of reproduction – sexual copulation – and communication – audio-visual perception and speech – compared to the rest of quadruped animals. This story is constructed around principles of scarcity, sacrifice and competition defining an individual adaptation selected by natural conditions. In particular, the savannah theory claims that two major factors accelerated this notorious evolutionary change. On the one hand, the climatic change that eradicated the forest of the African continent induced the emergence of a vast area of plain grass. On the other, this unsteady climate urged a change in diet, gradually constraining the apes to become meat-eaters. Hence, hominids are descendent from those apes that left the trees and moved out onto the grassy plains or savannah where they turned from quadruped into bipedal, from vegetarians into meat-eaters and finally hunters. The modifications of the body of the ape into the hominid shape are a direct result of plain dwelling and land hunting. The ape learned to stand up straight on two legs in order to see the prey over the plains. He also learned to run faster after the prey while carrying weapons with his now free hands. His body became hairless and smooth so as to keep him cool while chasing the prey in the sunshine. The orthodox savannah theory ascribes the ape–hominid transformation to a gradual, harmonious and convenient adaptation to a new environment.

The assumption of gradual development and advantageous modifications of the hominid body stands in strong contrast with Elaine Morgan's theory of the *Aquatic Ape*. Drawing on the work of the marine biologist Alisteer Hardy, Morgan analyses the relations between the hominid body and aquatic mammals. Her investigation suggests that the morphology and physiology of the hominid body are profoundly different from the rest of terrestrial mammals, but strikingly akin to most aquatic mammals. The Aquatic Ape theory observes that the morphological transformations of the hominid body stem from a divergence in evolution: a destratification (deviation) from the (terrestrial) bio-geological and social order of quadrupeds' development. This destratification is linked to the outbreak of drastic changes in the ecosystem that impacted upon the ape's modes of reproduction and communication unleashing an intensive mutation of the body–sex. Morgan argues that only a leap from a terrestrial to an aquatic environment can explain the unique modifications of the hominid body. The morphological, reproductive and communicative modifications of this body indicate the marine memories of an ape that was forced to migrate out of land and dwell in an aquatic environment for twelve million years, during the notorious yet obscure period between the Miocene and the Pliocene. By challenging the savannah belief in favourable evolution, the Aquatic Ape theory highlights the non-linear impact between intra- and extra-molecular bodies where modifications indirectly correspond to a virtual action of the environment on the body.

In her books *The Descent of Woman* (1972), *The Aquatic Ape* (1982) and *The Scars of Evolution* (1990), Morgan sustains the argument that drastic and rapid changes in the ecosystem led the ape to migrate towards the sea. Far from being advantageous or gradual, these changes are regarded as biophysical and bio-social shocks that affected the entire morphological, perceptual and socio-cultural organizations of the ape body. Instead of denoting a passive subjection of the ape to the marine environment or suggesting a psychoanalytical trauma, these shocks above all entail a material transfer of matters-functions marking the virtual impact or affective relation between the environment and the body. By increasing the gap between the time of reception and action, this impact unfolds a delay between the stimuli received and the responses emitted producing a veritable mutation of contents and expressions of reproduction and communication. By trans-situating the modifications of the hominid body in the field of differential correspondences (non-linear tendencies) between codes and milieus, the Aquatic Ape theory points to the geo-physical and bio-social mutations of the 'body of the earth', where a body is always already in contact with an environment of bodies.

In primate literature, it is hypothesized that sometime between six and seven million years ago – during the Miocene period – and three-and-a-half million years ago – during the Pliocene era – somewhere in north-east Africa in the region of the Red Sea, certain anthropoids suddenly became bipedal. The obscure link between the ape and the hominid maps onto the geological shifts that occurred between the

Miocene and the Pliocene eras. According to Morgan, this link can be explained in relation to the geological dynamics suggested by the theory of Continental Drifts (1990: 52). Not only the drift of continents but also atmospheric pressures pushed the ape to immerse in a marine milieu. The mild temperature, the heavy rainfall and the flourishing of the forests in the Miocene was followed by the Pliocene drought that lasted twelve million years. The Pliocene saw the parching of the forests, starting from the centre of Africa and rapidly pushing mammals to migrate towards the sea. Many Miocene apes were wiped out, but the bipedal Australopithecines – Lucy – appeared.

These shifts in the ecosystem rendered the dwelling on the plain quite hostile for the ape. According to Morgan, during the Pliocene drought, the almost quadruped and fruit-eater ape landed on the plain. Nevertheless, she found it impossible to adapt to terrestrial life, eating grass and meat and competing with faster quadrupeds. For this still hairy ape, the sea rather than a terrestrial cave, remained the most imminent environment to escape to. This immersion in the water was not a result of gradual and convenient adaptation, but it implied fast and brusque changes of bodily functions.

Morgan explains that it was a female ape that first latched onto a marine milieu. Protected from terrestrial predators that would not venture into the sea – such as feline predators – this female ape started to eat shrimps, to collect eggs and invent tools to open shells. Walking slowly in the water urged her spine and the hind limbs to align in one straight line, moving away from the 90 degrees angle of a land-dwelling quadruped in order to breathe. She lost her body hair and webbed her digits in order to swim more smoothly, learning to move the spine like a fish. The sea became her unnatural environment where an abstruse disarray of organs on her body altered forever the hominid's modes of communication and reproduction. The legs elongated, the buttocks grew as a protective feature – a sort of mobile cushion – for sitting on the beach and the vagina migrated forward from a rear quadruped position and inward, folded within the body cavity and covered by a protective membrane, the hymen.

Morgan's theory argues against the androcentric view of evolution according to which the transformation and dislocation of female sexual organs are induced by a will to attract male sexual attention or by a necessity to develop more successful adaptations for sexual reproduction. She points out that not only did the vaginal migration render copulation technically more difficult, but it also concealed signals of female fertility and arousal, rendering oestrus imperceptible.

Mating behaviour itself changed. The most common habit for sexual mating in quadrupeds involves a rear-mounting position – the female primate vagina is exposed on the surface allowing an easy rear penetration. In this early aquatic phase, the hominid was not yet equipped with his specific larger penis compared to other terrestrial primates. The enlargement of this organ did not originate as a way to make sex sexier or as a pleasurable reward to the male apes in need of extra satisfaction after hunting. Rather, it became a necessary transformation to afford copulation once the female vagina moved out of easy reach. This morphological alteration designates a destratification from the bio-social reproductive order of quadruped mammals exposing the capacity of the ape's body to be affected by the impact of a marine sphere. The abilities to receive and respond to aquatic stimuli define the biophysical and biocultural potential of a body–sex to become. The migration and enveloping of the vagina compelled the apes to substitute a rear approach to sex common to all land primates with a ventro-ventral proximity that is only common to humans and aquatic mammals (whales, dolphins, dugongs and manatees, etc.).

The aquatic environment also forced oestrus (sexual and reproductive peaks) to fade away. Clear sexual signals – olfactory, visual or behavioural – regulating sexual activities are not a feature of human sex. Ovulation does not correspond to any peak of desire in the aquatic-hominid mammal and is therefore undetectable by the male. Orthodox theories speculating on the disappearance of oestrus assume that this specific hominid modification of sexual communication is a reaction against a natural predicament among quadrupeds, a sort of exception that confirms the rule. Conversely, Morgan sustains that this disappearance is not a random occurrence, but is related to the becoming aquatic of the ape. In an aquatic environment, the pheromonal message transmitted by the female during oestrus – a scent signal – would be washed away. Similarly, in the waters visual signals would be less effective. In short, oestrus vanished because it ceased to communicate the distinct message of copulation and sexual desire. It became immersed in the noise of the sea, where male copulating behaviour could no longer be regulated by the rhythms of the female cycle. Hence, copulation became disentangled from feminine sex. Destratified from the scent of oestrus, this sex-desire became ambivalent and imperceptible. Yet, as Morgan specifies, the aquatic deviation from oestrus also rendered feminine desire irrelevant to species survival. Male apes were sufficiently active to ensure that females would reproduce their kind without necessary consent to copulation.

The ventro-ventral copulation defines one of the most drastic modifi-cations of reproduction in the mammal world distributing a new muta-tion of sex on the biocultural strata. This modification shaped the new relationship between the female and the male ape. In the animal world, a frontal proximity with an adult male indicates aggressive and confrontational intentions. Yet aquatic males had to learn to approach females frontally in order to copulate. Morgan believes that the female aquatic mammal reacted to this frontal approach by adopting a position of defence, lying on the floor with the hands covering her face. This gesture conveys a signal of submission and retraction from the conflict informing the attacker to let the prey go. Yet, the male hominid 'lost the capacity to release a victim whose subjection has been made apparent' (Theweleit 1987: 293). Rather than letting the prey go, the male forced his frontal approach onto the female hominid, turning the act of copulation into an unusual act of violence, an unnatural form of aggression linked with this new mode of reproduction.

This tension between copulation, sexuality and aggression is a mark of the unpredictable ways in which variations in the ecosystem affect the hominid capacities of reception and action. The aquatic impact on the zones of perception of a body involves the increasing and decreasing intensification of reception and action that induce the shut-ting down of some and the activation of other organs. Such vacillating degrees of intensification expose a biophysical and biocultural destrati-fication of acquired modes of reproduction out of which the new entanglement between penetration and aggression eventuates a reterri-torialization of sex on the strata.

As Theweleit reports, Sandor Ferenczi in his formulation of a genital theory in psychoanalysis focuses on the conjunction between the female body–sex and water (1987: 292). With Morgan, he argues that living species first evolved out of the sea. The U-turn out of the sea onto land, turned women 'into oceans': masses or quanta of flowing waters, carriers of the sea. To Ferenczi, the relation between the sea – the immense floods of fluids – and the female body is not a represen-tation. It does not correspond to an identification of the female repro-ductive body – represented by the womb – with the sea. Instead of relying on the linguistic signifier woman, where the sea always already symbolizes the uterine mother, the link between the sea and femininity primarily defines a virtual resonance of anti-climactic dynamics irredu-cible to the Oedipal economy of pleasure, in which flows are chan-nelled towards sexual reproduction or filiation.

In order to explain the emergence of male aggression in sexual behaviour, Ferenczi adopts Morgan's theory of the Aquatic Ape that explains the convergence between biophysical and social changes of sexual behaviour. He adds that the frontal penetration forced onto female hominids in order to copulate resonates with the male aggressive act of rape. Far from being an isolated phenomenon, this aggression is enmeshed with the drastic biophysical and biocultural changes entailing the ape becoming aquatic, the marine mutations of the terrestrial orders of information transmission. These changes are marks enfolded in the hominid body as memories of abrupt morphological, reproductive and communicative modifications. Sexual aggression evokes a reterritorialization of the hydrodynamics of the sea enveloped in the female body–sex. According to Ferenczi, this is a reaction directed against the marine fluctuations of the female sex, where the circulation of desire no longer is visible to naked eyes and no longer is attached to sexual organs.

When the rain started to fall, the Pliocene merged in the Pleistocene and the aquatic ape moved out of the waters onto the lands incorporating the amniotic memories of the sea, the non-climactic fluctuations of desire. According to Morgan, male aggression eventually decreased to seduce the female hominid into copulation. Her non-localized desire, no longer visible sex, forced the male hominid to invent new tactics of affection to reassure and please her (1990: 109).

In Morgan's Aquatic hypothesis, female sexual selection does not account for individual survival, competition, and filiative heredity. The devastating shifts of continents, atmospheric pressures, sudden inundations and droughts jeopardised the animal and plant populations and introduced the anomalous opportunity for the terrestrial ape to become aquatic. This becoming unfolds a destratifying machine of sex, the continual declination of sex from biophysical and biocultural states of equilibrium. Far from opposing the natural to the social environment of sex, the Aquatic Ape theory suggests that female sexual selection depends upon variable relations of milieus and codes where the social order of sex intersects with the affects of an aquatic milieu on the hominid capacities of perception and action. This new relation between the woman's body and the aquatic ape does not aim to engender a genealogy of sexual difference and identification. The enfolding of waters in the womb does not point to a return to a primitive femininity, but to an ocean of molecular fluctuations disclosing the potential becomings of a body–sex. The impact of the aquatic environment on the ape body abstracts desire from sexual organs distributing an aquatic mutation of sex on the biophysical and biocultural strata.

TURBO SEX

Is not everything interwoven with everything? Is not machinery linked with animal life in an infinite variety of ways? The shell of a hen's egg is made up of delicate white ware and is machine as much as an egg-cup.

S. Butler (1985: 199)

[. . .] 'unidentifiable microbes,' the small screen said. It was able to show him tiny, spiderlike organisms in her flesh, some of them caught in the act of reproducing along with her cells – *as part of her cells*. They were not viruses. According to the computer, they were more complete, independent organisms. Yet they had made themselves at home in human cells in a way that should not have been possible – like plasmids invading and making themselves at home in bacteria. But these were more complex organisms that had sought out higher game than bacteria and managed to combine with it without killing it. They had changed it, however, altered it slightly, subtly, cell by cell. In the most basic possible way, they had tampered with Meda's genetic blue print. They had left her no longer human.

O. E. Butler (1984: 48–9)

On the plane of consistency, the mutation of reproduction and sex intercepts all levels of order – biophysical, biocultural, biodigital – through a molecular connection of matters-functions of bodies diverging from steady states. Hence, mutations are not relevant to one stratum but their effects distribute across all layers of stratification. For example, the emergence of technical machines able to connect, convert and capitalize on information does not only affect the biocultural modes of connection, but also the biophysical capacities of cellular and multicellular reception and action of a body. Far from determining mutations, these technical machines transmit and reproduce information like natural machines.

Marshall McLuhan pointed to the relation between the body and technologies by discussing the changes provoked by electronic technologies.[8] His formula, 'The medium is the message', outlines the emergence of an imploded mediascape, from electric wires to telephony, when electronic technology in the post-war world invested economy and culture through the revolution of information transmission. The implosion of the media does not correspond to a new monopolistic organization of all media where technology dominates society. This implosion most strikingly displays the communicating modifications of a body no longer defined by an organic essence, but by a web of extendable parts – such as ear, mouth, foot, hands, eyes – diffusing on an electronic global scale. Electronic and satellite networks, radio and television broadcasts, cellular phones and Internet nodes, map the electronicization (and digitalization) of the senses. Instead of suggesting a mere analogy between the body and technology, implying a sterile extension of human parts onto the media sphere, technical machines operate a virtual action on the capacity of the body to change. These machines do not mainly add layers of emotional responses and cognitive associations to perception, but above all detract the senses from the sensible by shedding light on the relation between matter, memory and perception.[9] Perception is not defined by subjective experience but by an activity of selection in a vast field of kinetic particles clashing on the body and stimulating sensory responses. In this sense, McLuhan's hypothesis of 'the extension of man' runs the risk of anthropomorphizing technical machines – where organic unity determines machines – but also of equating perception to an induced function – passively driven by technical changes – rather than defining the loop of reception and action of a body. Besides these risks, McLuhan's work crucially suggests the reversible relations between the body and technology where the impact of new media unleashes an unprecedented metamorphosis of a body's sensory zones (and organs) of perception.[10]

As Deleuze and Guattari affirm, technical machines do not constitute isolated phenomena of transformation, but primarily expose the dynamics of a socio-technical collective machine, which establishes what is a technical element at a given moment, what is its usage, extension, comprehension, etc. Technical machines are always consistent with machinic assemblages – biochemical, bio-social and bio-economical assemblages – that select, qualify and invent technical elements in a given combination. In *Erewhon* (1872; 1985), Samuel Butler provides many examples of machinic assemblages of reproduction. He argues that there is no formal essence that determines the way a technical machine operates a signal and the way a human being communicates. There is no specific or personal unity of the organism or structural unity of the machine. The assumptions that a technical machine cannot reproduce itself and can only be exteriorly individualized are not dissimilar from the assumption that the organization of limbs defines a human being according to one centre of reproduction. As Butler explains, there is no centre of reproduction, but only a continuously scattered connection of machines of reproduction, related and mixed with each other. For example, the egg of a butterfly becomes a caterpillar, which then becomes a chrysalis, which then produces a new butterfly (Butler 1985; 198–211). The butterfly is a machine that affords the egg ways to make another egg: a machinic production. Unlike McLuhan, Butler does not believe that machines are an extension of the human organism, but argues that machines are the limbs and organs of a society whose identity is always distributed into parts of distinct engineering machines. Machinic connections designate everywhere the continual variations of information transmission that intermingle all levels of organization of matter.

The bio-socio-technical assemblage of reproduction entails a continual destratification of the biophysical and biocultural orders (meiotic sex, the law of entropic sex and filiation). Thus, the emergence of biodigital sex is not an extension of nineteenth-century technologies, the organic and parthenogenic sex of industrial reproduction that we discussed in Chapter 3. Rather, it marks the diffusion of a new (turbulent) assemblage of reproduction and communication: a symbiotic mixture of microbodies and information technologies. Biodigital machines tap into the molecular variations of sex unfolding the potential of mixed assemblages of information to impact on the biophysical (meiotic sex) and biocultural (two-parent sex) organizations of the body. The engineering of nucleic DNA, cytoplasm, bacteria, viruses, egg cells, stem cells, sex cells, embryos exceeds the binary order of sex deploying a warfare of bacterial recombination, viral communication and non-filiative reproduction.

Transgenic sex, the recombination of genetic material from two or more cellular bodies, constitutes the most ancient mode of genetic transfer on the biophysical stratum: bacterial sex. During the Lower Precambrian times, three billion years ago, transgenic sex provided a way for bacterial cells to repair their DNA damaged by intense solar radiations. Margulis and Sagan define the emergence of sex as the coming into contact of heterogeneous bacterial cells trading their genetic material; a sort of microsurgical operation where non-damaged DNA served to repair enzymes burned by intense radiation (1997). With the tiny opening of the bacterial cell wall and membrane, genes floated to the surface to reach a new bacterial cell. This brief contact to send genes is defined as conjugation, when two bacterial cells merge by way of proximity, and transfection or transduction when genetic material is traded through a virus.

In genetic engineering, transduction is the most common procedure of cellular and genetic modification. Viruses attack bacteria and inject their genetic material into the cell. They hijack the bacterial genetic system and start viral replication. The bacterial cell eventually reaches a critical point, a threshold of change by breaking apart, and new viruses, produced by the combination of bacterial and viral genes, will spread into a new bacterium host. Such a virulent sex corresponds to bacterial abilities to trade genes by developing a variety of metabolisms – including the use of metals – of which plants and animals have learned to use only few. Bacterial sex not only breeds new genes, but also manipulates the genetic composition of the bacterial body itself. Bacterial promiscuity defines a hyper-computational broadcasting of information across the globe, incorporating the most dangerous anti-bacterial genes and vaccines and transferring immunity across all the bacterial population. Transgenic sex puts up no resistance to mutations and affords no protection from contagion.

In genetic engineering, transgenic sex includes the insertion of pigs' genes in human cells to improve organs and cell transplants, the repro-gramming of genes in bacteria to make genetically engineered insulin, the culture of human pluripotent stem cells to produce new cells and tissues to be used for 'cell therapies'. This genetic and cellular re-engineering entails the immanent connection of matters-functions of information cutting across biophysical machines of reproduction by facilitating horizontal transfer and rampant recombination of genetic material across species barriers and favouring the emergence of new viruses and pathogenic bacteria. Genetic engineering modulates (i.e. captures the virtual tendencies of) bacterial sex to re-programme cellular bodies that have come to define new generations of mutant microbes, viruses, vegetables, insects, fishes, reptiles, sheep and humans. This re-programming intensifies the reversible potential of retroviruses and micro-mutations where the non-linear recombination of chemical elements and molecular aggregates, genetic sequences and cellular compounds defines the turbulent dynamics of information.

Not only transgenic sex, but also mammal cloning deploys a turbu-lent destratification of the biophysical and biocultural orders of sex and reproduction. In mammal cloning, the double fusion of mitochondrial DNA from the recipient and the donor cytoplasms in the egg cell points to the non-linear relation between nucleic and non-nucleated mutations: mitochondria unfold the capacity of the cytoplasmic body to affect nucleic structures. Thus, mitochondrial fusion does not only signal the potential of new genetic variations but also intensifies the reversal potential of mitochondrial mutations to affect the nucleic germline, unleashing the capacity of the genotype to mutate beyond prediction. Far from reprogramming the same nucleic instructions and structures, cloning lays open a reverse causality: an act of future mutations on the present (the potential emergence of unpredictable variations) and of present mutations on the past (the genetic deviation from acquired variations). The turbulent recombination of mitochondria indicates a reversible relation between bacterial (biophysical) and engineered (biodigital) assemblages of desire out of which a new sex will eventuate.

Mammal cloning defines a new point of declination from meiotic sex, heterosexual mating, and the entropic entanglement between sex, reproduction and death. Yet, it does not simply denote the perfect control of the body–sex or the ultimate triumph of disembodiment. Rather, mammal cloning exposes a body–sex to a matter-matrix of continual variations composing an immanent plane of nature. This 'kinematics of the egg', as Deleuze inspired by Lucretius calls it (1994: 214), designates a *mechanosphere* of bodies–sexes where symbiotic recombinations de-identify genetic material and accelerate the unpredictable mutations of desire.

HYPERNATURE

In this chapter, I have produced a diagram of the destratification of sex and reproduction intersecting the biophysical, biocultural and biodigital organizations of a body–sex. This diagram defines hypernature as a plane of consistency: the parallel mutations of sex and reproduction that compose a symbiotic body. Microbial sex, aquatic sex and turbo sex partake of an engineering nature that does not distinguish the organic from the inorganic, the pure from the artificial, the biological from the technological. Hypernature unfolds an ecosystem of microrelations between bodies that defines the potential of a body–sex to become.

Hypernature subtracts nature from the Cartesian transcendent God governing bodies from above and from afar, imposing on bodies an identity, a predetermined idea and form. The erection of God above the 'body of the earth' is at the core of all principles of morality that attribute all manifestations of nature to one unextended entity creating without being created. This God is the expression of pure good that does not know evil and mediates the distinction between reality and fiction, natural and contaminated by opposing a mutable and extended universe to an immutable and eternal substance. For Spinoza, this conception of nature fails to explain the capacity (potentia) of a body to change, to be affected and to affect bodies.

Far from moral principles, this Spinozist hypernature defines an ethics-ethology of bodies colliding and mutating. Spinoza's God does not presuppose principles of good and evil, humane and inhumane. This ethology explains that poison and evil, destruction and sadism are dimensions of God emerging and proliferating through encounters or mixtures between bodies that do not agree. These encounters include the incorporation of microbial bodies in the nucleic macromolecule, the capture of mitochondria in the meiotic order of sex, the copulation between modified hominid bodies combining sex and aggression, the entropic entanglement of sex and death, the micro-fascist capture of genetic identification and genetic design.

Instead of being harmonious and advantageous, evoking a sort of altruism between individuals, these encounters are symbiotic assemblages of desire between diverse bodies involving diverse conditions. These assemblages unleash a necessary yet unpredictable mutation of the modes participating in the composition that coincides with the intensive mutations of substance. Although evil and sadness are dimensions of God (i.e. intensive matter), they do not define the primary engineering of bodies emerging from joyful encounters or anti-climactic fluctuations of desire: the increasing capacity of a body to be affected and affect new bodies. For example, the symbiotic association between the female ape and the aquatic environment increases the capacity of a body to modify swerving from its acquired state of reproduction and communication. Similarly, the assemblage between genetic engineering and bacterial cloning increases the power of bacterial sex to be affected and distribute across new unnatural compositions.

Even if assemblages can decrease the mutating capacity of a body, it does not follow that desire is negative. Quite the contrary, negativity is only a dimension of a primary productive desire. Negativity points to the blockage of flows of connection in closed loops of abolition that decrease the potential of a body to act: negating desire through principles of lack and need. The economy of pleasure, for example, entraps flows in the constant cycle of accumulation and discharge. It negates the symbiotic connection of bodies by imposing transcendence on flows separating the body from an immutable mind (or God). This economy is embedded in the Cartesian metaphysics of nature that denies motion and mutation to matter: the potential of bodies to generate new bodies. This economy understands nature as lacking the capacity of organization and therefore needing to be governed, managed and controlled.

As Deleuze and Guattari argue, assemblages of desire define the primacy of lines of flight (positive flows of production) in relation to an economy of pleasure that represses energy by isolating bodies.[11] Assemblages of desire are without finality but entail the parallel combination of intensive or virtual bodies and extensive or actual modes of reproduction (biophysical, biocultural and biodigital sex). Preindividual bodies do not coincide with their actualization.

On this machinic hypernature, nothing is ever completely actualized. The virtual is partially siphoned into the actual, but in doing so the process itself kick-starts a re-virtualization of the actual: the proliferation of mutant desire swerving from peaks of equilibrium. Thus, preindividual bodies are inseparable from the variations of bodies–sexes composing a hypernature of intensive extensions where each actual desire responds to a virtual desire (immanent consistency).

For Spinoza, a body – an existing mode – is an assemblage of bodies partaking of a potential essence or degree of power (God or Substance). This degree of power is defined as *conatus*: 'a tendency to maintain and maximize the ability to be affected' of a body entering relations of forces with other bodies able to destratify (drift away) the body from gravitating points of stability (*Ethics* VI: 38). Conatus involves an effort to maintain intensity in existence, preserve anti-climactic relations of motion and rest between modal bodies.[12] This effort is dictated neither by an internal will nor by a necessity to adapt to an external power. Rather, it entails a chance assemblage of bodies that expands the capacities of mutation of a body. Hence a body–sex 'to be preserved requires a great many other bodies by which it is, as it were, continually regenerated' (*Ethics* II, Lemma, Scholium). These symbiotic mergings are not additions of parts but point to the micro-variations of desire, the intensive expansion of the tendencies of a body to mutate coinciding with an 'affirmation of essence [God] in existence [bodies]' (Deleuze 1988c: 102). This engineering of molecular particles defines the *intensive essence* of a body: the ceaseless mutations of hypernature. This nature mutates while being mutated by new assemblages of sex and reproduction.

The biodigital mutations of sex and reproduction are not opposed to nature, as they are not engendered by an external power (technology, mind, culture and the law of the phallus). Genetic engineering partakes of an engineering nature composed of symbiotic assemblages of microbial and multicellular bodies, the social body and the body politics, the capitalist body and the body of technologies. On this hypernature, the entanglement of sex with sexual reproduction (meiotic sex) constitutes a phase of order in wider processes of modification that include the biodigital mutations of sex. Rather than a linear genealogy, symbiotic modifications expose the unprecedented mutations of sex and reproduction emerging from a fluctuating ecosystem of bodies–sexes.

The biodigital assemblage indicates the emergence of a new symbiotic modification, increasing or decreasing the conatus (desire or appetite) of a mutant body–sex to be affected and affect other bodies. This new symbiotic level does not simply reiterate the ultimate mastering of Man (the Cartesian disembodied mind) over nature or of capitalist technologies over natural bodies, food and animals. These assumptions operate to reinforce the tradition of representation of nature that reduces sex and reproduction to organic integrities and filiative genealogies. The emergence of biodigital sex and reproduction rather marks the acceleration of a symbiotic mutation of a body–sex spreading through the turbulent dynamics of an engineering nature. This mutation hints at an ethics-ethology of the body that defines a new relation between nature, technology and feminine desire: micro-feminine warfare.

Notes

1 For Spinoza there is a single order of nature: *natura naturans* (as substance and cause) and *natura naturata* (as effect and mode) which is one and the same Nature marked by mutual immanence between two levels of constitution and production. Whereas in the first level the cause remains in itself in order to produce, in the second the effect or product remains in the cause. See *Ethics*, I, 29, Schol.; Deleuze 1988c: 92; Deleuze 1990b: 14; 49; 99–100. However, Spinoza's concept of *natura naturans* and *natura naturata* is often considered problematic for the supposed deterministic model it implies. Lloyd discusses some of the criticisms of this model through a confrontation with Spinoza's text. See G. Lloyd, 1996: 43–8. It is important to point out that our reading of Spinoza stems from Deleuze's engineering analysis, which highlights an immanent composition and expression of substance constituted and produced by singular multiplicities. Furthermore, this reading exposes the fundamental lines of Deleuzian immanence which refers neither to an object or belongs to a subject, but 'is immanent to itself and notwithstanding, it is in movement'. In both Deleuze and Spinoza, immanence entails that the desire of the self-cause coincides with the desire of a mode to preserve oneself (*conatus*), that is, with the *potentia* of matter itself.

2 On the distinction between matter and substance in Deleuze and Guattari, see B. Massumi 1992: 152. While the former indicates the plane of consistency or BwO, the latter constitutes a given type of substance according to a singular mode of composition. See G. Deleuze and F. Guattari 1987: 153. See also Deleuze 1988c: 109.

3 See DeLanda 2002: 9–43.

4 Nomad or minor sciences follow the singularities of matter where variables are placed in a state of continuous variations rather than being ordered through the form–matter duality (Royal science). See Deleuze and Guattari 1987: 361–674.

5 On sex selection, see M. Ridley 1994. See also K. Sigmund 1993: 124–53.

6 On the 'Mitochondrial Eve', see D. C. Dennett 1995: 97. See also R. L. Cann *et al.*, 1987: 31–6.

7 Another important theory in primate literature is the Neoteny theory. See S. J. Gould 1977: 21–70. On the critique of this theory, see E. Morgan 1982: 17.

8 On McLuhan's theory of cultural communication, see M. McLuhan and B. R. Powers 1989. See also M. A. Moos 1997.

9 On the relation between the senses, perception and memory, see B. Massumi, 2001.

10 McLuhan's theory of metamorphosis of perception is echoed by David Cronenberg's film *Videodrome* (1982). In this film, the emergence of technologies of communication and reproduction of images points to the process of metamorphosis of bodily senses and the formation of new organs of perception through the diffusion of pathologies and diseases. On the importance of McLuhan's perception in Cronenberg's *Videodrome*, see S. Shaviro 1993.

11 As Deleuze and Guattari argue, pleasure implies the stopping of the flow of desire, the channelling of desire towards a climax. Desire is prior to pleasure (one mode of organization of desire). Desire is neither good, as it is what primarily invests the micro-fascism of destruction and abolition, nor bad, as it lays out the primacy of the continual variation and connection of productive flows. It is neither passive, as it moves, nor active, as it declines and spills in and out of directionality. See Deleuze and Guattari 1987: 530, note 39. See also Deleuze and Guattari 1983: 333.

12 On the importance of conatus as a non-transcendent desire-power in Spinoza, see T. Negri, 1991a: 144–182.

Conclusion

MICROFEMININE WARFARE

[. . .] the regime of the war machine is [. . .] that of affects, which relate only to the moving body in itself, to speeds and compositions of speed among elements. Affect is the active discharge of emotion, the counterattack, whereas feeling is an always displaced, retarded, resisting emotion. Affects are projectiles just like weapons.

Deleuze and Guattari (1987: 400)

Recent debates about cybersex (prosthetic sex) and the bio-technological changes of human reproduction (cloning) problematically reiterate the binarism between the material (embodied) and immaterial (disembodied) body. These debates tend to reinforce the patriarchal economy of pleasure that opposes passive (disordered) nature – the feminine – to active (ordered) culture or technology – the masculine. This economy operates as a closed system maintaining constant balance by accumulating and discharging energy outside. In this way, a technology–mind composite detaches itself from external disorder and from carnality. The cybernetic longing for disembodiment defines the new human relation with technology, an extension of the mind ruling the body. The proliferation of biodigital technologies then corresponds to the ultimate dream of disembodiment: the triumph of the patriarchal model of sex.

On the other hand, the post-gender world of the cyborg has claimed the autonomy of feminine desire from nature by building a new relation between women and technologies. Challenging Cartesian essentialism (body–mind dualism), the post-gender cyborg has pointed to the artificial construction of nature on behalf of shifting scientific discourses about the body–sex. The relation between technology, nature and desire remains contained in the tradition of representation that organizes reality by reducing all material signs (genetic, cellular, behavioural, gestural, attitudinal, technical) to the closed circle of meaning.

By separating feminine desire and technology from nature, these debates reinforce the mind–body dichotomy. The latter implies that nature-matter-body is unable to produce and reproduce without the intervention of a transcendent power (the mind or the signifier). By oscillating between disembodiment (the masculine liberation from biological ties) and embodiment (the cultural signification of the cyborg), such debates reiterate an organic conception of the body: a self-enclosed, inert and individuated whole.

Abstract sex proposes a third route out of this dominant dichotomy. The bio-technological mutations of bodies expose the non-linear dynamics of matter: the potentials of the micro and macro organizations of a body (from the unicellular body to the bio-technical body) to connect beyond the inorganic–organic dualism.

From this standpoint, we previously asked, is cloning natural? What is the relation between feminine desire and sexual reproduction? In which ways are new bio-technologies connected with feminine desire and nature?

In Chapter 2, a biophysical map of sex defines cloning and bacterial sex as the most ancient mode of sex and reproduction. Challenging the genealogical concept of evolution (linear development), bacterial sex defines the emergence of new machines of sex and reproduction (mito-chondrial hypersex, meiotic sex) enfolded in all multicellular bodies through the entanglement of sex, reproduction and death (human sex).

In Chapter 3, a biocultural organization of the body defines the relation between sexual reproduction and feminine desire beyond the essentialism and constructivism dichotomy. This relation points to the emergence of a *genital-less* reproducibility (parthenogenic sex) that exceeds the bio-disciplinary order of Sex (Oedipal reproduction and entropic pleasure) and the organic composition of industrial capitalism.

In Chapter 4, the biodigital organization of sex defines bio-technologies as immanent to the molecular field of the body-nature. Beyond the embodiment and disembodiment dualism, this organization exposes the virtual potential of a body–sex to become. This biodigital assemblage (biological and digital cloning) maps the tendencies of the bio-informatic phase of capitalism (the capitalization of all information) exposing a reversible (non-linear) parasitic relation between absolute recombination (unpredictable mutations) and absolute control (nano-modulation) of molecular sex and reproduction.

In Chapter 5, the endosymbiotic diagram of the microbial, aquatic and turbulent modes of sex and reproduction connects the biophysical, biocultural and biodigital organization of a body–sex on a plane of consistency (the intensive connection of all bodies). These modes fall out of the strata and designate the machinic composition of nature: hypernature. This symbiotic recombination of sex and reproduction lays out an intensive (abstract) essence of a mutant body and reproduction.

Drawing on Spinoza's ethics-ethology of nature, hypernature entails the construction of a *schizogenesis* irreducible to the Cartesian model of nature determined by the mind–body division. Hypernature defines the relation between feminine desire, technology and nature through immanent (without negation) relations of affect between the biodigital body–sex and the biophysical and biocultural organization of the body. In this sense, cloning is not opposed to nature but unfolds in a conti-nuum with unicellular and multicellular modes of sex and reproduc-tion. This continuum does not imply analogy or resemblance between nature and technology.

Conversely, it indicates the metastable relation between auto-generating compositions partaking or belonging to a vaster process – a virtual or abstract phylum that encompasses critical knots of change or intensive differentiations. This continuum delineates the potential becomings of matter: the power of nature-matter-body to mutate, to be affected by new assemblages of bodies (a bacterium, a human being, an egg cell, a microchip) that in turn affect the organization of society, culture, economics and politics. Thus, bio-technology is not simply natural. It partakes of the hypernatural capacities of a body to become.

This becoming does not correspond to the progressive and individual development of one integrated whole. Rather, it maps the assemblage of bodies (endosymbiosis) producing unpredictable mutations (declina-tions) from acquired (stable) forms and functions of sex and reproduc-tion. Out of these assemblages a new dynamics of desire emerges across the fluctuating levels of a body: from the micro (bacterial sex, hypersex, meiotic sex) to the macro (hominid sex, disciplinary sex, parthenogenic sex) to the micro again (biodigital sex, cloning, trans-genic sex). This dynamics exposes the reversal of affects from one level to another, the capacity of biodigital cloning to be affected by bacterial cloning and the capacity of bacteria to affect the biocultural order of sex.

If bio-technologies partake of this hypernature of potential muta-tions, then the detachment of feminine desire from nature risks reiter-ating the old dualism between passive nature (femininity) and active culture-technology (masculinity). By dismissing nature-matter as always already signified by scientific discourses, the new pervasive power of bio-technologies reinstates the ultimate mastering of Man over (inert) nature. Hence feminine desire remains separated not only from nature but also from the potential dynamics of stratification of sex (the turbulent organization of the body).

Abstract sex furthers the autonomy of feminine desire from the organic and entropic orders of nature by highlighting that a body is composed of a thousand modes of sex and reproduction. This composition defines neither a harmonious nor a disordered state of nature driven by altruist or individual aims of survival. It entails auto-generating dynamics of association constituting a symbiotic ecosystem of bodies (plane of consistency) out of which new orders of sex and reproduction emerge (stratification) under certain gradients and degrees of pressure.

The relation between feminine desire, nature and technology entails a symbiotic dynamics of order and mutation going beyond the good (liberation from nature) and the bad (mastering of matter). This relation primarily involves a reversible parasitism between rigid (nuclear) organizations and turbulent (bacterial) bodies.

This parasitism points to a microfeminine warfare lodged in the strata, colliding with the nucleic order of pleasure and genealogical reproduction investing the biophysical (meiotic sex), biocultural (human sex), biodigital (designed sex) levels of a body. This warfare is not a reaction to stratification: the assimilation of bacterial sexes in meiotic sex, the sadism of biopower, the entropy of pleasure and genetic identification. Strata do not generate warfare. Rather, they appropriate or capture warfare by imposing a transcendent (nucleic) power on the immanent (symbiotic) aggregation of bodies.[1] Microfeminine warfare emerges and proliferates through a hypernature of intensive recombination between bodies–sexes, escaping (preceding and exceeding) rather than resisting stratification.

Microfeminine warfare is primarily a micropolitics that defines the molecular composition of all molar organizations of sex (meiotic sex, sexual reproduction and genetic modulation).[2] This warfare designates the tendencies of mutation of a body rather than focusing on stable levels of difference. Outside the regime of identity, this micropolitics deploys the power of molecular sexes never finalized to the establishment of one difference. Difference becomes as it were under construction, to be continuously attained by drifting from sexual identity: the localization of desire on sexual organs, the blocking of feminine desire in the organic and discursive body.

This microfeminine warfare can be related to Deleuze and Guattari's 'becoming-woman'. Becoming-woman does not correspond to a mere imitation of woman 'as defined by her form, endowed with organs and functions, and assigned as a subject' (1987:275). Rather, becoming-woman entails 'particles that enter in the relation of movement and rest, or zones of proximity, of a microfemininity [. . .] that produce in us a molecular woman, create the molecular woman' (275).

For Deleuze and Guattari, becoming-woman is the first step towards a destratification (declination) of the body from the sexed and gendered organism, subject and signifier. Becoming-woman is a tactic to unblock desire from the economy of pleasure (the patriarchal model of sex) based on lack, scarcity, individual competition, species survival and filiative reproduction.[3] Unlike the becoming-animal and becoming-intense, becoming-woman entails a micropolitics that goes beyond the male–female, man–woman binarism. Yet, this micropolitics involves men and women.[4] It is directed against the repressive organization of desire dominated by pleasure (climactic sex) extending across all levels of order (biophysical, biocultural, bio-political, bio-economical, biodigital).

The importance of becoming-woman for the micropolitics of a body is to be related to the repressive (negating) power of the economy of pleasure. The latter imposes the fundamental binarism of sex on the body that gives way to the nature and culture, biology and technology, individual and society, passive and active dichotomies. This binarism primarily acts on the body through the Oedipalization of the girl, who lacking the penis, the most valued member in the patriarchal organization of the body, is gendered as a castrated boy. The girl becomes an example of castration for the boy, the bio-social threat of losing power, identity, and value in the politico-economic regime of order. For the economy of pleasure the girl is a chromosomal anomaly: she is neither a-sexed nor is she ready for sexual reproduction. The girl escapes the biocultural imperative of binary sexes, the sex-gender axis of Oedipal identification that confines desire to sexual filiation and genital sex. This is why becoming-woman is fundamental to all processes of becoming.[5]

The economy of pleasure thus separates the body from the ecosystem of bodies–sexes. It constructs nature as a battlefield of individual competition and survival of the fittest ensured by the successful insemination of the semen, the genealogy of the species. Pleasure represses all divergent flows from the cycle of accumulation and discharge, the imperative of the climax: the channelling of all relations towards the aim of self-satisfaction, the enclosing of all flows in the circle of identity (based on lack and scarcity, the negation of productive desire).

The notion that one can 'become a woman' or 'becoming-woman' has met a good degree of resistance within feminism. This hostile response is probably due to the uneasy distinction between molar politics (women's rights and identity power) and micropolitics (processes of mutations) defined by the unspecific (non-identified) body of the becoming-woman.[6] Becoming-woman precedes and exceeds all politics of identity that equates affects (the potential body) to feelings (subjective emotions). This autonomy from the identity of the body seems to imply that the Deleuze–Guattarian becoming-woman evokes the dissipation not only of feminist politics, but also of all kinds of political force.

However, as argued by some Deleuzian feminists, the process of becoming-woman deploys an important tactics of differentiation of a body beyond the tradition of representation. Becoming is no longer subjected to 'being' (the law of identity), but directs itself against man or the human as the origin of all concepts and politics. Thus, the task that challenges feminism in its confrontation with Deleuze and Guattari's philosophy of becoming is whether a becoming-woman 'can be made to work'.[7] For feminism, this becoming does not propose a becoming of the subject woman, but a becoming towards differentiation, the challenge of inventing new virtual (potential) bodies.[8] The importance of becoming-woman for feminism must be related to the crucial problematization of the dynamics of pleasure in Deleuze and Guattari: the Oedipal principle of reality that subsumes desire to the imperative of possessing and lacking the phallus. This principle is not to be considered as a psychoanalytical discourse but as an event: a singular organization of desire that invests all spheres of organization of power (biocultural, bio-political, bio-economical).

Is it possible to hold onto a microfeminine politics of desire without falling into the homogeneity of all differences? What is at stake in arguing that becoming-woman is only a step towards a becoming-animal, becoming-imperceptible (the becoming-intense of all affects) where the molecularization of sex challenges feminine difference altogether?

In the first instance, it can be argued that becoming-woman in Deleuze and Guattari is not undifferentiated. Rather, it is intensively differentiated: potential micro mutations rather than individual difference. Unlike the becoming-animal and the becoming-intense, becoming-woman defines the autonomy of non-climactic desire from the economy of pleasure, the consistency of potential desire cutting across all levels of organization of a body. In the second instance, becoming-animal and becoming-intense do not entail the nullification but the intensification of becoming-woman: the expansion and not the termination of molecular femininity. Thus, the dissolution of micro-femininity in an undifferentiated intensity will entail the negation of non-climactic desire: the blockage of molecular sexes into the binarism of the sexes, the dismissal of the multifaceted micropolitics of a body–sex by reiterating rather than challenging the primacy of pleasure over mutant desire.

Microfeminine warfare disentangles feminine desire from organic, innocent and inert nature, connecting singular modifications of sex and reproduction to the machinic networks of hypernature. This warfare does not re-essentialize feminine desire through a new analogy between organic nature and feminine sex, biological identity and power of reproduction. On the contrary, it becomes a vector of inten-sification of non-climactic (mutant) desire. This molecular femininity is important not only for feminism, but also for all micropolitics of the body: the micro variations of a body (skin, sex, perception, attitudes, gestures . . .) drifting from the individual body (fixed difference).

As recently argued, for feminism micropolitics is not detached from macropolitics.[9] The non-linear relationship between the micro and the macro levels of order exposes a pragmatics of affects where minimal causes in a system (e.g. the biodigital mutation of sex) unchain unpre-cedented effects in another (the biophysical and biocultural mutations of meiotic sex and human sex). Yet, this positive feedback does not completely explain the pragmatics of becoming-woman or micro-feminine warfare.

How do you build a microfeminine war machine? How do you diffuse this micropolitics of non-climactic desire? How do you produce a pragmatics of mutations?

The Spinozist ethics-ethology of local encounters sets for us some crucial criteria for this micropolitics: the construction of *common notions* between bodies and the extension of *conatus* (desire or appetite) of a body.[10] In the *Ethics*, common notions constitute the unity of composition of nature, something common to all bodies–minds, for instance extension, relations of motions and rest that define the agree-ments or disagreements between bodies on the basis of their immediate encounter. For example, the encounter between a nucleic body and a bacterial body entails a direct disagreement that decreases the power of bacteria to proliferate. For Spinoza, this is a sad encounter blocking the production of common notions or joyful associations, the potential expansion of affirmative desire. Bodies that agree and produce a reciprocal intensification of their potential to be affected and to affect other bodies instead produce joyful encounters. For example, the encounter between bacteria and mitochondria increases the power of microbial bodies to affect other bodies by trading genes across all multicellular bodies.

This increasing power of microbial bodies to affect defines the *conatus* of a bacterial colony. Conatus corresponds to the preservation of intensive potential in existence. Yet, the preservation of this potential requires the proliferation of new alliances between bodies that agree. For example, the immediate assemblage between bio-technologies and bacterial recombination defines the expansion of the power (conatus) of bacterial sex to preserve non-nuclear modes of reproduction through the emergence of new symbiotic mutations. Rather than individual progression (nuclear organization), this bacterial conatus implies a symbiotic association of bodies of all sorts unleashing the potential of a body to mutate on a hypernature of contagious encounters.

Abstract sex extends these criteria by defining a method, a mode and an instantiation of warfare. The endosymbiotic conception of a body–sex builds up a method for connecting variations. The bacterial mode of recombination, reversible parasitism and viral transduction exposes the biodigital zones of mutation between bodies–sexes. The instantiation of endosymbiosis to all levels of stratification maps the intersection of the biological, economical and cultural body. These criteria encourage the expansion of a microfeminine war machine outside the strata (the nuclear logic of pleasure): the emergence of a new body–sex that connects the mutations of desire to the potential becomings of hypernature.

This pervasive warfare hints at new imminent questions: what is the impact of abstract sex on digital culture? What is the relation between molecular perception and the biodigital architecture of virtual reality? How does bacterial sex affect digital kinaesthetics?

These are urgent questions. Biodigital mutations are not merely producing new cultures and new species, they primarily designate the proliferation of a new nature that encompasses all scales of matter. Abstract sex is seeping into your everyday life. Trade is the only option.

Notes

1 On the exteriority of the war machine in relation to the strata, see Deleuze and Guattari 1987: 351–423.

2 On the difference between micropolitics and macropolitics, see Deleuze and Guattari 1987: 213–14.

3 On the difference between desire and pleasure, see Deleuze and Guattari 1987: 530, note 39. See also Deleuze and Guattari 1983: 333. See also Deleuze 1997: 183–95.

4 On the micropolitical importance of becoming-woman for men and women, see E. Grosz 1994: 176–7. As Grosz highlights, becoming-woman includes the parallel importance of molar politics for feminism, which is, however, counter-balanced by a warning about the reduction of politics to a finalized project for the re-installation of the subject. Thus, also a woman has to become-woman or becoming-minoritarian, a rupture from the molar capture of identity.

5 Deleuze and Guattari note that in order to fabricate the organism, the body is first stolen from the girl, then from the boy to whom the castration of the girl is indicated as a threat, and her body displayed as object of his pleasure. The girl is the first Oedipal victim. 'This is why, conversely, the reconstruction of the body as a Body without Organs, the anorganism of the body, is inseparable from a becoming-woman, or the production of a molecular woman' (1987: 276). As Grosz also suggests, this girl's body coincides neither with a virgin nor with a representative body. The girl is the 'site of a culture's most intensified disinvestments and recastings of the body' (1994: 175). Similarly, Irigaray questions the oedipalization of the girl within the patriarchal economy. The girl's body is impossible to categorize through the binary machine of sex, where there is only one and the same sex. The girl is neither a boy nor a gendered woman. She is outside the sex/gender, man/woman, heterosexual/bisexual binarism. Irigaray, 1985a: 167.

6 On the critique of Deleuze and Guattari's becoming-woman, see A. Jardine 1985: 208–26. See also R. Braidotti 1991: 111–12; 114; 125; 1994: 111–23. See also L. Irigaray 1993: 83–94; 1985b: 140–1. On the feminist debate about becoming-woman, see Grosz 1994: 160–83. See also, Pelagia 1999: 97–120. See also, M. Gatens 1996a: 162–87.

7 On the importance of Deleuze and Guattari's concept of becoming-woman for feminist politics, see I. Buchanan and C. Colebrook 2000: 11–12; 110–27.

8 On the body politics of the future for Deleuzian feminism, see E. Grosz 2000: 214–34.

9 On the dynamics of molecular and molar power in relation to becoming-woman, see J. A. Flieger 2000: 38–63.

10 On common notions see Spinoza, *Ethics*, 1992, II: 29, schol.; II, prop. 37-40; II: 11, 12, 19, 24, 25; II, def. 4; III, def. 2; IV, def. 30. On the explanation of the dynamics of common notions, see G. Deleuze 1988c: 54–5; 103; 1990b: 145–54; 255–88. On the definition of conatus, see *Ethics*, III, def. of desire; III: 7; IV: 38;

II: 13, schol.; V: 39. On the explanation of the dynamics of conatus, see Deleuze 1988c: 97–104. On the importance of conatus as collective power-potentia, see T. Negri 1991a. Negri points to the radical difference of Spinoza's approach to the ontological determination of power in terms of *conatus* and *cupiditas*. In particular, he specifies that '[c]onfusing this ontological determination with the morality of individualism is, at best, myopic. Here, the effect, the dynamism and the articulation of individuality have constructed an irreversible constitutive mechanism. This is a collective and materialistic horizon: Individuality returns neither as a principle nor as a value, but simply as an element of the structure of being that continually spreads toward and across sociability' (1991a: 152).

Glossary

abstract machine: the diagrammatic interconnection between heterogeneous composite bodies that synthesizes without exhausting their potential.

abstract sex: the abstract machine of endosymbiosis.

bacteria: microbodies composed of a single cell without a distinct nuclear membrane.

bacterial sex: the trading of genetic particles (viruses) among different bacteria and across lineages (also called transgenesis). Bacterial sex is independent from bacterial reproduction (cloning and budding) (Margulis).

biocultural sex: the anthropomorphic (human) organization of meiotic sex.

biodigital sex: assemblage of genetic, cellular and technical processes that decodes and recombines information.

biophysical sex: the bacterial and eukaryotic symbiotic process of producing new cellular and multicellular bodies.

capital: the nucleic capture and investment of/in the body of a cell. The investment of bio-economic power in the field of abstract sex (endosymbiosis).

content: a substance–form composite. The form of content is a form of containment in which affects are actualized. A substance of content exhibits these actualized qualities (Massumi).

cloning: the copying of genetic material by bacteria, egg cell (parthenogenesis), eukaryotic cells. Bio-technological animal and human cloning involves the copying of nucleic genes and the double fusion of cytoplasmic material.

desire: anticlimactic distribution of energy flows.

destratification: immanent trading of information falling outside strata or emerging in the cracks between strata.

ecumenon: terrestrial biosphere. The regime of common principles organized by strata as distinct from Planomenon or machinic plane of consistency (which has no regime).

endosymbiosis: ecological term defining a physical association between different bodies: the condition of one body residing within another (Margulis).

entropy: thermodynamic term which defines the degree of disorder in a system. The tendency of a system to accumulate and discharge energy-flows.

eukaryote: an organism composed of cells with a distinct nucleic membrane.

evolution: descent with modification (Darwin).

expression: a substance–form composite. The form of expression is an order of functions (the actualizations of selected functions). The substance of expression is what embodies these selected functions (Massumi).

feedback: reciprocal communication between a system and the environment. Negative feedback (balance); positive feedback (out of balance).

genome: digital map of DNA.

hypernature: potential ecosystem of engineered bodies or immanent relations of connection and affection between bodies (the Planomenon) preceding and exceeding nuclear organizations. It coincides with Spinoza's nature.

hypersex: permanent symbiogenesis leading to the emergence of a new cell, organs or organisms by irreversible physical association between different kinds of bodies. It is the process that led to the emergence of the eukaryotic cell through the association between different bacteria (Margulis).

machinic assemblage: potential concatenation of heterogeneous compositions of bodies.

matter: unformed or intensive substance (Deleuze and Guattari). Nature or God (Spinoza's substance).

meiotic sex: cell division that leads from cells with two sets of chromosomes (diploid) to those with only one (haploid). This process precedes sexual reproduction and sexual mating. The cellular entanglement of sex, reproduction and death (Margulis). The linear transmission of germs through the death of the somatic body.

microfeminine warfare: endosymbiotic field of desire. A war without object.

mutation: heritable DNA change. Intensive variation emerging from symbiotic assemblages. See also *transduction*.

parthenogenic sex: state of development in which unfertilized eggs develop into offspring without mating (sperm) (Margulis). The autonomy of reproduction from the logic of filiation (the preservation of genetic information through sexual coupling).

pleasure: a climactic process of heat (energetic) distribution (Freud). The capture of desire into a closed system.

replication: process that increases by copying the number of DNA or RNA molecules. Molecular duplication process (Margulis).

reproduction: a process involving the increase in the number of bodies. A single body (unicellular organism) reproduces (binary fission and budding). Sexual reproduction involves two parents (Margulis).

reverse causality: the future acting on the past or effects acting on causes.

sex: the union of genetic material from more than one source to produce a new body or the passing of genetic material into a cell from a virus, bacterium or any other source (Margulis).

stratification: organization and selection of bodies into stochastically ordered layers and structures.

substance: formed matter (Deleuze and Guattari); Nature or God (Spinoza).

symbiogenesis: the origin of new cells, organs or organisms by association between different kinds of being (Margulis).

symbiosis: enduring physical combination between two or more organisms belonging to different species, lineages and phyla. It can be behavioural, metabolic, genetic (Margulis).

transduction: the transfer of small particles (viral or plasmid DNA) from an organelle or bacterium to another organelle or bacterium mediated by a virus. The change of energy from one form to another (e.g. mechanical energy to heat) (Margulis). The intensive process of individuation (Simondon).

turbulence: far-from-equilibrium system theory term. The swerving from linear trajectory. The intensive emergence of unpredictable mutations.

virus: ultramicroscopic infectious agent that replicates itself within cells of living hosts. A software used to infect other programmes.

Bibliography

Aldridge, Susan, 1996. *The Thread of Life. The Story of Genes and Genetic Engineering*. Cambridge: Cambridge University Press.

Alexander, Brian, 2001. '(You)^2', *Wired*, 9–02 (February): 120–35.

Alliez, Eric, 2001. 'On Deleuze's Bergsonism', in Gary Genosko (ed.), *Deleuze and Guattari: Critical Assessments of Leading Philosophers*, Vol. 1, Part II, 2001, pp. 394–411.

Ansell Pearson, Keith, 1997a. *Viroid Life: Perspectives on Nietzsche and the Transhuman Condition*. London and New York: Routledge.

_____ (ed.), 1997b. *Deleuze and Philosophy: The Difference Engineer*. London and New York: Routledge.

_____ 1999. *Germinal Life: The Difference and Repetition of Deleuze*. London and New York: Routledge.

_____ 2001. 'Thinking Immanence: on the Event of Deleuze Bergsonism', in Gary Genosko (ed.), *Deleuze and Guattari: Critical Assessments of Leading Philosophers*, Vol. 1, Part II, pp. 412–41.

Ball, Philip, 1999. *H₂O. A Biography of Water*. London: Phoenix.

Balsamo, Anne, 1996. *Technologies of the Gendered Body: Reading Cyborg Women*. Durham, NC: Duke University Press.

Bateson, Gregory, 1973. *Steps to an Ecology of Mind*. St Albans: Paladin.

_____ 1979. *Mind and Nature, A Necessary Unity*. New York: E. P. Dutton.

Baudrillard, Jean, 1993. *The Transparency of Evil: Essays on Extreme Phenomena*. New York: Verso.

_____ 1994a. *The Illusion of the End*, trans. C. Turner. Cambridge: Polity Press.

_____ 1994b. *Simulacra and Simulation*, trans. S. Faria Glaser. Ann Arbor: University of Michigan Press.

Baught, Bruce, 2001. 'Deleuze and Empiricism', in Gary Genosko (ed.), *Deleuze and Guattari: Critical Assessments of Leading Philosophers*, Vol. 1, Part II, pp. 357–75.

Bear, Greg, 1985. *Blood Music*. London: Legend.

_____ 1999. *Darwin's Radio*. London: HarperCollins.

Beaumont, P. and Willan, P., 2002. 'Woman to give birth to clone, claims scientist,' *Observer*, 26 May.

Bell, Daniel and Kennedy, Barbara (eds), 2000. *The CyberCulture Reader*. London: Routledge.

Benjamin, Walter, 1968. *Illuminations*, Hannah Arendt (ed.), trans. H. Zohn. New York: Schocken Books.

Bergson, Henri, 1983. *Creative Evolution*, trans. A. Mitchell. Lanham: University Press of America.

_____ 1991. *Matter and Memory*, trans. N. M. Paul and W. S. Palmer. New York: Zone Books.

Birke, Lynda, 1986. *Women, Feminism and Science: The Feminist Challenge*. Brighton: Wheatsheaf.

Birke, Lynda, Himmelweit, Susan and Vines, Gail (eds), 1990. *Tomorrow's Child, Reproductive Technologies in the 90s*. London: Virago Press.

Bogard, William, 1996. *The Simulation of Surveillance*. Cambridge: Cambridge University Press.

Bosma, Josephine, Van Mourik Broekman, Pauline, Byfield, Ted, Fuller, Matthew, Lovink, Geert, McCarty, Diana, Schultz, Pit, Stalder, Felix, Wark, McKenzie and Wilding, Faith (eds), 1999. *Readme! Filtered by Nettime: ASCII Culture and the Revenge of Knowledge*. New York: Autonomedia.

Bosteels, Bruno, 1998. 'From Text to Territory: Félix Guattari's Cartographies', in Eleanor Kaufman and Kevin Jon Heller (eds), *Deleuze and Guattari. New Mappings in Politics, Philosophy and Culture*. Minneapolis and London: University of Minnesota Press, pp. 145–74.

Bouchard, Jr: J. Thomas, 1997. 'Whenever the Twain Shall Meet', *The Sciences*. September–October: 52–7.

Braidotti, Rosi, 1991. *Patterns of Dissonance*, trans. E. Guild, Cambridge: Polity Press.

_____ 1994. *Nomadic Subjects: Embodiment and Difference in Contemporary Feminist Theory*. New York: Columbia University Press.

Braudel, Fernard, 1973. *Capitalism and Material Life, 1400–1800*. New York: Harper & Row.

_____ 1986. *The Wheels of Commerce*. New York: Harper & Row.

Buchanan, Ian and Colebrook, Claire (eds), 2000. *Deleuze and Feminist Theory*. Edinburgh: Edinburgh University Press.

Butler, E. Octavia, 1984. *Clay's Ark*. London: VGSF.

_____ 1987. *Dawn*. New York: Warner Books.

_____ 1989. *Imago, Xinogenesis III*. London: Gollancz.

Butler, Judith, 1990. *Gender Trouble: Feminism and the Subversion of Identity*. London: Routledge.

_____ 1993. *Bodies that Matter: On the Discursive Limits of Sex*. London: Routledge.

Butler, Samuel, 1985. *Erewhon*. Harmondsworth: Penguin Books.

Cadava, Eduardo, 1997. *Words of Light. Theses on the Photography of History*. Princeton: Princeton University Press.

Cann, Rebecca L., Stoneking, M. and Wilson, A. C., 1987. 'Mitochondrial DNA and human evolution', *Nature*, 325, January: 31–6.

Cavallaro, Dani, 2000. *Cyberpunk and Cyberculture. Science Fiction and the work of William Gibson*. London: Athlone Press.

Chatin, Gregory J., 1999. *The Unknowable*. Springer-Verlag.

Cibelli, Jose B., Lanza, Robert P., West, Michael D. and Ezzell, Carol, 2002. 'The First Human Cloned Embryo', *Scientific American*, January: 43–9.

Coghlan, Andy, 1997. 'One Small Step for a Ship', *New Scientist*, March: 4.

Coghlan, Andy and Concar, David, 1997. 'How the clock of life was turned back', *New Scientist*, March: 5.

Cohen, Philip, 1998a. 'We Ask. They Answer. The Clone Zone: A Special Report', *New Scientist*, May: 26–30.

_____ 1998b. 'Clone Alone. The Clone Zone', *New Scientist*, May: 32–7.

_____ 2000. 'The Force', *New Scientist*, February: 30–5.

Coleman, William, 1977. *Biology in the Nineteenth Century. Problems of Form, Function, and Transformation*. Cambridge: Cambridge University Press.

Corea, Gena, 1985. *The Mother Machine, Reproductive Technologies from Artificial Insemination to Artificial Wombs*. London: The Women's Press.

Crary, Jonathan, 1998. 'The Camera Obscura and its Subjects', in N. Mirozeff (ed.), *The Visual Culture Reader*. London: Routledge, pp. 245–52.

Daniel, Kevin. J. and Hood, L. (eds), 1992. *The Code of Codes: Scientific and Social Issues in the Human Genome Project*. Cambridge, MA: Harvard University Press.

Darwin, Charles, 1888. *The Descent of Man and Selection in Relation to Sex*, Vol. 1, (2nd edn), London: Clowes.

_____ 1993. *The Origin of Species, By Means of Natural Selection or The Preservation of Favoured Races in the Struggle for Life*. New York: The Modern Library.

Dawkins, Richard, 1983. *The Extended Phenotype*. Oxford: Oxford University Press.

_____ 1989. *The Selfish Gene*. Oxford: Oxford University Press.

_____ 1991. *The Blind Watchmaker*. Harmondsworth: Penguin.

_____ 1995. *River out of Eden*. London: Basic Books.

DeLanda, Manuel, 1992. 'Nonorganic Life', in Jonathan Crary and Sanford Kwinter (eds), *Incorporation*, Zone 6. New York: Zone Books, pp. 129–67.

_____ 1997. *A Thousand Years of NonLinear History*. New York: Zone Books.

_____ 2002. *Intensive Science and Virtual Philosophy*. London and New York: Continuum.

Deleuze, Gilles, 1972. *Proust and Signs*, trans. R. Howard. New York: Allen Lane: The Penguin Press.

_____ 1983. *Nietzsche and Philosophy*, trans. H. Tomlinson. London: Athlone Press.

_____ 1986. *Cinema 1. The Movement-Image*, trans. H. Tomlinson and B. Habberjam. London: Athlone Press.

_____ 1988a. *Bergsonism*, trans. H. Tomlinson and B. Habberjam. New York: Zone Books.

_____ 1988b. *Foucault*, foreword by Paul Bové, trans. S. Hand. Minneapolis and London: University of Minnesota Press.

_____ 1988c. *Spinoza: Practical Philosophy*, trans. R. Hurley. San Francisco: City Lights Books.

_____ 1989a *Masochism. Coldness and Cruelty*; Sacher-Masoch *The Venus in Furs*, trans. J. McNeil (reprint). New York: Zone Books.

_____ 1989b. *Cinema 2. The Time-Image*, trans. H. Tomlinson and R. Galeta. London: Athlone Press.

_____ 1990a. *The Logic of Sense*, trans. M. Foster with C. Stivale, (ed.) Constantin V. Boundas. London: Athlone Press.

_____ 1990b. *Expressionism in Philosophy: Spinoza*, trans. M. Joughin. New York: Zone Books.

_____ 1991. *Empiricism and Subjectivity. An Essay on Hume's Theory of Human Theory*, trans. and introduction by C.V. Boundas. New York: Columbia University Press.

_____ 1993. *The Fold, Leibniz and the Baroque*, trans. T. Conley. London: Athlone Press.

_____ 1994. *Difference and Repetition*, trans. P. Patton. London: Athlone Press.

_____ 1995. *Negotiation*, trans. M. Joughin. New York: Columbia University Press.

_____ 1997. 'Desire and Pleasure', trans. D.W. Smith, in A. I. Davidson (ed.), *Foucault and his Interlocutors*. Chicago: University of Chicago Press, pp. 183–95.

Deleuze, Gilles and Félix, Guattari, 1983. *Anti-Oedipus, Capitalism and Schizophrenia*, preface by Michel Foucault, trans. R. Hurley, M. Seem and H. R. Lane. London: Athlone Press.

_____ 1986. *Kafka. Toward a Minor Literature*, trans. D. Polan. Minneapolis: University of Minnesota Press.

_____ 1987. *A Thousand Plateaus, Capitalism and Schizophrenia*, trans. B. Massumi. London: Athlone Press.

_____ 1994. *What is Philosophy?*, trans. G. Burchell and H. Tomlinson. London: Verso.

Dennett, Daniel C., 1995. *Darwin's Dangerous Idea: Evolution and the Meanings of Life*. London: Allen Lane.

Di Berardino, Marie and Mckinnel, G. Robert, 1997. 'Backward Compatible', *The Sciences*, September–October: 32–7.

Di Filippo, Paul, 1996. *Ribofunk Anthology*. New York and London: Four Walls Eight Windows.

Farquhar, Dion, 1997. *The Other Machine, Discourses and Reproductive Technologies*. New York and London: Routledge.

Fausto-Sterling, Anne, 1992. *Myths of Gender: Biological Theories about Women and Men*, (2nd edn) New York: Basic Books.

Flagan, Mary and Booth, Austin (eds), 2002. *Reload, Rethinking Women and Cyberculture*. Cambridge, MA and London: MIT Press.

Flieger, Jerry A., 2000. 'Becoming-Woman: Deleuze, Schreber and Molecular Identification', in Ian Buchanan and Claire Colebrooke (eds), *Deleuze and Feminist Theory*. Edinburgh: Edinburgh University Press, pp. 38–63.

Foucault, Michel, 1972. *The Archeology of Knowledge*, trans. A. Sheridan. London: Tavistock.

_____ 1977. 'Theatrum Philosophicum', in *Language, Countermemory and Practice*, trans. D. F. Bouchard and S. Simon. Oxford: Basil Blackwell, pp. 165–99.

_____ 1980. *Power/Knowledge: Selected Interviews and Other Writings, 1972-77*, C. Gordon (ed.). Brighton: Harvester Press.

_____ 1989. *Foucault Live, Collected Interviews, 1961-1984*, S. Lotringer (ed.), trans. L. Hochroth and J. Johnston. New York: Semiotext(e).

_____ 1990. *The History of Sexuality*, Vol. 1, *An Introduction*, trans. R. Hurley. London: Penguin Books.

_____ 1991. *Discipline and Punish: the Birth of the Prison*, trans. A. Sheridan. London: Allen Lane.

_____ 1994. *The Birth of the Clinic. An Archeology of Medical Perception*, trans. A. Sheridan. New York: Vintage Books.

Freud, Sigmund, 1905. 'Three Essays on the Theory of Sexuality', *The Standard Edition of the Complete Psychological Works of Sigmund Freud*, Vol. VII. London: Hogarth Press.

_____ 1920. 'Beyond the Pleasure Principle', *The Standard Edition of the Complete Psychological Works of Sigmund Freud,* Vol. VIII. London: Hogarth Press.

Gatens, Moira, 1988. 'Towards a Feminist Philosophy of the Body', in Barbara Caine, Elizabeth A. Grosz and Marie de Lepervanche (eds), *Crossing Boundaries: Feminism and the Critique of Knowledges.* Sydney: Allen and Unwin, pp. 59–70.

_____ 1996a. 'Through a Spinozist Lens: Ethology, Difference, Power', in Paul Patton (ed.), *Deleuze: A Critical Reader*, Oxford and Malden: Blackwell, pp. 162–87.

_____ 1996b. *Imaginary Bodies, Ethics, Power and Corporeality.* London and New York: Routledge.

Genosko, Gary, 1998. 'Guattari's Schizoanalytic Semiotics: Mixing Hjelmselv and Pierce', in Eleanor Kaufman and Kevin Jon Heller (eds), *Deleuze and Guattari. New Mappings in Politics, Philosophy and Culture.* Minneapolis and London: University of Minnesota Press, pp. 175–90.

Gould, Stephen Jay, 1977. *Ontogeny and Philogeny.* Cambridge, MA: Harvard University Press.

_____ 1991. *Ever Since Darwin.* Harmondsworth: Penguin.

_____ 1996. *Full House: The Spread of Excellence from Plato to Darwin.* New York: Harmony Books.

_____ 1997. 'Individuality. Cloning and the discomfiting cases of Siamese Twins', *The Sciences*, September–October: 14–16.

Graham-Rowe, Duncan, 2000. 'Speedy Sex. A bit of evolution will work wonders for the Internet', *New Scientist*, 7 October (http://www.newscientist.com/hottopics/ai/speedy.jsp).

Gray, Chris Hables, (ed.), 1995. *The Cyborg Handbook.* London and New York: Routledge.

Grosz, Elisabeth, 1994a. *Volatile Bodies, Toward a Corporeal Feminism.* Bloomington and Indianapolis: Indiana University Press.

_____ 1994b. 'A Thousand Tiny Sexes. Feminism and Rhizomatics', in Constantin Boundas and Dorothea Olkowski (eds), *Gilles Deleuze and The Theatre of Philosophy.* New York: Routledge, pp. 187–210.

_____ 1995. *Space, Time, and Perversion, Essays on the Politics of Bodies.* New York and London: Routledge.

_____ 2000. 'Deleuze's Bergson: Duration, the Virtual and a Politics of the Future', in Ian Buchanan and Claire Colebrooke (eds), *Deleuze and Feminist Theory*. Edinburgh: Edinburgh University Press, pp. 214–34.

Guattari, Félix, 1984. *Molecular Revolution: Psychiatry and Politics*, trans. R. Sheed. New York: Penguin.

_____ 1995. *Chaosmosis: an ethico-aesthetic paradigm*, trans. P. Bains and J. Pefanis. Sydney: Power Publications.

_____ 2000. *The Three Ecologies*, trans. I. Pindar and P. Sutton. London and New Brunswick, NY: Athlone Press.

_____ 2001. 'Machinic Heterogeneities', in D. Trend (ed.), *Reading Digital Culture*. Oxford: Blackwell, pp. 38–51.

Guattari, Félix and Tony, Negri, 1990. *Communists like Us: New Spaces of Liberty, New Lines of Alliance*, trans. M. Ryan. New York: Semoi-text(e).

Haraway, Donna, 1985. 'A Manifesto for Cyborgs: Science, Technology, and Socialist Feminism in the 1980s', *Socialist Review*, 80: 65–108.

_____ 1989. *Primate Visions: Gender, Race, and Nature in the World of Modern Science*. London and New York: Routledge.

_____ 1991. *Semians, Cyborgs and Women*. London: FA Books.

_____ 1992. 'When Man^{TM} is on the Menu', in Jonathan Crary and Sanford Kwinter (eds), *Incorporation*. New York: Zone Books, pp. 36–43.

_____ 1995. 'Cyborgs and Symbionts: Living Together in the New World Order', in C. H. Gray (ed.), *The Cyborg Handbook*, London and New York: Routledge, pp. xi–xx.

_____ 1997. *Modest Witness@Second_Millenium, FemaleMan©_Meets_ Onco Mouse. Feminism and TechnoScience*. London and New York: Routledge.

Harding, Sandra, 1991. *Whose Science? Whose Knowledge?* Ithaca, NY: Cornell University Press.

Hardt, Michael, 1993. *Gilles Deleuze, An Apprenticeship in Philosphy*. London: UCL Press.

_____ 1998. 'The Withering of Civil Society', in Eleanor Kaufman and Kevin Jon Heller (eds) *Deleuze and Guattari. New Mappings in Politics, Philosophy and Culture*. Minneapolis and London: University of Minnesota Press, pp. 23–39.

Hardt, Michael and Negri, Tony, 2000. *Empire*, Cambridge, MA: Harvard University Press.

Hayles, Katherine N., 1999. *How we Became Posthuman*. Chicago and London: University of Chicago Press.

Hjelmslev, Louis, 1969. *Prolegomena to a Theory of Language*, trans. F. J. Whitfield. Madison: University of Wisconsin Press.

Holland, Eugene W., 1997. 'Marx and Postructuralist Philosophies of Difference', in Ian Buchanan (ed.), *A Deleuzian Century*, Special Issue, *The South Atlantic Quarterly*, 93(3) (Summer): 525–42.

Hubbard, Ruth, 1990. *The Politics of Women's Biology*. New Brunswick, NJ and London: Rutgers University Press.

Irigaray, Luce, 1985a. *Speculum of the Other Woman*, trans. G. C. Gill. Ithaca, NY: Cornell University Press.

————— 1985b. *This Sex which is not One*, trans. C. Porter. New York: Cornell University Press.

————— 1987. 'Is the Subject of Science Sexed?', *Hypatia*, 2 (Fall) 65–87.

————— 1991. *Marine Lover: of Friedrich Nietzsche*, trans. G. C. Gill. New York: Columbia University Press.

————— 1993. *An Ethics of Sexual Difference*, trans. C. Burke and G. C. Gill. London: Athlone Press.

Jacob, François, 1973. *The Logic of Life*, trans. B. E. Spillman. New York: Pantheon.

————— 1974. *The Logic of Living Systems, A History of Heredity*, trans. B. E. Spillman. London: Allen Lane.

Jameson, Fredric, 1984. 'Postmodernism, or the Cultural Logic of Late Capitalism', *New Left Review*, 146 (July–August): 53–92.

Jardine, Alice, 1985. 'Becoming a Body without Organs: Gilles Deleuze and His Brothers', in *Gynesis: Configurations of Woman and Modernity*. Ithaca: Cornell University Press pp. 208–26.

Jay, Martin, 1993. *Downcast Eyes: The Denigration of Vision in Twentieth-Century French Thought*. University of California Press.

Kahn, Axel, 1997. 'Clone Mammals . . . clone man?', *Nature*, 386 (13), March: 119.

Kapsalis, Terry, 1997. *Public Privates, Performing Gynecology from Both Ends of the Speculum*. Durham and London: Duke University Press.

Kaufman, Eleanor and Kenvin, Jon Heller (eds), 1998. *Deleuze and Guattari. New Mappings in Politics, Philosophy and Culture*. Minneapolis and London: University of Minnesota Press.

Kauffman, Stuart A., 1993. *The Origins of Order. Self-organization and Selection in Evolution*. New York and Oxford: Oxford University Press.

Keller, Evelyn, Fox, 1985. *Reflections on Gender and Science*. New Haven and London: Yale University Press.

————— 1992. *Secrets of Life, Secrets of Death, Essays on Language, Gender and Science*. London and New York: Routledge.

_____ 1995. *Refiguring Life Metaphors of Twentieth Century Biology*. New York: Columbia University Press.

_____ 1996. 'The Biological Gaze', in *FutureNatural, Nature, Science, Culture*, G. Robertson *et al.* (eds), London and New York: Routledge, pp. 107–21.

Kelly, Kevin, 1994. *Out of Control: the New Biology of Machines, Social Systems, and the Economic World*. Reading, MA: Addison-Wesley.

Kirkup, Gill, Jones, Linda, Woodward, Kath and Hovenden, Fiona (eds), 2000. *The Gendered Cyborg, A Reader*. London and New York: Routledge and The Open University.

Langton, C. Christopher, 1992. 'Life at the Edge of Chaos', in C. G. Langton, J. D. Farmer, S. Rasmussen, and C. Taylor (eds), *Artificial Life II. A Proceeding Volume in the Santa Fe Institute Studies in the Sciences of Complexity*, Vol.10. Reading, MA: Addison-Wesley.

Laqueur, Thomas, 1990. *Making Sex, Body and Gender from the Greeks to Freud*. Cambridge, MA: Harvard University Press.

Latour, Bruno, 1993. *We Have Never Been Modern*. Hemel Hempstead: Harvester.

Lazcano, Antonio, Fox, George E. and Orò, John F., 1992. 'Life before DNA: The Origin and Evolution of Early Archeon Cells', in R. P. Mortlock (ed.), *The Evolution of Metabolic Function*. Boca Raton, FL: CRC Press, pp. 237–95.

Lazzarato, Maurizio, 1996. *Videofilosofia. La Percezione del Tempo nel Postfordismo*. Roma: il Manifestolibri.

_____ 2002. *Puissance de L' Invention, La Psychologie Economique de Gabriel Tarde contre L'Economie Politique*. Paris Xe: Les Empêcheurs de Penser en Rond.

LeVay, Simon, 1994. *The Sexual Brain*. Cambridge, MA: MIT Press.

Levi, Primo, 1981. *Lilith e altri racconti*. Torino: Einaudi.

Levy, Pierre, 1998. *Becoming Virtual. Reality in the Digital Age*, trans. R. Bononno. New York and London: Plenum Trade.

Lewin, Roger, 1992. *Complexity, Life at the Edge of Chaos*. New York: Macmillian.

Lewontin, Richard C., 1997. 'The Confusion Over Cloning', *New York Review of Books*, XLIV (16) 23 October.

_____ 2000. *It Ain't Necessarily So. The Dream of the Human Genome and Other Illusions*. London: Granta Books.

Lloyd, Genevieve, 1996. *Spinoza and the Ethics*. London and New York: Routledge.

Lucretius, 1994. *De Rerum Natura. On the Nature of the Universe*, trans.

R. E. Latham, revised with an Introduction and notes by John Godwin. Harmondsworth: Penguin.

Lyotard, Jean François, 1993. *Libidinal Economy*, trans. I. Hamilton Grant. Bloomington: Indiana University Press.

McKie, Robin, 2002, 'Dolly the Sheep creator turns to humans', *Observer*, 13 October.

McLuhan, Eric and Zingrone, Franz, (eds) 1995. *Essential McLuhan*, London and New York: Routledge.

McLuhan, Marshall, 1964. *Understanding Media, the Extension of Man*. London: Routledge.

McLuhan, Marshall and Powers, Bruce, R., 1989. *The Global Village*. Oxford: Oxford University Press.

McMenanim, Mark and Dianne, 1994. *Hypersea*. New York: Columbia University Press.

Maddox, Brenda, 2002. *Rosalind Franklin: the Dark Lady of DNA*. London: HarperCollins.

Mae-Wan, Ho, 2001. 'The Human Genome Sellout and Beyond' in Tech Flesh 8, *C-Theory*, September. (*http://gd.tuwien.ac.at/soc/ctheory/articles/Tech_Flesh_8:_The_Human_Genome_Sellout_and_Beyond*_by_Mae-Wan_Ho_.html*.)

Malgaroli, Francesco, 2001. 'Oggi a Washington il piano per la clonazione umana', Scienza e Morale, *La Repubblica*, 7 August: 10–11.

Margulis, Lynn, 1970. *Origin of Eukaryotic Cells*. London and New Haven: Yale University.

_____ 1971. 'Symbiosis and Evolution', in *Scientific American*, 225 (2), (August): 3–11.

_____ 1981. *Symbiosis in Cell Evolution*. San Francisco: W.H. Freeman.

_____ 1998. *The Symbiotic Planet. A New Look at Evolution*. London: Weidenfeld & Nicolson.

Margulis, Lynn and Sagan, Dorion, 1985. 'The Riddle of Sex', in *The Science Teacher*, 52 (3), (March): 185–91.

_____ 1986. *Origins of Sex*. New Haven: Yale University Press.

_____ 1991. *Mystery Dance: On the Evolution of Human Sexuality*. New York: Summit Books.

_____ 1995. *What is Life?* London: Weidenfield & Nicolson.

_____ 1997. *What is Sex?* New York: Simon & Schuster.

Marsh, Margaret and Ronner, Wanda, 1996. *The Empty Cradle. Infertility in America from Colonial Time to the Present*. Baltimore, MD: Johns Hopkins University Press.

Marx Karl, 1954. *Capital. A Critique of Political Economy*, Vol. 1, trans.

from the 3rd German edn by S. Moore and E. Aveling and edited by Frederick Engels. London: Lawrence & Wishart.

_____ 1973. *Grundrisse. Foundations of the Critique of Political Economy*, trans. M. Nocolaus. Harmondsworth: Penguin Books.

Massumi, Brian, 1992. *A User's Guide to Capitalism and Schizophrenia*. Cambridge, MA: MIT Press.

_____ 1996. 'The Autonomy of Affect', in Paul Patton (ed.), *Deleuze: A Critical Reader*. Oxford: Blackwell, pp. 217–39.

_____ 1998. 'Requiem for Our Prospective Dead (Toward a Participatory Critique of Capitalist Power)', in Eleanor Kaufman and Kevin Jon Heller (eds), *Deleuze and Guattari, New Mappings in Politics, Philosophy and Culture*. Minneapolis: University of Minnesota Press, pp. 23–76.

_____ 2000. 'Too-Blue: Colour Patch for Expanded Empiricism', in *Cultural Studies*, 14 (2): 185–210.

_____ 2001. 'Sensing the Virtual, Building the Insensible', in Genosko, Gary (ed.), *Deleuze and Guattari, Critical Assessments of Leading Philosophers*. Vol. 3, Part VIII. London and New York: Routledge, pp. 1066–84.

_____ 2002. *Parables for the Virtual, Movement, Affect, Sensation*. Durham: Duke University Press.

Maturana, Humberto R. and Varela, Francisco J., 1980. *Autopoiesis and Cognition: The Realization of the Living*. Dordrecht: D. Reidel.

Mayr, Ernest, 1982. *The Growth of Biological Thought*. Cambridge, MA: Belknap Press.

Mirowsky, Philip, 1991. *More Heat than Light. Economics as Social Physics, Physics as Nature is Economics*. New York: Cambridge University Press.

Monod, Jacques, 1972. *Chance and Necessity, An Essay on the Natural Philosophy of Modern Biology*, trans. A. Wainhouse. London: Collins.

Moos, Michael A. (ed.), 1997. *Marshall McLuhan Essays. Media Research: Technology, Art and Communication*. Amsterdam: Overseas Publishers Association.

Morgan, Elaine, 1972. *The Descent of Woman. The Classic Study of Evolution*. London: Souvenir Press.

_____ 1982. *The Aquatic Ape, A Theory of Human Evolution*. New York: Stein & Day.

_____ 1990. *The Scars of Evolution: what our bodies tell us about human origins*. Harmondsworth: Penguin.

Musselwhite, David, 1987. *Partings Welded Together: politics and desire in the nineteenth-century English novel*. London: Methuen.

Negri, Tony,1991a. *Marx Beyond Marx: Lessons on the Grundrisse*, Jim Fleming (ed.), trans. H. Cleaver, M. Ryan and M. Viano. New York: Autonomedia.

_____ 1991b. *The Savage Anomaly, The Power of Spinoza's Metaphysics and Politics*, trans. M. Hardt. Minneapolis and Oxford: University of Minnesota Press.

Olkowski, Dorothea, 1991. 'Semiotics and Gilles Deleuze', in T. A. Sebeok, Jean Umiker-Sebeok and E. Young (eds), *The Semiotic Web*. Berlin: Mouton de Guyter, pp. 285–305.

Oudshoorn, Nelly, 1994. *Beyond the Natural Body, An Archeology of Sex Hormones*. London and New York: Routledge.

Pace, Norman R., 1991. 'Origin of Life, Facing Up to the Physical Setting', in *Cell*, 65, 17 May: 531–3.

Parisi, Luciana, 2000a. 'The Microbial Circuit of a Body', *Tekhnema, Journal of Philosophy and Technology*, 6 (Fall): 90–109.

_____ 2000b. 'Essence and virtuality: the incorporeal desire of Lilith', *Anglistica, Aion New Series, Interdisciplinary Journal*, Naples: I.U.O. 4 (1): 191–214.

Parisi, Luciana and Terranova, Tiziana, 2000. 'Heat Death: emergence and control in genetic engineering and artificial life', *CTheory, Theory, Technology and Culture*, 23 (1–2), Article 84[I] (5 October) (*http://www.tao.ca/fire/ctheory/0119.html*).

_____ 2001. 'A Matter of Affect: videogames and the cybernetic rewiring of vision', *Parallax 21*, 7 (4), October–December: 121–8.

Patton, Paul (ed.), 1996. *Deleuze: A Critical Reader*. Oxford: Blackwell.

Pelagia, Goulimari, 1999. 'A Minoritarian Feminism? Things to do with Deleuze and Guattari', *Hypatia* (14) 2: 97–120.

Pennisi, Elisabeth and Williams, Nigel, 1997. 'Will Dolly Send in the Clones?', *Science*, 275, 7 March: 1415–16.

Pfeffer, Naomi, 1993. *The Stork and the Syringe. A Political History of Reproductive Medicine*. Oxford: Blackwell.

Plant, Sadie, 1997. *Zeros and Ones*. London: Fourth Estate.

_____ 1998. 'Coming Across the Future', in *Virtual Futures 1995*. New York and London: Routledge, pp. 30–6.

_____ 2000. 'On the Matrix: Cyberfeminist Simulations', *The Gendered Cyborg, A Reader*, Kirkup, Gill *et al.* (eds) London and New York: Routledge and The Open University, pp. 265–75.

Prigogine, Ilya, 1997. *The End of Certainty. Time, Chaos, and the New Laws of Nature*. New York: The Free Press.

Prigogine, Ilya and Stengers, Isabelle, 1984. *Order Out Of Chaos, Man's*

New Dialogue with Nature, foreword by Alvin Toffler. New York: Bantam Books.

Rabinow, Paul, 1996. *Making PCR: A Story of Biotechnology*. Chicago and London: University of Chicago Press.

Reik, Theodor, 1949. *Masochism in Sex and Society*, trans. M. H. Beigel and G. M.Kurth. New York: Grove Press.

Ribalow, M. Z., 1997. 'Take Two. How have movies about cloning prepared us for the real thing', *The Sciences*, (September–October): 38–41.

Ridley, Matt, 1994. *The Red Queen: Sex and Evolution of Human Nature*, NewYork: Macmillan.

Robins, Kevin, 1996. *Into the Image: Culture and Politics in the Field of Vision*. London and New York: Routledge.

Sagan, Dorion, 1992. 'Metametazoa: Biology and Multiplicity', in Jonathan Crary and Sanford Kwinter (eds), *Incorporation*. New York: Zone Books, pp. 362–85.

Sapp, Jan, 1994. *Evolution by Association: A History of Symbiosis*. Oxford: Oxford University Press.

Serres, Michel, 1982. *Hermes: Literature, Science, Philosophy*. Baltimore, MD: Johns Hopkins University Press.

———— 1995. *Genesis*, trans. G. James and J. Nicelson. Ann Arbor: University of Michigan Press.

———— 2000. *The Birth of Physics*, trans. J. Hawkes, D. Webb (ed.). Manchester: Clinamen Press.

Shaviro, Steven, 1993. *The Cinematic Body. Theory out of Bounds*. Minneapolis: University of Minnesota Press.

Shelley, Mary, 1993. *Frankenstein or the modern Prometheus*, M. Butler (ed.). London: Pickering & Chatto.

Shildrick, Margrit, 1997. *Leaky Bodies and Boundaries: Feminism, Postmodernism and (Bio)Ethics*. London and New York: Routledge.

Shostak, Stanley, 1999. *Evolution of Sameness and Difference. Perspective on the Human Genome Project*. Singapore: Harwood Academic Publishers.

Shröndinger, Erwin, 1944. *What is Life?* London: Cambridge University Press.

Sigmund, Karl, 1995. *Games of Life, Explorations in Ecology, Evolution and Behaviour*. London: Penguin.

Simondon, Gilbert, 1992. 'The Genesis of the Individual', in Jonathan Crary and Sanford Kwinter (eds), *Incorporation*. New York: Zone Books, pp. 296–319.

Sims, J. Marion, 1873. *Gynecological Surgery for Fertility, Clinical Notes* on *Uterine Surgery with Special Reference to the Management of the Sterile Condition*. New York: Wood.

Spinoza, Baruch, 1992. *Ethics, Treatise on the Emendation of the Intellect* and *Selected Letters*, trans. S. Shirley, S. Feldman (ed.). Cambridge and Indianapolis: Hackett.

_____ 1995. *The Letters*, trans. S. Samuel, Introduction and Notes by Steven Barbone, Lee Rice, and Jacob Adler. Indianapolis and Cambridge: Hackett.

Springer, Claudia, 1995. *Electronic Eros: Bodies and Desire in the Post-industrial Age*. Austin: University of Texas Press.

Squires, Judith, 1996. 'Fabulous Feminist Futures and the Lure of Cyberculture', in J. Dovey (ed.), *Fractal Dreams: New Media in Social Context*. London: Lawrence & Wishart, pp. 194–216.

Stengers, Isabelle, 1997. *Power and Invention: Situating Science*, trans. P. Bains. Minneapolis: University of Minnesota Press.

Stone, Allucquere Rose, 1991. 'Will The Real Body Please Stand Up?', in *Cyberspace: The First Steps*, M. Benedikt (ed.). Cambridge, MA: MIT Press, pp. 88–118.

Tarde, Gabriel, 1999. *Monadologie et Sociologie*, Vol. I, Préface d'Éric Alliez, Postface de Maurizio Lazzarato. Institut Synthélabo: Les Empêcheurs de Penser en Rond.

Terranova, Tiziana, 2000. 'Free Labor: producing culture for the Digital Economy', *Social Text*, 63 (Summer): 33–58.

Thacker, Eugene, 2000a. 'Redefining Bioinformatics: A Critical Analysis of Technoscientific Bodies', *Enculturation, Post-Digital Studies*, 3 (1) (Spring) (*http://enculturation.gmu.edu/3_1/toc.html*).

_____ 2000b. 'The Post-Genomic Era Has Already Happened', *Bio-policy* Journal, 3 (1) (PDF Document formatted for Bioline International website, *http://www.bioline.org.br/*).

Tuana, Nancy (ed.), 1989a. *Femininsm and Science*. Bloomington: Indiana University Press.

_____ 1989b. 'The Weaker Seed: the sexist bias of reproductive theory', *Hypatia*, 3 (1): 35–59.

Turkle, Sherry, 1995. *Life on the Screen: Identity in the Age of the Internet*. New York: Simon & Schuster.

Theweleit, Klaus, 1987. *Male Fantasies*, Vol. I and II. Cambridge: Polity Press.

Varela, Francisco, 1991. 'Organism: A Meshwork of Selfless Selves', in A. Taber, (ed.), *Organism and the Origins of Self*. Boston: Kluwer Academic Publishers, pp. 79–107.

Vines, Gail, 1997. 'One giant step into the unknown', *Scientist*, 1 March: 5.

Virilio, Paul, 1997. *Speed and Politics*. New York: Semiotext(e).

Waldby, Catherine, 2000. *The Visible Human Project. Informatic Bodies and Posthuman Medicine*. London and New York: Routledge.

Weibel, Peter, 1999. 'On the History and Aesthetics of the Digital Image', in Timothy Druckrey with Ars Electronica (eds), *Ars Electronica: Facing the Future*. Boston, MA: MIT Press, pp. 51–65.

Weismann, August, 1882. *Studies in the Theory of Descent*, 2 vols, trans. R. Medola, prefatory note by Charles Darwin. London: Sampson Low, Marston, Searle & Rivington.

Whitford, Margaret, 1991. *Luce Irigaray: Philosophy in the Feminine*. London and New York: Routledge.

Wiener, Norbert, 1961. *Cybernetics, or Control and Communication in the Animal and the Machine*. Cambridge, MA: MIT Press.

_____ 1989. *The Human Use of Human Beings: Cybernetics and Society*. London: Free Association Books.

Worringer, Wilhem, 1963. *Abstraction and Empathy. A Contribution to the Psychology of Style,* trans. M. Bullock. New York: International University Press.

Zammito, John H., 1992. *The Genesis of Kant's Critique of Judgment*. Chicago and London: University of Chicago Press.

Index

Lightning Source UK Ltd.
Milton Keynes UK
UKOW06f0603120416

272057UK00001B/61/P